Contents

Faculty Work

Confronting the Current Job Market

Letters ‖ 242

From the Editor

Initiated in 1977 to provide "a publication through which language and literature teachers can debate what are usually called 'professional matters'" (Brod and Neel iii), *Profession* seems to have filled its purpose in a modest way and now stands as a record of evolving professional issues in the field. For twenty years MLA members have debated the relative soundness of a series of intellectual and curricular developments, responses to shifting foreign language enrollments, strategies for coping with institutional adversity, and ways of influencing the academic job market.

As you will see, the subjects discussed in this issue of *Profession* have much in common with those found in earlier volumes. The Presidential Forum, which Herbert Lindenberger organized for the 1997 convention, calls attention to the value of interdisciplinary work. Linda Hutcheon and Michael Hutcheon, Edward W. Said, Marshall Brown, Jeffrey T. Schnapp, and Susan Howe demonstrate how studies of art, music, and literature illuminate our understanding of particular works of art. The next group of essays also concerns intellectual and curricular issues. Henry R. Cooper, Jr., traces the history of Slavic studies, Nelly Furman proposes reshaping the French curriculum, and Peter Hohendahl considers the history and current situation of German studies in the United States. David Mazella describes a recent change in the major that the University of Houston English department approved because the department lacked the faculty to staff required courses. Lauren Berlant and Lori Schroeder Haslem take up issues concerning cultural and multicultural studies that are the source of tensions in many language and literature departments.

The essays clustered under the rubric of "Faculty Work" touch on a variety of subjects. Mara Holt and Leon Anderson wish to initiate a field-wide conversation about the increased pace of academic life; Michael Selmon, responding to the report written by the MLA Commission on Professional Service that appeared in *Profession 1996*, examines the causes of ambivalent attitudes toward service. Guadalupe Valdés takes up the sensitive question of what constitutes near-native speaking ability in foreign languages, Barton R. Friedman reflects on changing expectations over the course of his career regarding effective teaching and student achievement, and Bruce E. Graver reports on what he learned from his work on an electronic edition. Two authors focus on religion: Patricia Michaelson questions the role of faith in her professional life, and Regina M. Schwartz shows how religion and profession can come together. The last article in this section is by Zack Bowen, who describes how, as department chair, he learned to "construct helpful dialogical self-narratives—or simply split personalities that work to advantage in solving administrative problems." Lest you think Bowen's approach is entirely light, I quote from his tough conclusion:

> The point is that, as chairs, the lowest, most functionary level of university administration, we have been and are in some measure to blame for letting our institutions get away with it [using fear to undermine academic values]. If we submit to corporate fear or to some aspiration to join exalted ranks by willing submission, we have let our faculties and our profession down. To whatever extent we are able to resist unwarranted incursions into the rights of our faculty members, their economic well-being, or the health of our programs, I think we are obligated to do so. Many chairs may be surprised at how much weight their simple refusal to go along will carry. If chairs don't give the power structure maximum grief over some arbitrary or inhuman scheme, nobody else will.

This year's cluster of essays about the job market includes a description by Linda K. Karell of a successful, though roundabout, academic job search; an account by Geoffrey T. Wilson of why new PhDs are reluctant to consider employment opportunities outside the academy; and a review of events leading to what Robyn R. Warhol considers an improvement in the job security of non-tenure-track faculty members at her institution. Warhol concludes with a comment from Brian Kent, a non-tenure-track colleague, who presents a less sanguine view of the situation. Finally, Sandra M. Gilbert memorializes a friend who served on the MLA Committee on Professional Employment and died in November 1997 before the report reached MLA members. Gilbert's account "Bob's Jobs" deserves the attention of both new PhDs and their advisers.

I wish to thank the members of the *Profession* Advisory Committee—Klaus L. Berghahn, John Guillory, Walter D. Mignolo, and Jacqueline Jones Royster—who evaluated the submissions for *Profession 1998*. Thanks are also due my colleagues on staff, who read and comment on *Profession* essays—David Laurence, director of English programs and the Association of Departments of English, and Elizabeth Welles, director of foreign language programs and the Association of Departments of Foreign Languages. In addition, Laurence and Welles make recommendations about which articles from the *ADE Bulletin* and *ADFL Bulletin* might be reprinted in *Profession*.

For the next issue of *Profession*, committee members seek essays about professional matters that are on MLA members' minds. They also wish to open a new discussion that may help the association reenvision the goals of studying and teaching the humanities in a global context. The committee therefore invites writers, scholars, and teachers who live and work outside the United States or who are visiting the United States to send essays about how the humanities are taught and studied in their countries. In addition, committee members are interested in what these individuals think about issues that concern scholars and teachers in the United States regarding literary and cultural studies, the teaching of foreign languages and bilingual education, the crisis facing area studies, the corporatization of academic institutions in the United States and abroad, the widespread study of English in non-English-speaking countries, national language policies, and the impact of globalization. On these and other topics the views of MLA members in the United States are also welcome.

Committee members hope that readers of *Profession 1998* will forward this invitation to participate in an international conversation to colleagues in other countries. The committee invites essays of 1,800 to 5,000 words, which must reach the MLA office by 1 March 1999. Manuscripts may be faxed to 212 533–0961 or sent by e-mail to the managing editor of the journal, Carol Zuses (carol.zuses@mla.org).

Phyllis Franklin

WORK CITED

Brod, Richard I., and Jasper P. Neel. "From the Editors." *Profession* 77. New York: MLA, 1997. iii–iv.

Breaking Boundaries, Making Connections

HERBERT LINDENBERGER

The following essays, originally presented at the 1997 MLA Presidential Forum under the title "Indisciplinarity: Art, Literature, Music," share a common concern: the breaking of disciplinary boundaries as a means of enabling new territorial arrangements to meet current-day concerns.[1] As Jeffrey Schnapp explains near the beginning of his presentation, "The disjunction between [art history and literary history] was the product of a distinctively Western institutional history, a history readily traceable to a taxonomy of disciplines first incubated in nineteenth-century German universities." Each of these essays can be seen as an attempt to test and remap these boundaries.

In an era during which it has become fashionable to view even one's gender as a social construction, it scarcely seems daring to speak of the various disciplines we practice as products of an ongoing social process. Yet academic disciplines have traditionally functioned much like literary genres: while pretending that the rules and procedures governing them have been naturally ordained, the disciplines have often suppressed the motivations and the contingencies that shaped their development into their present state.

When I started graduate work many years ago, nearly all my instructors discouraged any questioning of the procedures their students were ex-

The author is Avalon Foundation Professor of Humanities in the Department of Comparative Literature and the Department of English at Stanford University and a past president of the Modern Language Association.

pected to practice. Except for required courses in bibliography and the history of literary theory, every course was centered on a particular period within a single national literature. My instructors generally confined themselves to their own scholarly worlds, encompassing what counted at the time as the significant literature of that period—literature that we were expected to examine within the limits of the methodology in which the individual instructor had been trained.[2]

To escape these limits, I sought ways of breaking boundaries, and I was able to do so because I was following a degree program not in a single national literature but in that relatively new and also still suspect field comparative literature. Although the individual courses I needed to take were drawn from offerings in the traditional national literatures, I eagerly took advantage of the freedom to imagine my own structures cutting across periods, national literatures, and methodologies. Indeed, throughout my career, I used the license granted me as a practitioner of comparative literature to continue making connections, eventually seeking to cross the boundaries among art forms and the particular academic disciplines associated with these forms.

It scarcely seems accidental that four of the authors of these essays exploring interdisciplinarity took their doctorates in comparative literature. Another author, Michael Hutcheon, is a medical professor who also works in medical history. Susan Howe is at once a poet and a specialist in early American literature and intellectual history.

It is also no coincidence that these authors have backgrounds in other art forms. Marshall Brown and Edward Said came close to professional status on musical instruments, the former on the cello, the latter on the piano. Linda Hutcheon has been trained on the piano and Michael Hutcheon on the trumpet. Schnapp, as he mentions at the start of his essay, practiced conceptual painting. Howe pursued a career as a visual artist before turning to poetry.

Like many scholars today, no one of these scholars quite fits the usual categories defined for our profession. For instance, the published work of each cuts across several of the divisions that the Modern Language Association has set up as a means of organizing its convention activities. When asked—as I often am by people both within and without the profession—what my specialty is, I'm hard put, as any of these writers would be, to give a precise answer. To say "Interdisciplinary" would be begging the question; to say "Comparative literature" inevitably leads to the question of what I compare; to resort to "I'm not very specialized," as I sometimes do, invites accusations of dilettantism; and to answer, as I also sometimes do, "I specialize in whatever I happen to be working on at the moment," sounds unnecessarily aggressive.

It seems appropriate that a group of essays seeking connections among art forms should include two essays on opera. Doubtless the only major genre whose principles were theorized before they were put into practice, opera was intended from the start to combine a variety of forms. Linda Hutcheon and Michael Hutcheon's essay on Richard Strauss's *Salome*, moreover, not only considers the various arts—literature, music, dance, visual art—that are brought together within this opera but also stresses the sharp disjunctions between the opera and the earlier works in various media—Gustave Moreau's many drawings and paintings of the Salome story, Joris-Karl Huysmans's novel *A rebours*, Oscar Wilde's play, not to speak of Jules Massenet's earlier opera, *Hérodiade*, on the same narrative.

The disjunctions depicted here among the distinct manifestations of a single narrative are mirrored in other essays by a concern for marking differences between particular periods. For Said, for example, Beethoven's celebration of conjugal fidelity in *Fidelio* defines the gap separating a new postrevolutionary world from the seemingly amoral treatment of sexual relationships in the opera upon which Beethoven is implicitly and disdainfully commenting, namely, Mozart's *Così fan tutte*, composed the year that the French Revolution began. The differences among the worlds of these operas are clearly marked for the audience, Said shows, in the way that Beethoven echoes yet also rethinks Fiordiligi's second-act aria "Per pietà" in Leonore's aria "Komm Hoffnung." Yet Said does not rest content with a simple confrontation between two antithetical works; he demonstrates that the earlier opera actually problematizes the later one, serving, he tells us, as "a destabilizing force that does not stop bothering, if not infecting and undermining, the imposing structure of *Fidelio*."

Brown takes a single genre, the fugue, within a single art form; he depicts the transformation the fugue undergoes when Mozart, composing at a time when the genre had come to seem antiquated, reworks a piece by Bach within the new classical style. For Brown, music, since it is largely free of representational elements, provides the ideal means of defining the formal properties that link the various arts during a particular period. As he wrote in an earlier essay on the parallels between musical and narrative forms, "If we are interested in the formal sense of a period or a movement, we may well look to its music for the clearest, most easily describable examples" (221). In the present essay he is able to oppose what he calls the "artisanal ethos" of the Bach fugue, with "the three instruments [having] absolutely equal status," to the "aristocratic refinement" and "dramatic contrasts" among the instruments evident in Mozart's rewriting of this fugue. The examples that music provides the analyst thus could serve as examples to illuminate similar differences in period styles within other art forms.

Whereas Brown seeks models to illuminate the changes that genres undergo from one generation to the next, Schnapp's essay exemplifies a generational change in critical method. By reexamining a painting by René Magritte to which Michel Foucault had devoted a short book in 1973,[3] Schnapp offers a materialist view to contest Foucault's structuralist reading. For Foucault, a linguistic emblem such as "This is not a pipe," which explicitly contradicts the pictorial sign directly above it, works to "rout the object, revealing its filmy thinness" (41)—with the result that Magritte, despite the meticulously representational nature of individual objects within his paintings, in his own way approaches the nonrepresentational mode Foucault describes in Kandinsky (34–35). Thus, Magritte's combination of picture and contradictory accompanying text works to confirm a structuralist program "bring[ing] pure similitudes and nonaffirmative verbal statements into play within the instability of a disoriented volume and an unmapped space" (53–54).

Employing a deliberately materialist metaphor, Schnapp contrasts what he calls Foucault's "structuralist mulcher" with his own "art/lit combine" that "sifts and sorts" according "to the particularity and materiality of each and every medium." To demonstrate his point, Schnapp presents a thickly described context for Magritte's pipe: the presence, as well as the diversity of uses, of pipes in other Magritte paintings and also in the artist's life; the role of pipes in the work of earlier figures such as Balzac, Baudelaire, and Courbet; the history of the briar pipe as "a distinctive product of the era of industry"; the pipe's presence within a key text of architectural theory by Le Corbusier, in whose circle Magritte moved. In place of Foucault's grandscale context, which encompasses the history of representation in the West, Schnapp gives us a set of concrete, seemingly heterogeneous phenomena that provide a new context within which to locate Magritte's painting.

The diverse interdisciplinary practices evident in the essays described thus far find a parallel in the intergeneric boundary breaking of Susan Howe's contribution. By using the word *contribution* I avoid the question of its precise genre. As with Howe's earlier writings, such as "A Bibliography of the King's Book" (*Nonconformist's Memorial* 45–82) and "Thorow" (*Singularities* 39–57), one can call this piece a poem, if only because, when faced with the need to classify herself professionally, Howe refers to herself as a poet.

One could of course resort to *mixed genre*, a term often used in treatises of poetics to avoid committing oneself to still another classification.[4]

Or one could use the contemporary label *performance piece* to indicate the fact that, like many of her writings, this one is intended for oral (and visual) performance as well as for the printed page. Or, as Howe put it at one point to describe the theatricality motivating her work, "Sometimes I think what I'm doing on the page is moving people around on a stage" (qtd. in Keller 13).

Symptomatic of the generic uncertainty of this piece are the varying functions of its title. The label "Renunciation Is a P[ei]rcing Virtue" constitutes at once the first two lines of the Dickinson poem serving as Howe's epigraph, the title that editors have customarily attached to this poem, a pun on the name of the historical figure on whom Howe's text is centered, and a hint as to how one might go about interpreting the cryptic manuscript reproduced at the end of this text. And what role does this manuscript play within the piece as a whole? Should we describe it as a postmodern appropriation comparable to the way painters from Robert Rauschenberg and Andy Warhol on include earlier visual images in their work? Moreover, to what genre do we assign this Dickinson fragment? Written on the flap of an envelope, as her poems sometimes are, can it also aspire to the status of poem?

And how to classify the Charles Sanders Peirce manuscript pages reproduced here? Are they visual art, calligraphy, or philosophy—philosophy being the category to which Peirce is relegated today despite the difficulties he encountered, as Howe tells us, in gaining acceptance within that profession in his own time? And what of Howe's own narrative about the various tribulations that Peirce suffered in the academic profession? Do we count it as biographical or historical writing, or both of these at once?

"History and fiction have always been united in my mind," Howe once stated in an interview. "It would be hard to think of poetry apart from history" (qtd. in Foster 17). As a recent analyst of her work, Peter Nicholls, puts it, "Howe regards herself as first and foremost a poet, but she is also a freelance historian in a long and distinguished line which includes writers such as Ezra Pound and Charles Olson" (586).

Yet the characters peopling Howe's histories—Mary Rowlandson (*Birth-Mark* 89–130), Thoreau (*Singularities* 39–57), Melville (*Nonconformist's Memorial* 83–146), Dickinson (*My Emily Dickinson*)—are, like the Peirce portrayed here, also among the lonely, banished (often self-banished) figures of American literature. Can one perhaps view them also as images of the avant-garde writer in our own time? Howe herself hints at this connection when, speaking of the problems encountered by what she calls "experimental writers," she asks, "Why is it that their work is almost completely shut out of magazines with larger distribution networks? Why are they shut out of jobs in creative writing programs?" (qtd. in Keller 22).

Howe's boundary breaking has long been noted as central to her endeavors. Placing her within a larger American experimental poetic tradition, Peter Quartermain writes, "Howe's work, from the very title of her first book (*Hinge Picture*) on, treads borders, boundaries, dividing lines, edges, invisible meeting points" (186). Yet in their own linguistically and visually radical way, her texts are also emblematic of the boundary breaking and the genre bending that many contemporary literary scholars, like the other authors of these essays, have felt the need to practice to make sense of the artifacts they seek to illuminate. Challenging traditional disciplinary and generic borders above all enables us to establish new connections and, one hopes, to encourage supportive institutional arrangements within our profession.

NOTES

[1]Russell Berman, warning against a tendency to value interdisciplinarity for its own sake, has written of "interdisciplinarity [. . .] as a transitional phase [. . .] and not an end in itself. Overcoming interdisciplinarity would then imply a refounding of the field as a discipline with redefined goals and evaluative norms" (67). My purpose in organizing this forum was to provide some models by means of which literary study can stimulate and institutionalize inquiry into the relations among art forms.

[2]A notable exception among my graduate instructors was Northrop Frye. For a detailed description of how his teaching made me rethink earlier assumptions, see Lindenberger 374–76. Since the seminar I took with him needed a period title to accord with departmental policy, it was called English Romantic Poetry. In actuality Frye used this seminar to think out the larger theory that eventually resulted in his classic work *Anatomy of Criticism*.

[3]Foucault's book-length version resulted from the controversy that his original essay on this painting, published in 1968, generated.

[4]See, for instance, the section entitled "Generic Mixture" in Fowler (181–83).

WORKS CITED

Berman, Russell A. "Reform and Continuity: Graduate Education toward a Foreign Cultural Literacy." *Profession 1997*. New York: MLA, 1997. 61–74.

Brown, Marshall. *Turning Points: Essays in the History of Cultural Expressions*. Stanford: Stanford UP, 1997.

Foster, Edward. "An Interview with Susan Howe." *Talisman: A Journal of Contemporary Poetry and Poetics* 4 (1990): 14–38.

Foucault, Michel. *This Is Not a Pipe*. Trans. and ed. James Harkness. Berkeley: U of California P, 1982.

Fowler, Alastair. *The Kinds of Literature: An Introduction to the Theory of Genres and Modes*. Cambridge: Harvard UP, 1982.

Frye, Northrop. *Anatomy of Criticism*. Princeton: Princeton UP, 1957.

Howe, Susan. *The Birth-Mark*. Hanover: Wesleyan UP, 1993.

———. *My Emily Dickinson*. Berkeley: North Atlantic, 1985.

———. *The Nonconformist's Memorial*. New York: New Directions, 1993.

———. *Singularities*. Hanover: Wesleyan UP, 1990.

Keller, Lynn. "An Interview with Susan Howe." *Contemporary Literature* 36 (1995): 1–34.

Lindenberger, Herbert. "Presidential Address 1997: Teaching and the Making of Knowledge." *PMLA* 113 (1998): 370–78.

Nicholls, Peter. "Unsettling the Wilderness: Susan Howe and American History." *Contemporary Literature* 37 (1996): 586–601.

Quartermain, Peter. *Disjunctive Poetics: From Gertrude Stein and Louis Zukofsky to Susan Howe*. Cambridge: Cambridge UP, 1992.

"Here's Lookin' at You, Kid":
The Empowering Gaze in Salome

LINDA HUTCHEON and MICHAEL HUTCHEON

While it may seem obvious that the staged body is central to any form of theatrical representation (Roach 101), the almost disembodied voice has come to dominate discussions of opera, especially since the advent of technological advances in audio recording and radio transmission. But a staged operatic performance presents more than just audible music: it includes a verbal text and a staged, dramatized, visualized narrative for which that music was specially written. As a literally embodied art form, opera arguably owes its undeniable affective power to this overdetermination of the verbal, the visual, and the aural—and not to the aural alone. This broader-based power is, in fact, openly thematized in operas such as Richard Strauss's *Salome*, specifically in the strange scene where the singer does not sing at all: she dances, and for almost ten minutes the orchestra supports her moving body, not her voice. As audience members, we look as well as listen; the consequences of that act of gazing provide the focus for this brief study of the intersection of the verbal, visual, and musical arts.

Strauss's 1905 opera was based on the somewhat earlier Oscar Wilde play of the same name and represents the fin-de-siècle, decadent revision of the biblical story (Mark 6.14–29; Matt. 14.1–12) of the beautiful (and very young) princess of Judea who dances for the lustful Herod in order to possess and, in this version, to kiss the decapitated head of John the Baptist,

Linda Hutcheon is University Professor of English and Comparative Literature at the University of Toronto. Michael Hutcheon is Professor of Medicine at the University of Toronto. A version of this paper was presented at the 1997 MLA convention in Toronto.

the object of her newly awakened passion. It was shocking then;[1] it still manages to shock today. Wilde's lyrically lush libretto (even in German translation) contributed to that shock as much as did the powerful, radically new sounds of Strauss's music. Together, the dramatic narrative, the text, and the music worked to position the body of Salome front and center, where the audience members (like Herod) could not take their eyes off her.

Salome's body was decidedly the obsession of late-nineteenth-century European culture, especially French culture.[2] Indeed, the exotic dancing princess became the subject of operas,[3] ballets, poems, stories, plays, sculptures, decorative objects, and paintings. No painter was more obsessed with the corporeal Salome than Gustave Moreau, who left hundreds of oils, watercolors, and drawings as testimony to his visual fascination (Kaplan 58–67). He anticipated and in part created the tastes of a generation of writers, from Jules Laforgue to the young Proust, from J.-K. Huysmans to Oscar Wilde (see Mathieu, *Moreau* 16, 250; "La religion" 16–17). Two of Moreau's paintings from the year 1876 stand out from all the others precisely because Huysmans immortalized them in his novel *A rebours* (*Against Nature*). Huysmans's hero, a dandy named Des Esseintes, purchases these works in order to contemplate Salome's charms and dangers. One is an oil painting entitled *Salomé dansant devant Hérode* and pictures the princess in an exotic, orientalized setting.[4] Curiously, Huysmans's depiction of Salome's body puts the static painted image into motion: "[E]lle commence la lubrique danse qui doit réveiller les sens assoupis du vieil Hérode; ses seins ondulent et, au frottement de ses colliers qui tourbillonnent, leurs bouts se dressent; sur la moiteur de sa peau les diamants, attachés, scintillent" '[S]he begins the lascivious dance which is to rouse the aged Herod's dormant senses; her breasts rise and fall, the nipples hardening at the touch of her whirling necklaces; the strings of diamonds glitter against her moist flesh' (*A rebours* 143; *Against Nature* 64). For Des Esseintes, Salome becomes more than a biblical character or even a pornographic delight: she is "la déité symbolique de l'indestructible Luxure, la déesse de l'immortelle Hystérie, la Beauté maudite [. . .] la Bête monstrueuse" 'the symbolic incarnation of undying Lust, the Goddess of immortal Hysteria, the accursed Beauty [. . .] the monstrous Beast' (144–45; 66).

Moreau's watercolor called *L'apparition* disturbs Des Esseintes even more, though not for the obvious reason, that is, that the head of John the Baptist appears floating before the terrified dancer. This Salome upsets him because she is "vraiment fille; elle obéissait à son tempérament de femme ardente et cruelle [. . .]; elle réveillait plus énergiquement les sens en léthargie de l'homme, ensorcelait, domptait plus sûrement ses volontés, avec son charme de grande fleur vénérienne, poussée dans des couches sacrilèges, élevée dans des serres impies" 'a true harlot, obedient to her passionate and cruel female temperament [. . .]; here she roused the sleeping senses of the male more powerfully, subjugated his will more surely with her charms—the charms of a great venereal flower, grown in a bed of sacrilege, reared in a hot-house of impiety' (48; 68).

Such disconcerting remarks may well seem overblown (not to say misogynistic) today, in terms of both sentiment and rhetoric. Yet we need to remind ourselves of two things: first, the strategic value of exaggeration in the decadent aesthetic; and second, the astonishing impact of this description on all subsequent representations of Salome, especially the one by Oscar Wilde, whose character Dorian Gray saw in Des Esseintes a prefigurement of himself.[5] Huysmans's description of Moreau's disturbing paintings has been called the "principal engenderer" of Wilde's play *Salomé*, from which Strauss composed his opera (Ellmann 321).[6] But there is something equally disconcerting about the very physical composition of Moreau's oil paintings of this period: there is a radical disjunction between the large background blocks of color, which were developed in advance to get the chromatic harmony right, and the superimposed drawing of fine detail, often in India ink (Mathieu, *Moreau* 122, 200; Lacambre 34). What strikes the eye is that the superimposed drawing does not always coincide with the color blocks: the delicate tracery is almost independent of the colored form it appears intended to define. Likewise, to draw an analogy, Wilde's delicate, "bejewelled" text (Murray, "Strauss" 569) seems at odds with the strong, powerful music Strauss composed for it. However, as with Moreau's compositions, it is precisely the lack of fit between text and music that gives the work disturbing power. Without Strauss's music, Wilde's play remains an ornate, extended lyric (Lewis 127) or maybe a ballad, but it is not, on its own, very dramatic: for that, it needs the uneasy conjunction—and disjunction—with the music's emphatic and dramatic vocabulary of harmonies, rhythms, and instrumentation.[7] And when the two opposites come together, as in Moreau's paintings, the power to disconcert lies to a great extent in their aesthetic noncoincidence.

There is a direct analogy here with the disjunction within the disconcerting character of Salome herself, as she gradually and progressively comes to embody on the stage a psychic lack of fit. It is this lack of fit that makes her, by the end, so powerful and terrifying. Wilde intended his Salome to be both the embodiment of sensuality *and* a virgin (Ellmann 232, 255); but she soon became, to use Lawrence Kramer's term, "everyone's favorite *fin-de-siècle* dragon lady" (271). Yet this is a femme fatale with a difference: as Ken Russell captured so well in his film *Salome's Last Dance*, she is also a very young adolescent and a virgin.[8] The audience comes to see the contradictions only as the opera progresses, as her character is unveiled as surely as the famous Dance of the Seven Veils reveals her body. The medical discourses of the pathological female available at the time of the play and opera provided the rest of the context for her demonization: Salome was seen from the start as the hysteric, the necrophiliac, or simply (given the text's obsession with the moon) the menstruating, pubescent woman medically connected with loss of control, mobility of emotion, increased sexuality, and a penchant for violence.[9]

Yet the Salome of the opening is a beautiful, young, impulsive, spoiled child who must have her own way, a pampered princess who lives very much in her own world, as befits the narcissism of the young. This same pubescent girl, however, soon develops an obsessive and lethal passion to kiss the lips of Jochanaan (the opera's Germanic-Hebraic name for John the Baptist). Indeed, on first seeing his body, she sings a hymn of praise to its beauties that is most sensual and rare in opera.[10] Opera is a genre that is always ready to talk of love but extremely reticent when it comes to frank expressions of physical desire (Goldet 64–65).

Though young, Salome knows the meaning of power. Her dance is a calculated move in a game of exchange with Herod in which she offers her body as a sensual, sexual spectacle to his eyes, in return for a promise that will fulfill both her childlike willful stubbornness and her consuming sexual obsession to kiss the mouth of the resistant prophet. The Dance of the Seven Veils is undoubtedly the best-known part of the opera. Wilde's text, like the Bible, leaves the dance undescribed,[11] but the opera music is explicitly descriptive. And, in one critic's words, "its Hollywood-exotic contours, bedizened with motifs from the opera proper, sometimes tempt directors to make an elaborate production number, far beyond the rather chaste little scenario that the composer sketched to guide himself" (Murray, "Salome" 147). In that scenario, Strauss posed Salome as in the Moreau painting *Salomé dansant devant Hérode* and then provided her with a rather stylized choreography—"menacing steps or lively paces"—to go with certain bars of the music (see Puffett, *Strauss* 165–66). Strauss came to feel that many productions went "beyond all bounds of decency and good taste. [. . .] Salome, being a chaste virgin and an oriental princess, must be played with the simplest and most restrained of gestures." He felt that the music offered quite enough "turmoil," and so the acting should be "limited to the utmost simplicity" (Strauss, "Reminiscences" 151). At least in Strauss's eyes, this was not intended to be what Kramer calls "the first operatic striptease in history" (281).

The dance is the moment in the opera when the sensual is made visible as well as audible (Banks 15). In turn-of-century Europe, though, dance had a particular cultural resonance that contributed to the especially memorable quality of Salome the dancer. Not only did dance (in general) become an emblem of the perfect work of art that fuses sensuousness and thought into one (Kramer 279), but it also took on more medicalized and pathological meaning through its association with hysteria. This is one of the reasons, argues Felicia McCarren, that there was such a fashion for dancing Salomes: popular dancers like Loïe Fuller and Maud Allan commissioned modern ballets on the theme, and European audiences flocked to them.[12] While the dance of Strauss's Salome could be (and indeed has been) interpreted as a Dionysian dance of the body, it is also explicitly presented in the opera as a corporeal token in an economy of exchange (Koritz 81): Salome uses her dancing body as a means to an end.

That body clearly becomes the focus of the attention—and the literal eye—of both audience and characters. As dancer, Salome is without a doubt the object of the gaze—particularly Herod's male gaze.[13] As Martin Jay has argued, ocularcentrism—or the dominance of the visual—has a long and complex history in Western culture, where the visual has been considered superior to the other senses, in part because it is detached from what it observes (21–82; see also Berger; Bryson). Through distancing, the observer has the potential power of objectifying what is observed, of mastering and controlling it. Because of this connection between power and the act of seeing, the privilege of vision has been linked to sexual privilege (Owens 58): the gaze has thus been gendered male, leaving women as the objects of the gaze, either as exhibitionists or as passively displayed bodies. The representations of women in opera and visual art, as in film, as Laura Mulvey famously argued, are "coded for strong visual and erotic impact so that they can be said to connote *to-be-looked-at-ness* (11). This coding means that to be looked at is a negative, a position of powerlessness.

Salome the character and *Salome* the opera turn this now widely accepted theory on its head. Here, to be the object of the gaze is to have ultimate power; it is the position of being looked at that conveys mastery and control. This is certainly an opera obsessed with the act of looking and even staring. It opens with the Syrian guard, Narraboth, staring at Salome; the soldiers on guard watch Herod, wondering what he is looking at; Salome enters, staring at the moon and worrying about why Herod stares at her the way he does.[14] The verb *ansehen* 'to look at' dominates the text. The one person who evades anyone's gaze at this point is Jochanaan, who has been imprisoned deep in a cistern by Herod; Herod obviously knows the power of being seen and wants to deny it to his enemy and harshest critic.

But Jochanaan's voice evokes in Salome the desire to see Jochanaan. To this end, knowing the erotic force of being looked at, Salome attempts to seduce Jochanaan's guard, Narraboth, with the promise of a future glance at him. This is a young woman who is not objectified by the gaze but empowered by it: she finally compels Narraboth to look at her, and when he does, he gives in at once to her request to bring Jochanaan out of the cistern, against Herod's orders. But Jochanaan too knows the power of the visual and refuses to look at the staring Salome. The power is in the one beheld and not in the beholder. Jochanaan refuses to give Salome the power that would result from his gaze.

Salome's dance is her best revenge, as all of us—audience as well as Herod—bestow power on her as we gaze. Salome does not reverse the centrality of the male gazer as powerful (Riquelme 596); rather, she alters the power dynamics of the gaze itself. Therefore, when we as audience members gaze, we set up the tragedy of both Salome and the man whose life she demands as her reward for dancing. Finally addressing his decapitated head with its closed eyes, she asks why he never looked at her when alive (why, in other words, he never granted her the power that others did). The tragic in this, for Salome, lies in her belief that, had he looked at her, he would have loved her. Such was indeed the experience of the beautiful young princess until now.

In arguing that Salome gains power through being gazed at both by Herod and by us, we are taking a position contrary to that of both Kramer, who sees Salome finally losing the power of the gaze that she usurped during the dance (277–78), and Carolyn Abbate, who sees Salome as a constant object of the gaze (254). Our argument is that the male gaze has not been usurped, because the power was never with it in the first place. Rather, in this case, to be the object of the gaze is to be empowered. As many have pointed out, *Salome* is an opera full of obsessive voyeurs and warnings of the dangers of looking; but in it, in stark reversal of the tradition, to look is to grant power to the one observed.

To render thus the visual as more complex in its empowering dynamics is to suggest the need to rethink the relation between the aural and the visual in operatic performance, especially from the point of view of the audience that is gazing at Salome's body as well as listening to her voice. As drama, the final scene functions in complicated ways for the audience. In it, Salome kisses Jochanaan's mouth; Herod, in disgust and terror, orders her death; and soldiers crush her body with their heavy shields. We may be shocked at his act as well as at hers, but given the growing horror that accompanied the gradual unveiling of Salome's character, her death may also allow the audience to experience some satisfying cathartic release: the embodiment of the terrifying femme fatale is no more. With the aid of what has been described as a music of "exposed nerve ends" (Schmidgall 281) that nonetheless has a strong erotic charge, the audience is both shocked and appeased. The audience is, above all, implicated.

In his novel, Huysmans had made his hero identify with Moreau's gazing Herod: "Tel que le vieux roi, des Esseintes demeurait écrasé, anéanti, pris de vertige, devant cette danseuse" 'Like the old King, Des Esseintes invariably felt overwhelmed, subjugated, stunned when he looked at this dancing-girl' (148; 68). Huysmans's construction of her as representing the predatory, hysterical, but irresistible temptation of the flesh suggests that Salome's appeal was in her progressive contradictoriness: as Gustave Klimt's paintings inspired by the opera suggest as well,[15] this deadly dancer was as much a degenerate object of misogynist fears as a sadomasochistic erotic ideal (Dottin 14).

Part of the unease of watching and listening to *Salome* even today may come from this implication of the audience in a relationship of empowerment that has fatal consequences. Over the decades audiences have kept going to see and hear this opera, watching (and figuratively causing) the deaths of Salome and Jochanaan over and over. Abbate argues that, at the end, Salome's "musical speech drowns out everything in range, and we sit as passive objects, battered by that voice" (254). But we are always affected by more than just the aural, and we are certainly not passive: we too have been active in the visual granting of power to this contradictory and complicated character—the vamp and the virgin—whose body we have stared at for almost the full ninety minutes of the opera. We watched her dance, but we also watched her die.[16] As a staged work, *Salome* does not allow the audience to remain passive or distanced: our gaze, like Herod's, does not objectify Salome. Instead, from our progressive empowering of her comes not only the sense of tragedy we feel but also the rising anxiety Salome continues to inspire.

NOTES

[1]The opera's critics seem to have found the opera more shocking than the audience at large, who greeted the first performance with thirty-eight curtain calls. There were fifty productions of the work within two years. Wilde's play was originally written in French in 1892 and then translated into English and famously illustrated by Aubrey Beardsley. A production with Sarah Bernhardt was banned in London in 1892 for portraying biblical characters on stage, but the play finally opened in Paris in 1896, the year following Wilde's famous trial and conviction. The German version premiered in 1901 in Breslau and found its perfect audience among the German avant-garde (who saw themselves as the supporters of an artist persecuted by English law and English aesthetic

conservatism): there were 111 performances in Germany in 1903 and 1904 alone. It was in Berlin at Max Reinhardt's Kleines Theater that Strauss saw the play in Hedvig Lachmann's prose translation (which he would go on to use for the libretto, instead of a poetic version prepared by Anton Lindner). When someone at the performance suggested to Strauss that it might make a good opera, he is said to have replied that he was already busy composing it (Puffett, Introduction 4).

The opera he completed a few years later suffered a fate at times not unlike that of Wilde's play: it too was banned, this time in Vienna (at the state theater) and for religious reasons. It had to be bowdlerized in order to play in London, where Sir Thomas Beecham claimed, "We had successfully metamorphosed a lurid tale of love and revenge into a comforting sermon" (qtd. in Jefferson 46). Indeed, no synopsis of this decadent plot appeared in the Covent Garden program until 1937. The New York production was closed down by the daughter of J. Pierpont Morgan on moral grounds; the press described the opera as having a "moral stench" (see Fludas 15). It would appear that the general taboo regarding respect for the bodies of the dead was broken too scandalously by Salome's necrophilic and almost cannibalistic kiss of the prophet's lips (Hamard 40).

[2]Pym offers statistical proof of this (312–13). Between 1860 and 1920, 82% of the existing Salome images (in various art forms) appeared, and Paris was the center of production of those images. The height of production was at the turn of the century. It has been argued that Salome's "prominence at the outset of the century was symptomatic of two major strains of cultural influence just then intersecting: orientalism, with its overtures of 1890s decadence, and feminism" (Bizot 85).

[3]Jules Massenet's 1881 opera *Hérodiade* is based on the Salome story as scripted by Paul Milliet and Henri Grémont (with A. Zanardini), but it eroticizes the plot (by increasing Herod's lust for Salome) and sentimentalizes it considerably: Salome seeks the mother who has abandoned her and falls in love with John the Baptist, who persuades her to love him chastely. He does eventually confess his love for her just before his execution, forbidding her to follow him in death. Massenet's Salome also dances, but does so in order to beg for mercy for a John the Baptist sentenced to death. When the execution takes place nonetheless, she attacks Hérodias with a dagger, but turns it on herself when she learns that Hérodias is the mother she has been seeking. An opera about lust and religion, erotic obsession and spirituality, it has some of the paradoxes of Strauss's opera, but Salome's relation to John here is chaste, spiritual, and sentimental—in short, a far cry from the one in Strauss's opera.

[4]Moreau did 120 drawings of this scene, 70 of them of Salome's body alone.

[5]"For years Dorian Gray could not free himself from the influence of this book. Or perhaps it would be more accurate to say that he never sought to free himself from it. [. . .] The hero, the wonderful young Parisian, in whom the romantic and the scientific temperaments were so strangely blended, became to him a kind of prefiguring type of himself. And, indeed, the whole book seemed to him to contain the story of his own life, written before he had lived it" (*Picture* 147). For more on the impact of Huysmans's descriptions of Salome, see Becker-Leckrone 239–40.

[6]Wilde's acquaintance with Mallarmé, who was writing his "Hérodiade" at the time, was another factor, as was Wilde's reading of J. C. Heywood's dramatic poem, published in England in 1888, which retold Heine's *Atta Troll* (where the phantom Herodias kisses the head of John the Baptist). Wilde studied many other visual representations of Salome (Ellmann 321–23).

[7]Dramatic effect is also the result, of course, of the cuts Strauss made to Wilde's text (or rather to Lachmann's German translation of it), reducing the subplots, repetitions, political maneuverings in the name of structural symmetries and formal groupings of events. See Tenschert; Carpenter 89–93.

[8]Bade, in fact, provocatively calls her "the paedophile's femme fatale" (16). See also McCracken on the links between the nineteenth-century notions of children and the twentieth-century Lolita figure. For him, Salome is the "Ur-nymphet."

[9]Control, according to Havelock Ellis, is "physiologically lessened at the menstral [sic] period even in health, while it is much more lessened in the neurotic and imbalanced" (256). In the light of this menstrual connection, the libretto's obsession with the moon takes on a new (and more sinister) meaning. It will also surprise no one that the woman whom Huysmans called "Goddess of immortal Hysteria" has indeed been interpreted as a hysteric or even a psychotic by post-Freudian critics (Newman 36; Kennedy 143–44; Tranchefort 127). But the more contemporaneous discourse—of Richard Krafft-Ebing and Havelock Ellis, not to mention Jean-Martin Charcot and Sigmund Freud himself—offered another context in which Salome could be constructed, in terms of pathological sexuality, as the suggestible, impulsive, sexually aroused hysteric, and, by the end, the degenerate nymphomaniac having no sense of shame or morality regarding the object of her desires (see Forel 227). Salome's character certainly caused Romain Rolland to write to his friend Strauss that Wilde's play "has a nauseous and sickly atmosphere about it: it exudes vice and literature. This isn't a question of middle-class morality, it's a question of health" (qtd. in Williamson 131). Rolland went on to call Salome "unwholesome, unclean, hysterical," as did many of the early critics of the opera, whose protests in the name of health likely also reflected the impact of Wilde's scandalous reputation and recent trial. The verbal signs of the influence of those medical discourses of pathological female sexuality are nonetheless present in that consistent vocabulary of hysteria and unhealthiness.

[10]She begins with an extravagant description that uses biblical similes of the whiteness of his body, of which she says she is enamored ("Ich bin verliebt in deinem Leib") and ends with a request to touch his body ("Lass mich ihn berühren deinen Lieb" [Strauss, *Salome* 35, 36]). At this point the motif of Herodias echoes in the music, identifying the daughter with the mother's condemned sexuality, as William Mann has explained (54). Jochanaan's response to Salome is an implicitly sexualized attack on womankind for first bringing evil into the world. His rejection causes Salome to respond with a series of, this time, hideous images of his body—which she now says she hates. The music shifts, offering "disturbingly heterogeneous orchestration, dissonant harmony and more angular vocal lines" (Banks 11). Having thus disposed of his white body, Salome turns her attention to his black hair. Her fulsome description and his subsequent rejection are followed, once again, by a revised depiction of his hair as a tangle of "black serpents writhing" around his neck. Her attention then becomes fixed on the redness of his mouth, and she concludes her praise by asking to kiss it. His continued rejection of her advances is met with her stubborn will: she insists she will kiss his mouth—and, of course, she eventually does.

[11]Marjorie Garber argues that "in its non-description, in its indescribability lies its power, and its availability for cultural inscription and appropriation" (341).

[12]See Mahling on Fuller's 1895 *Salome*, danced to Gabriel Pierné's music. In 1907, Florent Schmitt (on a libretto by Robert d'Humières) wrote a ballet for Fuller's troupe called *La Tragédie de Salomé*, in two acts with seven tableaux. Maud Allen's *Die Vision*

Salome was performed in Vienna in 1906, the year before Strauss's opera first played there. Elizabeth Dempster points out that these women, like Isadora Duncan and Ruth St. Denis, "constructed images and created dances through their own unballetic bodies, producing a writing of the female body which strongly contrasted with classical inscriptions. These dancers, creating new vocabularies of movement and new styles of presentation, made a decisive and liberating break with the principles and forms of the European ballet" (27–28). See also Conrad 156.

[13]See Garber on the "binary myth of Salome": "the male gazer (Herod) and the female object of the gaze (Salome); the Western male subject as spectator (Flaubert, Huysmans, Moreau, Wilde himself) and the exotic, feminized Eastern other" (340). On the gaze, see also Petitjean 132; Bucknell 515; Clément 125–26; Godefroid.

[14]Wilde's less innocent Salome says she knows why, but Strauss cut this line.

[15]Klimt's 1907 painting *Judith* was inspired by Salome, and some critics have also named it after Salome (di Stefano). Strauss himself said that in the world of Klimt he saw much of his own music, "especially *Salome*" (qtd. in Schmidgall 286).

[16]Salome's death has been seen as both a "misogynist anxiety dream" and a "patriarchal wish-fulfillment" (Kramer 279).

WORKS CITED

Abbate, Carolyn. "Opera; or, the Envoicing of Women." *Musicology and Difference: Gender and Sexuality in Music Scholarship*. Ed. Ruth A. Solie. Berkeley: U of California P, 1993. 225–58.

Bade, Patrick. *Femme Fatale: Images of Evil and Fascinating Women*. London: Ash, 1979.

Banks, Paul. "Richard Strauss and the Unveiling of 'Salomé.'" *Salome/Elektra*. London: Calder; New York: Riverrun, 1988. 7–21.

Becker-Leckrone, Megan. "Salome©: The Fetishization of a Textual Corpus." *New Literary History* 26 (1995): 239–60.

Berger, John. *Ways of Seeing*. London: BBC; Harmondsworth: Penguin, 1972.

Bizot, Richard. "The Turn-of-the-Century Salome Era: High- and Pop-Culture Variations on the Dance of the Seven Veils." *Choreography and Dance* 2.3 (1992): 71–87.

Bryson, Norman. *Vision and Painting: The Logic of the Gaze*. New Haven: Yale UP, 1983.

Bucknell, Bradley. "On 'Seeing' Salome." *ELH* 60 (1993): 503–26.

Carpenter, Tethys. "Tonal and Dramatic Structure." Puffett, *Strauss* 88–108.

Clément, Catherine. *Opera; or, The Undoing of Women*. Trans. Betsy Wing. London: Virago, 1989.

Conrad, Peter. *Romantic Opera and Literary Form*. Berkeley: U of California P, 1977.

Dempster, Elizabeth. "Women Writing the Body: Let's Watch a Little How She Dances." *Bodies of the Text: Dance as Theory, Literature as Dance*. Ed. Ellen W. Goellner and Jacqueline Shea Murphy. New Brunswick: Rutgers UP, 1995. 21–38.

di Stefano, Eva. *Il complesso di Salomè: La donna, l'amore e la morte nella pittura di Klimt*. Palermo: Sellerio, 1985.

Dottin, Mireille. "Le développement du 'mythe de Salomé.'" *Salomé dans les collections françaises*. Saint-Denis: Musée d'art et d'histoire, 1988. 13–16.

Ellis, Havelock. *Man and Woman: A Study of Human Secondary Sexual Characters*. London: Scott, 1899.

Ellmann, Richard. *Oscar Wilde*. London: Hamish Hamilton, 1987.

Fludas, John. "Fatal Women: Exploring the Eternal Mystique of the Femmes Fatales." *Opera News* Feb. 1977: 15–18.

Forel, August. *The Sexual Question.* Trans. C. F. Marshall. London: Rebman, 1908.

Garber, Marjorie. *Vested Interests: Cross-Dressing and Cultural Anxiety.* 1992. New York: Harper, 1993.

Godefroid, Philippe. "Le regard interdit." *Avant-scène opéra* 47–48 (1983): 146–49.

Goldet, Stéphane. "Commentaire littéraire et musicale." *Avant-scène opéra* 47–48 (1983): 53–110.

Hamard, Marie-Claire. "La femme fatale: *Salomé* et le *Yellow Book.*" *Cahiers victoriens et édouardiens* 36 (1992): 29–49.

Huysmans, J.-K. *A rebours.* Ed. Marc Fumaroli. 2nd ed. Paris: Gallimard, 1977.

———. *Against Nature.* Trans. Robert Baldick. London: Penguin, 1959.

Jay, Martin. *Downcast Eyes: The Denigration of Vision in Twentieth-Century French Thought.* Berkeley: U of California P, 1993.

Jefferson, Alan. *The Operas of Richard Strauss in Britain, 1910–1963.* London: Putnam, 1963.

Kaplan, Julius. *The Art of Gustave Moreau: Theory, Style, and Content.* Ann Arbor: UMI, 1982.

Kennedy, Michael. *Richard Strauss.* Oxford: Oxford UP, 1995.

Koritz, Amy. *Gendering Bodies / Performing Art: Dance and Literature in Early Twentieth-Century British Culture.* Ann Arbor: U of Michigan P, 1995.

Kramer, Lawrence. "Culture and Musical Hermeneutics: The Salome Complex." *Cambridge Opera Journal* 2.3 (1990): 269–94.

Lacambre, Geneviève. *Gustave Moreau: Maître sorcier.* Paris: Gallimard, 1997.

Lewis, Hanna B. "Salome and Elektra: Sisters or Strangers." *Orbis Litterarum* 31 (1976): 125–33.

Mahling, Christoph-Hellmut. "'Schweig' und tanze!' Zum 'tönenden Schweigen' bei Richard Strauss." *Die Sprache der Musik: Festschrift Klaus Wolfgang Niemöller.* Ed. Jobst Peter Fricke. Regensburg: Bosse, 1989. 371–79.

Mann, William. *Richard Strauss: A Critical Study of the Operas.* London: Cassell, 1964.

Mathieu, Pierre-Louis. *Gustave Moreau: Sa vie, son oeuvre.* Paris: Bibliothèque des arts, 1976.

———. "La religion dans la vie et l'oeuvre de Gustave Moreau." *Gustave Moreau et la Bible.* Nice: Musée national message biblique Marc Chagall, 1991. 15–24.

McCarren, Felicia. "The 'Symptomatic Act' circa 1900: Hysteria, Hypnosis, Electricity, Dance." *Critical Inquiry* 21.4 (1995): 748–74.

McCracken, Timothy. "Redeeming Salome: The Face in the Figure." Unpublished ms.

Mulvey, Laura. "Visual Pleasure and Narrative Cinema." *Screen* 16.3 (1975): 6–18.

Murray, David. "Richard (Georg) Strauss." Sadie 4: 565–75.

———. "Salome." Sadie 4: 146–49.

Newman, Ernest. *More Opera Nights.* London: Putnam, 1954.

Owens, Craig. "The Discourse of Others: Feminism and Postmodernism." *The Anti-Aesthetic: Essays on Postmodern Culture.* Ed. Hal Foster. Seattle: Bay, 1983. 57–82.

Petitjean, Martial. "Symbolisme et sacrifice." *Avant-scène opéra* 47–48 (1983): 132–37.

Puffett, Derrick, ed. *Richard Strauss:* Salome. Cambridge Opera Handbooks. Cambridge: Cambridge UP, 1989.

———. Introduction. Puffett, *Strauss* 1–10.

Pym, Anthony. "The Importance of Salomé: Approaches to a Fin de Siècle Theme." *French Forum* 14 (1989): 311–22.

Riquelme, J. P. "Shalom/Solomon/*Salomé*: Modernism and Wilde's Aesthetic Politics." *Centennial Review* 39 (1995): 575–610.

Roach, Joseph R. "Power's Body: The Inscription of Modernity as Style." *Interpreting the Theatrical Past*. Ed. Thomas Postlewait and Bruce A. McConachie. Iowa City: U of Iowa P, 1989. 99–118.

Sadie, Stanley, ed. *The New Grove Dictionary of Opera*. 4 vols. London and New York: Macmillan, 1992.

Salome's Last Dance. Dir. Ken Russell. Vestron, 1988.

Schmidgall, Gary. *Literature as Opera*. New York: Oxford UP, 1977.

Strauss, Richard. "Reminiscences of the First Performance of My Opera." *Recollections and Reflections*. Ed. Willi Schuh. Trans. L. J. Laurence. London: Boosey, 1953. 146–67.

———. *Salome*. *Salome/Elektra*. London: Calder; New York: Riverrun, 1988. 25–54.

Tenschert, Roland. "Strauss as Librettist." Puffett, *Strauss* 36–50.

Tranchefort, François-René. "Le mythe subverti." *Avant-scène opéra* 47–48 (1983): 127–31.

Wilde, Oscar. *The Picture of Dorian Gray*. London: Penguin, 1992.

———. *Salome: A Tragedy in One Act*. Trans. Alfred Douglas. New York: Dover, 1967.

Williamson, John. "Critical Reception." Puffett, *Strauss* 131–44.

Opera Opposed to Opera:
Così fan tutte *and* Fidelio

EDWARD W. SAID

The topic of influence and its anxieties, so rich in the history of literature, is less discussed in the history of music. Certainly the intimidating and inhibiting effect of Ludwig van Beethoven's Nine on subsequent symphonists (Brahms, Mahler, Bruckner) is much referred to, but the dynamics of an active, energizing struggle with an antecedent both disliked and respected have not often received much attention. This is a pity, since the case I want to consider here helps us make more sense of two popular and yet very problematic operas, one that I believe follows the other with considerable agitation. I have in mind Wolfgang Amadeus Mozart's *Così fan tutte*, first performed in 1790, and Beethoven's *Fidelio*, which went through three versions, 1805, 1806, and 1814–15. There are all sorts of reasons for Beethoven's difficulties with his only opera—his unfamiliarity with the form, his restless reconsideration and redoing of the work, his inability to satisfy himself—but one of them, I think, was the taunting antecedence of Mozart's most perfect and, unlike *Fidelio*, most effortless and, from Beethoven's rather staid point of view, most amoral performance.

Mozart has tried to embody an abstract force that drives people by means of agents (in *Così fan tutte*) or sheer energy (in *Don Giovanni*) without the reflective consent of their mind or will, in most instances. The intrigue in *Così fan tutte* is the result of a bet between Alfonso on the one hand and Ferrando and Guglielmo on the other, inspired neither by a sense of

The author is University Professor of English and Comparative Literature at Columbia University. A version of this paper was presented at the 1997 MLA convention in Toronto.

moral purpose nor by ideological passion. Ferrando is in love with Dorabella, Guglielmo with Fiordiligi; Alfonso bets that the women will be un-
faithful. A subterfuge is then enacted: the two men will pretend that they
have been called off to war. Then they will come back in disguise and woo
the girls, which is what happens. As Albanian (i.e., Oriental) men, the two
attempt to seduce each other's fiancée: Guglielmo quickly succeeds with
Dorabella; Ferrando needs more time, but he too is successful with Fiordiligi, who is clearly the more serious of the two sisters. Alfonso is helped in
the plot by Despina, a cynical maid who assists in her mistresses' downfall,
although she does not know of the bet among the men. Finally the plot is
exposed; the women are furious but return to their lovers, even though
Mozart does not specify exactly whether the pairs remain as they were at
the outset.

As many commentators have noted, the opera's plot has antecedents in
various "test" plays and operas, and, as Charles Rosen accurately says, it resembles "demonstration" plays written by Marivaux, among others. "They
demonstrate—prove by acting out—psychological ideas," Rosen adds, "and
'laws' that everyone accepted, and they are almost scientific in the way they
show precisely how these laws work in practice" (314). He goes on to speak
of *Così fan tutte* as "a closed system," an interesting, if insufficiently developed, notion, which does in fact apply to the opera.

We can learn a good deal here about *Così fan tutte* in the late-eighteenth-
century cultural setting by looking at Beethoven's reactions to the Lorenzo
da Ponte operas, which, as an Enlightenment enthusiast, Beethoven seems
always to have regarded with a certain amount of discomfort. Like many
critics of Mozart's operas, Beethoven is—so far as I have been able to discover—curiously silent about *Così fan tutte*. To generations of Mozart
admirers, including Beethoven, the opera seems to refuse the kind of meta-
physical, or social, or cultural significance found readily by Søren Kierkegaard and other luminaries in *Don Giovanni*, *Die Zauberflöte*, and *Le nozze di
Figaro*. There therefore seems very little to say about it. Most people concede that the music is extremely wonderful, but the unsaid implication is
that it is wasted on a silly story, silly characters, and an even sillier setting.
Significantly enough, Beethoven seems to have thought *Die Zauberflöte* the
greatest of Mozart's works (mainly because it was a German work), and he
is quoted by Ignaz von Seyfried, Ludwig Rellstab, and Franz Wegeler separately as expressing his dislike of *Don Giovanni* and *Figaro*; they were too
trivial, too Italian, too scandalous for a serious composer (Sonneck and
Martens). Once he expressed pleasure at *Don Giovanni*'s success, although
he was also said not to have wanted to attend his great older contemporary's
operas because they might make him forfeit his own originality.

These are the contradictory feelings of a composer who found Mozart's work as a whole unsettling and even disconcerting. Competitiveness is clearly a factor, but there is something else. It is Mozart's uncertain moral center, the absence in *Così fan tutte* of a specific humanistic message of the kind that *Die Zauberflöte* is so laboriously explicit about. What is still more significant about Beethoven's reactions to Mozart is that *Fidelio* can be interpreted as a direct, and in my opinion a somewhat desperate, response to *Così fan tutte*. Take one small but certainly telling example: Leonore's appearance at the outset disguised as a young man who comes to work as Rocco's assistant at the prison and engages the amorous attentions of Rocco's daughter, Marzelline. You could say that Beethoven has picked up a bit of the *Così* plot, in which the disguised lovers return to Naples and proceed to make advances to the wrong women, Ferrando coming on to Fiordiligi, Guglielmo on to Dorabella. No sooner does the intrigue start up than Beethoven puts a stop to it, revealing to the audience that young Fidelio is the ever-faithful and constant Leonore, come to Don Pizarro's prison to assert her fidelity and her *amour conjugal*, to use the exact title of Jean-Nicolas Bouilly's work, from which Beethoven took some of his material.

Nor is this all. Leonore's central aria, "Komm Hoffnung," is full of echoes of Fiordiligi's "Per pietà, ben mio" in act 2 of *Così*, which Fiordiligi sings as a last, forlorn plea to herself to remain constant and to drive away the dishonor she feels might be overcoming her as she suffers (and perhaps slightly enjoys) the impress of Ferrando's importuning: "Svenerà quest'empia voglia / L'ardir mio, la mia costanza, / Perderà la rimembranza / Che vergogna e orror mi fa" (I'll rid myself of this terrible desire with my devotion and love. I'll blot out the memory that causes me shame and horror). Memory for her is what she must try to hold on to, the guarantee of her loyalty to her lover, for if she forgets, she loses the ability to judge her present, timidly flirtatious, behavior for the shameful wavering it really is. And memory is also that which she must banish, as she recalls what she is ashamed about, her trifling with her real, but absent, lover, Guglielmo. Mozart gives her a noble, horn-accompanied figure for this avowal, a melody to be echoed in both key (E major) and instrumentation (horns) in Leonore's great appeal to hope, "lass den letzten Stern / Der Müden nicht erbleichen" (let this last star for the weary not be extinguished). But Leonore actually depends on hope and love; she does not doubt them, and although like Fiordiligi she has a secret, hers is an honorable one. There is no wavering, no doubting or timidity in Leonore, and her powerful aria, with its battery of horns proclaiming her determination and resolve, seems almost like a reproach to Fiordiligi's rather more delicate and troubled musings. Finally, Fiordiligi ends her aria on a note of regret, since she has already embarked on her course of betrayal, whereas of course Leonore is beginning her own ordeal of constancy and redemption on behalf of her still-missing husband.

One can see that fidelity and how to represent it is an issue of importance to Beethoven—an issue with which he wrestled in *Fidelio* independently of *Così*, but I think we have to grant that something about the world of Mozart's mature and greatest operas (with the exception of *Die Zauberflöte*) kept bothering Beethoven. One, of course, is their sunny, comic, and southern setting, which amplifies and makes more difficult to accept their underlying critique and implied rejection of the middle-class virtue that seems to have meant so much to Beethoven. Even *Don Giovanni*, the one da Ponte opera that twentieth-century reinterpretations have turned into a "northern" psychodrama of neurotic drives and transgressive passions, is essentially more unsettlingly powerful when enacted as a comedy of heedlessness and enjoyable insouciance. The style of famous twentieth-century Italian Dons like Ezio Pinza, Tito Gobbi, and Cesare Siepi prevailed until the 1970s, but their characterizations have given way to those of Thomas Allen, James Morris, Francesco Furlanetto, and Samuel Ramey, who represent the Don as a dark figure heavily influenced by readings in Kierkegaard and Sigmund Freud. *Così fan tutte* is even more aggressively southern in that all its Neapolitan characters are depicted as being shifty, pleasure-centered, and, with the exception of a brief moment here and there, selfish and relatively free of guilt, even though of course what they do is, by *Fidelio*'s standards, patently reprehensible.

Thus the earnest, heavy, and deeply serious atmosphere of *Fidelio* can be seen as a reproach to *Così*, which for all its ironies and beauties—well described by recent critics like Rosen and Scott Burnham—is grippingly without any kind of gravity at all. When the two pseudo-Oriental suitors are repulsed by Fiordiligi and Dorabella at the end of act 1, they drag the sisters into a broadly comic, false suicide scene. What transpires is based on the ironic disparity between the women's earnest concern for the men and the two suitors' amused playacting, with Despina's pretending to be a Mesmer-like "medico" whom the women can't understand ("Parla un linguaggio che non sappiamo") added on for good measure. Genuine emotion is thus undercut by the ridiculousness of what is going on. In act 2, where the disguises and playacting advance quite significantly into the emotions of the four main characters, Mozart extends the joke even further. The result is that the four do fall in love again, though with the wrong partners, and this undermines something very dear to Beethoven, constancy of identity. Whereas Leonore takes on the mask of the boy Fidelio, her disguise is designed to get her closer to, not further away from, her real identity as faithful wife. Indeed, all the characters in *Fidelio* are rigorously circumscribed in their unvarying essence: Pizarro as unyielding villain, Florestan as champion of good, Fernando as emissary of light, and so forth. This is at the opposite pole from *Così*, where disguises, and the wavering and wandering they foster, are the norm, constancy and stability mocked at as impossible. Despina puts it quite explicitly in act 2: "Quello ch'è stato, è stato, / Scordiamci del passato. / Rompasi omai quel laccio, / Segno di servitù" (What's done is done, and the less said, the better. Let's break all ties to the past, as a symbol of servitude).

Maynard Solomon notes that 1813 was an unproductive year for Beethoven, immediately after which he resorted to an "ideological/heroic" manner that yielded a series of noisily inferior works "filled with bombastic rhetoric and 'patriotic' excesses" that "mark the nadir of Beethoven's artistic career" (221, 223, 222). Such works as *Wellington's Victory* and several compositions written for the Congress of Vienna belong to the same period as the revisions to *Leonore* that resulted in the 1814 *Fidelio*. Solomon suggests that this ideological heroic style can be traced back to the 1790s in such works as the Joseph and Leopold cantatas, as well as Friedelberg war songs; yet in central works—Solomon in particular cites the Third and Fifth Symphonies, *Fidelio*, and the Incidental Music to *Egmont*—this aggressive and quasi-militaristic style "was sublimated into a subtle and profound form of expression" (223). It is therefore not surprising that *Fidelio*, the last work in this series, explicitly recalls some of its predecessors, perhaps as part of its obsession with the past. A well-known example occurs in the second scene of act 2: given permission by Don Fernando to release her husband from his chains, Leonore steps forward to perform the task of liberation. The music modulates from A major to F major and proceeds to a moving oboe solo and chorus borrowed almost literally from the *Cantata on the Death of Emperor Joseph II*: in the opera the episode bestows a majestic sense of order and calm on what has so far been a turbulent and confused scene. And—a second example—in the final scene of the opera it is hard not to hear echoes of the finale of the Fifth Symphony, animated and enlivened by words and voices. In both cases there is a similar, poundingly insistent use of C major to make affirmations and possess the tonic so as to dispel any lingering shadows.

Finally, *Fidelio* as a whole can be interpreted as an attempted counterblow to *Così fan tutte*, whose traces as an important antecedent are part of the past that Beethoven is working with. On the one hand, he incorporates the disguises, if not the malice, of *Così*; on the other, he uses unmasking as a way of asserting the virtues of the bourgeois matrimonial ideal of constancy in adversity. As I said earlier, memory in *Così fan tutte* is a faculty to be done away with in the pursuit of pleasure, whereas in *Fidelio* it is a vital part of character and, of course, constancy. Yet at the heart of the very thing that Beethoven is arguing for—persistence, the durability of fidelity, personal character as a source of continuity—there seems always to be a contradiction that will not disappear. It is lodged there as part of the very condition of its existence. Every affirmation, every instance of truth carries with it its own negation, just as every memory of love and conjugal fidelity also brings with it the danger and usually the actuality of something that will cancel it, annul it, obliterate it. Most critics who have written about Beethoven's powerfully heroic and teleological middle-period style seem to be more successful than Beethoven was in dispelling everything but the triumphalism with which he appears always to end his middle-period works. If we look a bit more closely at *Fidelio*, however, with its background of incorporated and canceled earlier versions in mind, we will see a more gripping, much more ambiguous and self-conscious struggle going on, a struggle that I believe makes *Fidelio* a more challenging opera than it usually appears to be.

Most commentators tend to treat the opening scene, in which Jaquino and Marzelline spar over their future together (which Marzelline dreads because she has already fallen in love with her father's assistant, Fidelio), as being on an inferior level of seriousness and importance. But the scene, like most things in opera, is a hybrid of elements that do not, because they cannot, blend; this produces a kind of volatility and tension that Beethoven throughout the opera is trying to represent. It derives at the outset from the incompatibility of desires and hopes: Jaquino's wanting at last to be alone with Marzelline, her pushing him away, Fidelio's interrupting their spat with insistent knocking. Each character has a conception of time that is different and doesn't mesh with those of the others; time is urgency for the eager young swain, hope for Marzelline, and, in Fidelio's case, anticipating and waiting. What is most symbolically freighted in the scene is Fidelio's first appearance, described meticulously by Beethoven: dressed as a young man, Fidelio carries a box of provisions on her back, a letter box on one arm, and, on her other arm, a collection of chains. We see the character, who is furnishing supplies and nourishment in the present, but also her encumbrances, which represent to her—as well as to her husband and perhaps the other prisoners—punishments brought on by past behavior.

Rocco's appearance gives Beethoven an opportunity to tie together the four characters of the opening sequence using a canon at the octave, also instigated by the second-act canon of *Così fan tutte*. The idea of the canon is similar in both works, a sort of *discordia concors* in which the characters express their incompatible sentiments in a rigorous, albeit meditative and even scholastic, form. "Mir ist so wunderbar" is significant for another reason, which takes us to Beethoven's problematic of representation in the opera and the kind of irreconcilability I mentioned earlier as hampering, and certainly rendering difficult, the affirmations he seems to be trying to make in this last version of his only opera. His choice of Bouilly's *Léonore, ou L'amour conjugal* as a story to set to music provided him, of course, with an entirely predictable rescue plot, in which wrongs are righted and the prisoners made free. One of the things we respond to in *Fidelio*, more in the last version than in the earlier versions, is the force and the authority with which one form of power is dislodged and a new, or at least much more acceptable, one is established in its place. Pizarro, the tempestuously bloody-minded tyrant, is replaced by Don Fernando, emissary of light and truth. No reason or logic is given for this salutary change except that it emanates from an offstage source of goodness and justice, concealed from and inaccessible to Florestan, Leonore, Pizarro, and the rest. Fernando makes clear to us that he has been dispatched by the monarch and is therefore a deputy, or substitute. In any event, unlike Don Alfonso, Fernando is supposed to produce a definitively salutary change in the turbulence of the social world depicted by Mozart as well as by Beethoven.

But Beethoven is not finally successful in convincing himself, or for that matter his attentive auditors, that the world of *Così* is so easily dispelled. Far from being stilled, the various doubts and uncertainties he experienced with *Fidelio* remain lodged at its heart, making the opera something more problematic, and interesting, than the simple paean to liberation and marital fidelity it is usually performed as. In part this ambiguity is an aspect of Beethoven's peculiar working through of affirmation and slump so characteristic of his other middle-period works, like the Fifth Symphony. But it is also the effect of Mozart's *Così fan tutte* gnawing away like a worm inside the sick rose, a destabilizing force that does not stop bothering, if not infecting and undermining, the imposing structure of *Fidelio*.

WORKS CITED

Burnham, Scott. *Beethoven Hero*. Princeton: Princeton UP, 1995.
Rosen, Charles. *The Classical Style: Haydn, Mozart, Beethoven*. New York: Viking, 1971.
Solomon, Maynard. *Beethoven*. New York: Schirmer, 1977.
Sonneck, Oscar George, and Frederick Herman Martens, ed. and trans. *Beethoven: Impressions of Contemporaries*. New York: Schirmer, 1926.

Why Music?

MARSHALL BROWN

My paper concerns the transformative power of music—what music does for culture and hence what it does for literature. I get to these matters at the end, through reflecting on a minute example of a particular issue in musical history. That issue is the origin of what historians of music call the classical style and historians of literature the romantic style. The example is a little-known work, probably by Mozart and catalogued as Köchel 404a. It consists of transcriptions for string trio of six Bach fugues, each preceded by a slow movement. Most of the slow movements were newly composed—perhaps a unique example of introductions by one composer to another composer's music. In each of the six pairs, a simpler-sounding, melodic composition—the technical term is *homophonic*—prefaces the interwoven texture of Bach's polyphony. My argument is that the origin of homophony out of polyphony illustrates the subverbal force of music. And while my conclusion doesn't explicitly draw the interdisciplinary lesson for literary study, the same kind of power should be felt and sought beneath the words of our verbal texts.

I start and end with a remark by Thomas Mann's Adrian Leverkühn: "Bach's problem [. . .] was this: how is harmonically meaningful polyphony possible? With the moderns the question presents itself somewhat differently. Rather it is: how is one to write a harmonic style that has the appearance of polyphony? Remarkable, it looks like bad conscience—the bad

The author is Professor of English and Comparative Literature and Adjunct Professor of Music at the University of Washington. A version of this paper was presented at the 1997 MLA convention in Toronto.

conscience of homophonic music in the face of polyphony" (*Doctor Faustus* 77; trans. modified). The first question poses the problem in formal terms: translated out of Leverkühn's technical language, it asks how a complex fugue could develop a clear and logical large-scale organization. The second question is similarly formalistic; the problem it poses is how a large-scale structure could develop the intricacy of a fugue. But then Mann, or his speaker, recasts the issue in psychological terms. Even more dramatically, in a famous study of Mozart that Mann read in English while working on the novel (*Story* 125), Alfred Einstein speaks of "a true crisis of creative activity [. . .] produced [in Mozart] by the encounter with a living polyphonic style" (153). Now there can be no doubt that Mozart encountered Bach as a remote and hallowed voice from the past, yet the relationship need not have been so agonized and agonistic as Mann and Einstein make it sound. The greatest living authority on the topic, Warren Kirkendale, perceives the situation quite differently. He writes, "The essential charm of classical fugato technique"—that is, of fugal devices within classical-period compositions—"lies in the way it traverses the styles of two different periods [and] imparts [a] historical charm to a work" (180). Confronting these different views, we might wonder what kind of charm is at play—delight, fascination, or mesmerization? Which masters the other when an assured fugue intrudes on a homophonic composition? How should we interpret the otherness of the historical predecessor at this juncture in the development of Western music?

While there are many theoretical frames available for approaching the Mozart-Bach confrontation, the most immediate of them is surely Lawrence Kramer's introductory essay "From the Other to the Abject," in his powerful recent book *Classical Music and Postmodern Knowledge* (33–66). Kramer begins by positing internal oppositions of content and form, or richness and unity, or movement and closure. These oppositions fashion a "logic of alterity" that, he says, is "far from stable" (34). Inherently "hierarchical" (37), binaries spread an infection of domination and submission. The casting may vary, but the roles are scripted; in Kramer's words, "many such reversals willy-nilly repeat the key terms of dominant structures in the very act of resisting them" (38). Hence, Kramer calls the musical other, in a term he borrows from the work of Julia Kristeva, "abject," which is to say, unhappily lacking an independent identity. Even before listening to a piece of music, we know that it will stage the triumph of formal identity over expressions in sound that are formless, or incompletely formed, or simply outmoded or inferior.

The unargued premise in Kramer's essay is that alterity entails hierarchy and domination. There are, however, other kinds of encounters with other

FIGURE 1 J. S. Bach, fugue from *Well-Tempered Clavier* 1, no. 8,
transcribed for string trio (Mozart K. 404a)

kinds of others. An important alternative, for instance, is the Hegelian
other, which does not challenge and undermine identity but precedes and
shapes it. Hegelian identity begins fluid, and the other is that through
which the self comes to determine and to know itself. Self and other, that
is, define themselves conjointly; the Hegelian other is as mysterious and as
open as the self, in a relation of mutual and ongoing accommodation and
regard. Hegel gives us one example of an othering that is transformative,
not objectifying.

The Bach fugue is a controlled transformational process. The subject of
the first of the fugues transcribed in K. 404a (fig. 1) has an unstable character
that fosters continuing movement rather than dramatic contrasts of keys.
Bach's fugues downplay the hierarchy of strong and weak beats that is fundamental to subsequent, classical-period music. Thus, while this fugue begins on the tonic D, the dominant A is both higher and longer, so that the D
sounds initially like a pickup to the A. At the start, as throughout the piece,
fugal entries come at unpredictable times as well as at varying distances in
pitch. The excitement of the piece derives from the steadily increasing pace
as entries get ever closer together and from the power of contrapuntal discovery of ever new ways of overlapping the subject with itself. The ethos,
however, remains artisanal; division of labor is not much in evidence, since
the three instruments have absolutely equal status and the structural contribution of the three voices is lucid at every point. The principle governing
the proliferating echoes is production rather than either aristocratic refinement or the dynamic mercantilism of classical-period balances of power.

The Mozartean introduction is remarkable for its absorption and renewal of Bach's compositional devices. It begins, as Bach does, with a single, unharmonized D (fig. 2). The cello answers the violin note for note in
the first bar, D-F-E-D, while in the second bar the two lower strings to-

FIGURE 2 Mozart, K. 404a, no. 1, introduction, mm. 1–5

gether outline the violin arpeggio: the viola has the higher notes, C# and E, while the cello has the lower A-C#-A. The first three bars initiate a classic cadence—tonic D minor, dominant A major, then renewed tonic D minor. Yet bar 3 quickly falls out of the tonic into G minor, and in fact the piece never rests on a full D-minor triad even where it asserts the tonic. The home key is always going or coming, never quite there. It all becomes preparation for the A-major chord that concludes the introduction and that makes Bach's D-minor beginning into a resolution, suddenly sounding more classically stable than has the introduction's D minor. The meter of the introduction is also fragile; it's rarely clear to the ear whether the principal stress falls on the first or the fourth beat of the bar. Bach's rhythmic and tonal freedom encourages a responding fluidity in the writing here. Voices multiply. First we hear one instrument, then two voices synchronized, then (first half of bar 2) overlapping voices, and finally, in bar 3, three independent voices (viola rising, cello falling, violin level). Through this composite of motivic echo and linear autonomy the piece acquires some of the texture of polyphonic music—a constant shifting around of consistent elements. Notable is the way the viola keeps changing allegiances, playing sometimes in tandem with the cello, sometimes with the violin, sometimes on its own. These variations are visible in the score even to those who don't read music, and throughout the piece the parallel voicing (viola playing in thirds or sixths with violin or with cello) resembles textures common in Bach. The introduction sounds radically different from Bach on account of its dramatic contrasts, such as that in bar 1 between the violin's dotted rhythms and the steady pace of the lower parts, yet it still resembles Bach in its regular alternation among solo voice, paired voices, and contrasting voices that creates the impression of interwoven polyphony.

In thus reconstituting polyphony as a texture that enriches classical organization, Mozart retroactively transforms its character. Structural in Bach, polyphony turns coloristic in Mozart; it becomes a device rather than a form. Bach draws out his fugue's subject, whereas Mozart, in a piece that changes mood every few bars, stresses the variable uses of fugal resources. Put in the simplest terms, while the Bach fugue *is* polyphonic and draws its power from its intellectual freedom, the Mozart introduction *feels* polyphonic and relies on expressive variation. Mozart gives Bach the stability of classical tonal structures and in return takes from him the intricate and flexible vivacity with which the slow tempo is handled. Introduction and fugue thus confront each other as two alternative conceptions of the nature of the musical work—as two selves, each identified as the other of its partner. Meaning, a relation of exterior sound to interior feeling, is at issue only in the introduction; in the fugue the issue is will in relation to its materials. Einstein and Mann speak of problems and anxieties, but Maynard Solomon's psychobiography of Mozart seems more judicious: contrasting Mozart's musical father to his oppressive biological father, Solomon calls the encounter with Bach "an opportunity to be grasped" rather than a threat to be warded off (121).

Building on these selected observations about the music, I return to the issue of otherness. When regarded as an instance of bad conscience or abjection, the historical other is treated as a personality invested with a role. In abjection, it would be said, Mozart meets an unfamiliar or unmastered psychological state in Bach's fugues, signaling a lack in himself; he subordinates his technique to Bach's, regresses into imitation, becomes hesitant, giddy, troubled. Kramer reports the condition as a reflex and a defense, "something within the subject that belongs to the sphere of fusion with the mother and must thus be cast violently out in order to maintain the subject's intactness" (58). On this account, art is most itself when most troubled, most contaminated; the demonic energy of wrestling with an incarnate fate is the true face of music and should be brought out in performance, "so that the music bec[omes] a tangible projection or articulation of bodily energy" (27; in a discussion of Mozart's Divertimento for String Trio, K. 563).

But I do not think that Kristeva herself views abjection as the unhappy detritus of psychological malfunction. Rather, abjection is a vertigo that precedes self-definition and remains polymorphous in its psychological manifestations. The abject often looks gruesome to us because, as Kristeva says, "corruption is its most common, most obvious appearance"; but that is only "the socialized appearance of the abject" and is not to be confused with its true nature (16). Emerging from what Kristeva calls the *chora*, the inchoate, disoriented space of the mother, the abject lies at the origin of individuation. It is a passing condition analogous to the *jouissance* of sexual excitement and, as Kristeva says, "confronts us [. . .] with our earliest attempts to release the hold of *maternal* entity even before existing outside of her, thanks to the autonomy of language" (13). Indeed, in "A Scription without Signs," a subsection in her book on abjection (73–75), Kristeva speaks of a writing that precedes language. In the Western cultural tradition, I need hardly point out, music is the preeminent example of such an expression that is written but not spoken. (Hence Kristeva speaks a couple of times of music as a "pure signifier" that is not semanticized [see 23 and esp. 49].) Working in the way Mozart works with Bach, music is the vehicle in Western culture of an abjection that is less conflictual, more enjoyable, more constructive, and more Hegelian than Kramer's account allows for.

Kristeva has two other terms for abjection; one fits K. 404a, the other does not. The term that does not fit is "the sublime." These are little pieces, seeking a natural accommodation with the past; they have their dramatic aspects, but it would stretch credibility to attribute flamboyance or transcendence to them. Sublimation is a cultural engagement involving the superego and the law; it is an identification with the other through which the self taps the mythic powers of the community at the expense of a certain repression or sacrifice of individual experience. The finale of Mozart's *Jupiter* Symphony is a sublime engagement with baroque counterpoint in this way. But in K. 404a there is neither fusion nor self-suppression. Mozart is finding his sea legs, not losing himself in the empyrean.

The Kristevan term that does fit is *flux*. Small in scale yet disjointed in sound, the introductions seem more a theater of rhetorical effects than patterned compositions. Mozart is coming to explore expressive possibilities, to recognize elements available for compositional forming, to know himself through knowing what he can make of the music of the past. It would not be too farfetched to term such minor writing (and I allude intentionally to Deleuze and Guattari here), with its attention to nuance, a deconstruction of earlier compositional practices. Indeed, it's time to introduce a pun that writers on music have surprisingly neglected and to say that Mozart here de-composes the resources of the fugue into local techniques of imitative echo and of accumulation. Still, to any of these formulations I prefer the term that is Hegel's alternative to sublimation and that evokes the primitiveness of the writing in K. 404a, the fracturing of effect, and the foundational character that goes along with the composition's fluid lack of identity. That Hegelian term is *Zugrundegehen* 'grounding through destroying.' Mozart here gets under Bach's skin in order to define and learn to know Bach and simultaneously to know and be himself more fully.

If we take our cue from the end of the Mann passage and erect K. 404a into a psychological confrontation, we hypostatize states of mind as preexisting conditions. But surely the effect of these quizzical little pieces is to explore and not to expose. There is nothing cathartic about them; they even seem to precede any narcissistic self-regard. Discursive utterances may never entirely loose themselves from engaged subjectivity. But music is not discursive and so can draw its power more directly from a realm that in worldly terms looks abject, corrupt, rotten, because it escapes self-definition but for that very reason is free of the anxieties that we attribute to persons. Bad conscience comes later than music. If, conversely, we return to the opening of the Mann passage and consider K. 404a a merely formal problem, we externalize and displace into the public realm a composition that was never an event, never published or performed in public. Really, these pieces are neither private nor public, for they preexist any such distinction of realms; they engage history from within the *chora* and hence neither express a psyche nor represent a culture. Rather, they come closer to what Theodor Adorno has called "the unconscious historiography of historical creation and miscreation" (506).[1] We have no adequate language for the musical space that precedes language. That is precisely why we need music.

NOTES

For their help in the preparation of musical examples, I would like to acknowledge the Center for Advanced Research Technology in the Arts and Humanities at the University of Washington.

[1]"Kunstwerke sind die bewußtlose Geschichtsschreibung des geschichtlichen Wesens und Unwesens." My rendering tries to reflect the untranslatable pun. The passage continues: "Understanding their language and reading them as such a historiography is the same thing. The path is indicated by the artistic technique, the logic of the image, its success or its fragility." This splendid brief text has not been translated and deserves to be better known.

WORKS CITED

Adorno, Theodor W. "Selbstanzeige des Essaybuchs 'Versuch über Wagner.'" *Die musikalischen Monographien. Gesammelte Schriften*. Vol. 13. Ed. Rolf Tiedemann. Frankfurt: Suhrkamp, 1971. 504–08.

Deleuze, Gilles, and Félix Guattari. *Kafka: Toward a Minor Literature*. Trans. Dana Polan. Minneapolis: U of Minnesota P, 1986.

Einstein, Alfred. *Mozart: His Character, His Work*. Trans. Arthur Mendel and Nathan Broder. London: Cassell, 1966.

Kirkendale, Warren. *Fugue and Fugato in Rococo and Classical Chamber Music*. Durham: Duke UP, 1979.

Kramer, Lawrence. *Classical Music and Postmodern Knowledge*. Berkeley: U of California P, 1995.

Kristeva, Julia. *Powers of Horror: An Essay on Abjection*. Trans. Leon S. Roudiez. New York: Columbia UP, 1982.

Mann, Thomas. *Doctor Faustus*. Trans. H. T. Lowe-Porter. New York: Knopf, 1948.

———. *The Story of a Novel: The Genesis of* Doctor Faustus. Trans. Richard Winston and Clara Winston. New York: Knopf, 1961.

Solomon, Maynard. *Mozart: A Life*. New York: Harper, 1995.

Art/Lit Combines; or, When a Pipe Is Only a Pipe

JEFFREY T. SCHNAPP

During the half decade of my graduate student years I lived with a painter, and when we fought, it was about the relation between visual and verbal artifacts. Deep in a formalist mood, she argued for the materiality of paint, for the intelligence of the trained eye and hand, for the rigors of a Cézanne-like model of figuration. She argued against the conceptualist bias of much contemporary art and against the excess "literariness" of work like the big abstract puzzle paintings that I had produced before my turn to literary studies. An unrepentant cerebralist, I defended conceptualism's and my honor. The separation between the visual and verbal domains was an arbitrary historical construct, I countered, proclaiming the pleasures of machine- and media-age art and the limits of a retinalism that I viewed, if not as a dead end, then as a throwback to the cult of handicrafts.

This argument, like most of its kind, wasn't always about what it pretended to be about. Nor was it meant to be resolved (though I eventually came around to seeing that she was right about my big puzzle paintings). In later years our ways parted, but our stances crisscrossed. She left behind the retina for affectively cool, computer-generated forms of collage that were very text- and theory-friendly. I went on to work in the interstices between art history and literature, shuttling back and forth between a premodern context, where text and image were so tightly wound around each other as to be inextricable, and a modern context, where

The author is Professor of Italian and Comparative Literature at Stanford University. A version of this paper was presented at the 1997 MLA convention in Toronto.

among my principal concerns were visual thinking and the seductive powers of new materials.

I begin with this anecdote only to state the obvious: namely, that the trajectories followed by the academic disciplines of art history and literary history have never been stable or predictable, certainly no more stable or predictable than the careers of their practitioners or the overlapping fields of objects that fall within their respective domains of inquiry. The disjunction between the two disciplines was the product of a distinctively Western institutional history, a history readily traceable to a taxonomy of disciplines first incubated in nineteenth-century German universities. And the same goes for postwar efforts to conjoin them under umbrellas as varied as semiology, the new cultural history, or visual culture studies. All are products of a parallel history and driven by new intra- and extrainstitutional pressures favorable to global, nondifferential approaches to art and literature. The now venerable machinery of disciplinary autonomy has thus come under repeated challenge from a new machine, the Art/Lit combine referred to in my title. It is this combine that I would like to talk about here from the perspective of a somewhat chastened ex-conceptualist. Too often the machine has been employed as a kind of mulching device that shreds every visual and verbal artifact into the same homogenized mulch of images and signs, so that, for instance, films can be read as if they were novels, language-based theorizations transposed over to pictures, bodies treated as texts, three-dimensional objects reduced to flat simulacra. But, as any Kansas farm boy can tell you, this ain't what a combine does best. A properly functioning one heads, threshes, and cleans the wheat; which is to say that it sifts and sorts. The quality of its yield depends on scrupulous attention to the particularity and materiality of each and every medium and to the signifying and symbolizing constraints and possibilities that attach to that medium. Words, images, and objects summon us in heterogeneous ways; in the following remarks, I scrutinize their workings in a single work: René Magritte's 1929 painting *The Betrayal of Images* (*La trahison des images*; fig. 1).

I have chosen this famous puzzle not just because I still delight in puzzle paintings but also because, like many of surrealism's visual products, it seems so emphatically to cast itself in a literary mold. Combining inscription and image according to the distinctive logic that Magritte would refine over the course of subsequent decades, the painting has long been considered something of a limit case in the productive coupling of image and word. Productive because, in the interpretation advanced by Michel Foucault in *This Is Not a Pipe*, what the work stages is a common failure of reference. According to Foucault's highly influential view, the work is a calligram whose verbal-visual alphabet Magritte constructs for purposes of

FIGURE 1 René Magritte, *The Betrayal of Images* (1929)

dismantling the oppositions between showing and naming, shaping and saying, reproducing and articulating, imitating and signifying, looking and reading.[1] Accordingly, the act of betrayal staged in *The Betrayal of Images* has as its target the mimetic regimen of Western metaphysics and assumes the form of a positive assertion of a simulacrum, which is to say, the affirmation of a syntagmatic axis of pure similitude emancipated from the paradigmatic axis of representation. Some features of this account are both accurate and insightful. But too much of the structuralist mulcher is at work here and too little of the combine. Magritte is not just a pictorial Raymond Roussel, as Foucault would have it; what gets mulched are those forms of signification and oblique reference that Magritte associated with his theme of themes: the mystery of objects.[2] What gets mulched is that dimension in which a pipe is only a pipe, an ordinary object endowed with everyday use-value and with a history that is at once private and public; a haunted and haunting object, therefore, that endures with its mute materiality in the company of related and unrelated families of objects.

That verbal play is assigned a key role in Magritte's art there can be little doubt. Titles, inscriptions, plaques, rebuses, and anagrams abound.[3] What is less self-evident is that the principal game in *The Betrayal of Images* hinges on the problem of visual-verbal (non-)(cross-)designation. This assertion is seemingly buttressed by Magritte's choice of title, though Foucault is careful to omit any mention of the title, fearing perhaps that the tight fit between title and work might undo an interpretation founded on the misfit among words, pictures, and things. There are good reasons for caution: the title was likely assigned some five or six years after the work was painted in 1929.[4] Caution is thrown to the wind, however, when it comes to dating—or, rather, backdating—the work to the year 1926: a gesture that conveniently places *The Betrayal of Images* right at the turning point when Magritte broke with the cubo-futurism and expressionism of his early years and emerged as himself, a leading pictorial interpreter of surrealism. The time shift permits a framing of Magritte's entire career (and by implication of surrealism itself) within the evolution of a single image and pictorial project. "The first version, that of 1926," the essay begins, only to leap immediately forward to 1966, the year before the artist's death: "The other version—the last, I assume—can be found in *Aube à l'antipodes*. The same pipe, same statement, same handwriting" (Foucault, *This Is* 15). Both the inaugural status granted the first version and its coupling with an "other" last version forty years later are at odds with the circumstances of Magritte's pictorial career—a career built around the reworking of a narrowly delimited universe of objects within which pipes recur obsessively, from beginning to end.

Far from inaugural, the pipe in *The Betrayal of Images* comes in the immediate wake of four pipe paintings, each of which explores the pipe's potential as a haunting object and each of which engenders a flurry of subsequent works: *The Future of Voices* (*L'avenir des voix*; 1927), *The Problem of Space* (*Le problème de l'espace*; 1928), *Pipe Camouflage* (*L'escamotage de la pipe*; 1928), and *Pipes Enamored of the Moon* (*Les pipes amoureuses de la lune*; 1928). The first, *The Future of Voices*, adopts what had already become a signature device: the hieroglyphic array or cabinet of object-obstacles, sometimes labeled, sometimes mislabeled, but more often unlabeled, that recurs in *The Alphabet of Revelations* (*L'alphabet des révélations*), *The Assignation* (*Le rendez-vous*), *Spontaneous Generation* (*La génération spontanée*), and *The Liberator* (*Le libérateur*). Whereas in the later works the array is cut into a single body, in *The Future of Voices* it floats loose against the sky and over a mountain landscape. Leaf, sponge, briefcase, and pipe hover like enigmatic voices (*voix*) in the wind that are also punning *voies* ("pathways") or *dévoies* ("detours"). Just what specific sort of celestial voice or pathway the pipe figures is hinted at in *The Problem of Space*, which portrays a pipe being smoked by a brick wall or, rather, smoked by a flat graffiti-like phantom who points to the illusionistic column to his side (fig. 2). The identity of the phantom and the nature of

FIGURE 2 René Magritte, *The Problem of Space* (1928)

his spatial magic become clear once we look at *The Barbarian* (*Le barbare*; 1927), in which he is revealed as Magritte's favorite doppelgänger, the dashing masked thief Fantômas, cast in the role of an illusionist. Fantômas, identified by his use of magical gadgets in both Pierre Souvestre and Marcel Allain's 1911 serial novel and Louis Feuillade's 1913 film, alternately towering above the city and blending into it, has the power of making objects and his person vanish and reappear in the service of artful crimes. His ability to elude even the most dogged detectives provided Magritte, the pictorial sleight-of-hand artist, with a model for his own light-fingered acts of levitation, piracy, disguise, and substitution. Hence the third in the series of pipe paintings, the biomorphic *Pipe Camouflage* (also known by the title *Première pipe*), in which label ("*la pipe*") and image correspond, though the blobby impasto that purportedly illustrates the inscription creates a sense of turbulence. Will the image grow into a pipe? Was it once a pipe (a failed "first" pipe)? To what degree is it mated to the pipe? Hence also successors like *The Littré Dictionary* (*Le Littré*; 1963), where the pipe is pulled out of a hat in the form of a rabbit; *Lady Beltham's Messengers* (*Les courriers de Lady Beltham*; 1964)—Lady Beltham was Fantômas's mistress—where the pipe appears as a cloud; *The Chorus of the Sphinxes* (*Le choeur des sphinges*; 1964), where the pipe is cut out of the forest; and *Musical Moments* (*Moments musicaux*) and

FIGURE 3 René Magritte, *The Philosophical Lamp* (1936)

Freedom of Worship (*La liberté des cultes*; both 1961), where the pipe pipes in music. The spell cast by the pipe appears celestial in the first instance, linked to vapors, perfumes, songs, and riddles; but, as already hinted in *The Problem of Space*, the pipe also serves as a conduit to and prolongation of a human body otherwise in hiding. The expression *casser la pipe*—literally "to break the pipe," figuratively "to die"—identifies smoking instrument with smoker's body, the body in question usually being masculine (though some sketches show clusters of pipes blossoming out of women's genitals and armpits, thereby designating the pipe also as a potential pipeline to or for feminine aromas).[5] Another pun helps explain the writhing bodies in *Pipes Enamored of the Moon*. *Faire une pipe*, after all, is street talk for fellatio. Magritte bravely explored the pipe's autoeroticism in a series of drawings of penis-pipes and penis-noses stuffing pipes, which came to a head in his 1936 *The Philosophical Lamp* (*La lampe philosophique*; fig. 3).[6] All of which brings the need for camouflage and denial out into the open. It is sometimes preferable that a pipe not be a pipe, especially when pipe making amounts to a hand or nose job.

The Betrayal of Images, in short, is neither a singular nor a definitive work. Even the versions enlisted by Foucault as "first" and "other" are parts of a complex sequence of workings and reworkings that appeared under various titles.[7] Which isn't to imply that my brief reconstruction of the pipe's private meanings has yet launched us fully outside the orbit of Foucault's axis of similitude, for these meanings have, in a sense, assumed the form of a nonhierarchical, mutually substitutable, potentially infinite series. But once the focus turns to the pipe's external history, I believe that it becomes clear why "Ceci n'est pas une pipe" is also the tag line for a bigger story: that of how the briar pipe was enshrined as a modernist signature object. Every single one of Magritte's pipes, from his 1920 cubo-futurist *Portrait of Pierre Bourgeois* (*Portrait de Pierre Bourgeois*) to later experiments like *The Sleepwalker* (*Le somnambule*), *Freedom of Worship*, and *The Possessive Pronoun* (*Le pronom possessif*), belongs to a distinctive category: the bent or straight briar pipe. This pipe is not just a cipher or a magical gadget that allows the pictorial Fantômas to escape the iconographic police and to fade away into the woodwork or brickwork. It corresponds to an actual object or, rather, to a set of objects that fed both a public image and an appetite. Like all pipe smokers, Magritte fetishized his pipes. They accompanied him from his youth through the final years of his life. They stood in for him in photographs, next to his wife; they were the mark of Magritte the modern man and the modern artist.[8] And he signed every one of them with his own corporate *griffe*, always scrawled in the same schoolboy hand.

The briar pipe is not any old pipe. It is a distinctive product of the era of industry, the result of up to thirty mechanical operations requiring precision tools and skilled tool operators. It combines a natural material, brier-root (*bruyère*), discovered in Corsica in the mid–nineteenth century thanks to patriotic pilgrimages to Napoleon's birthplace, with an artificial material, the early plastic vulcanite; both the wood and the plastic are baked, turned on lathes, finished, fitted, and polished.[9] First devised in the 1830s, popular only at the end of the century, the briar was far more resistant to breakage than its clay and meerschaum counterparts. But its success as a signature object was especially due to its clean lines, lines that translated into a cleaned-up image for the pipe smoker.

Tobacco had figured, alongside sugar, tea, coffee, and eau-de-vie, in Honoré de Balzac's 1838 *Traité des excitants modernes* as the most powerful of modern hyperstimulants:

> [Under its sway] you soar into a world of fantasy; like a child armed with a butterfly net racing across a meadow chasing fireflies, you snare your fluttering dreams [*délires*], dreams that surface in their ideal form such that one is readily inclined to make them into realities. The most glorious hopes prance by time and again, not as illusions, but bodies, bodies dancing like so many Taglionis and with such grace! You know what I'm

> talking about, fellow smokers! The spectacle enhances nature's beauty,
> all of life's difficulties vanish, life becomes effortless, intelligence lucid,
> the gray atmosphere of thought turns sky blue. Yet, odd as it may seem,
> the curtain falls on this opera as soon as hookah, cigar, or pipe goes out.
>
> (52–53; my trans.)

The cultivator of this practice was thought to be living fast and at the expense of his reproductive powers.[10] Marked as a decadent, the emblem of a modernity whose signage reads "No Exit" and "No Future," the mid-century pipe smoker is typified by Gustave Courbet's 1850 *Portrait of Baudelaire* (*Portrait de Baudelaire*) and by his *Self-Portrait* (*Auto-portrait*; commonly known as *Man with Pipe* [*L'homme à la pipe*]). The subject of the latter work was, in Courbet's own words, "a fanatic, an aesthete [. . .] a disillusioned man," and his social pigeonhole was the bohemian demimonde of Degas's *Absinthe* (1876), a marginal world evocative in turn of the lowly smokers, drinkers, and gamblers of seventeenth-century Dutch genre painting (qtd. in Ambrosini 34).[11] It was precisely these two universes—the bohemian demimonde and genre painting—that many generations of artists from Edouard Manet and Paul Cézanne to Theo van Doesburg set out to modernize, to virilize, and to heroicize, displacing, in the process, the old clay-pipe-smoking decadent subject with his briar-pipe-smoking industrial antitype (see Egbers). At the end of the genealogical line, we thus arrive at a new beginning: a man-machine for whom hyperstimulus translates into not dissipation but hyperproductivity and comfort. Such an individual is Fernand Léger's *Man with Pipe* (1920), whose pipe functions as the smokestack of a squeaky-clean factory-house (fig. 4).[12]

The shift may be reduced to the tale of two pipes. The first appears in a sketch left behind in Munich by Courbet in 1869. The legend accompanying this portrait of self as pipe reads "Courbet sans idéal et sans religion" ("Courbet without ideals and without religion" [Toussaint 97]).[13] The second appears atop the label "Coopérative la Pipe" on the final page of Le Corbusier's *Towards a New Architecture* (1923) and must also be taken as a self-portrait (fig. 5). There it hovers, alongside photographs of the rooftop autodrome of Fiat's Lingotto assembly plant, as the compacted sign of everything that has come before it in the course of the book's verbal-visual argument: the engineer, the plan, midwestern grain silos, the steamship, the airplane, the automobile, the house-machine. That it crystallizes the purist ideals and religion preached by Le Corbusier is made clear by the accompanying text:

FIGURE 4 Fernand Léger, *Man with Pipe* (1920)

> There reigns a great disagreement between the modern state of mind, which is an admonition to us, and the stifling accumulation of age-long detritus.
>
> The problem is one of adaptation, in which the realities of our life are in question.
>
> Society is filled with a violent desire for something which it may obtain or may not. Everything lies in that: everything depends on the effort made and the attention paid to these alarming symptoms.
>
> Architecture or Revolution.
>
> Revolution can be avoided. (288–89)[14]

The briar pipe embodies an architecture capable of providing technical solutions to modern problems. The pipe's pure lines, its freedom from ornament, its functionalism all signify an emancipatory rationalization of life and the democratization of mass comfort, consumption, and thrills. But they also figure the architect himself, the demiurge whose once hopelessly fluttering pipe dreams are now threatening to reengineer the real.

Towards a New Architecture was an epochal text. Both its sensibility and its catalog of machines for modern living permeate the visual environment of the subsequent decade. Among the many places where the book's presence can be felt is work of another man with a pipe: Piet Mondrian, the Dutch abstractionist and theoretician of neoplasticism. After long years devoted to elaborating an austere language of two-dimensional primary-colored planes, Mondrian decided to go three-dimensional in the 1920s. He transformed his Paris studio into a neoplasticist utopia: a "superhuman," "almost mathematically pure," hygienic space in which, anticipating a future cityscape in which beauty, health, and shelter would be ensured not by means of trees and flowers but "by opposing buildings and empty spaces in an equilibrated way," the individual can transcend his "petty personality" and "be uplifted through beauty toward universal life" (Postma and Boekraad 76).[15] Only two warm-bodied intruders are permitted into this glacially cool, smoke-free transformation chamber: a coal-burning stove and a briar pipe. The pipe's roving presence is signaled by the ashtray that appears in every site photograph, from the reconstruction done in 1989 to André Kertesz's famous 1926 photograph *Mondrian's Glasses and Pipe*. Like Léger's man-machine, the neoplastic superman needs his briar. Without it, his universal plans might go up in (nonproductive) smoke.

Towards a New Architecture's impact is even more direct on Magritte than on Mondrian. Magritte's ties to Le Corbusier date back to 1920 and involve the circle assembled around the Belgian revue *7 Arts*, among whose founders was the subject of Magritte's first pipe-smoker portrait, Pierre Bourgeois. The ties' apogee was reached in 1922, when Magritte coauthored

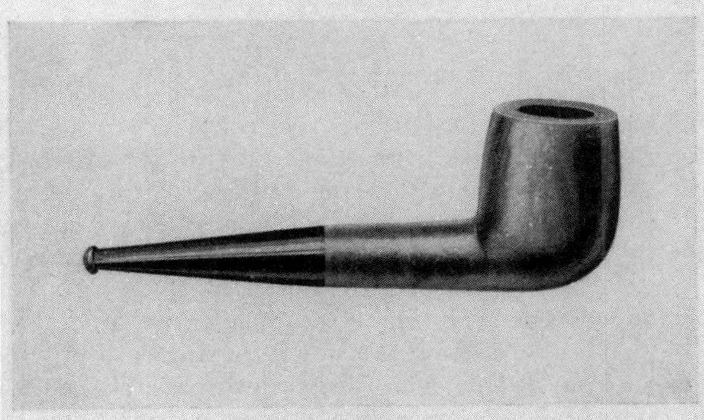

rement, logiquement, clairement, qui produit avec pureté des choses utiles et utilisables et, d'autre part, il se retrouve déconcerté, dans un vieux cadre hostile. Ce cadre, c'est son gîte; sa ville, sa rue, sa maison, son appartement se dressent contre lui et, inutilisables, l'empêchent de poursuivre dans le repos le même chemin spirituel qu'il parcourt dans son travail, l'empêchent de poursuivre dans le repos le développement organique de son existence, lequel est de créer une famille et de vivre, comme tous les animaux de la terre et comme tous les hommes de tous les temps, en famille organisée. La société assiste ainsi à la destruction de la famille et elle s'aperçoit, avec terreur, qu'elle en périra.

Un grand désaccord règne entre un état d'esprit moderne qui est une injonction, et un stock étouffant de détritus séculaires.

C'est un problème d'adaptation où les choses objectives de notre vie sont en cause.

La société désire violemment une chose qu'elle obtiendra ou qu'elle n'obtiendra pas. Tout est là; tout dépend de l'effort qu'on fera et de l'attention qu'on accordera à ces symptômes alarmants.

Architecture ou révolution.

On peut éviter la révolution.

FIGURE 5 Le Corbusier, final page from *Towards a New Architecture* (1923)

the purist treatise *L'art pur: Défense de l'esthétique*.[16] Subsequent years saw him drift away and out into the orbit of Dada, pursue advertising work, and abandon painting for nearly two years. Only in 1925 did Magritte resume painting, but reborn as a surrealist whose feeling for landscapes and objects had been reshaped by the work of Max Ernst and Giorgio de Chirico. The result was a turn away from conventional figuration to the dramas of objects with which this essay began. Much was jettisoned in the process of Magritte's conversion to surrealism, but not his membership in the Coopérative la Pipe. A prominent device in the family of devices that compose even his earliest hieroglyphic arrays, the briar pipe receives its first full-fledged portrait in 1929. This pipe that is not a pipe, as I hope has been amply demonstrated, shows up preannounced, accompanied by a great deal of figurative baggage. Still very much a briar pipe, still very much a *Magritte*, it arrives in all of its resplendent pipehood, a distinctive object of and instrument for modern desires. Yet, thanks to the intrusion of a verbal legend, it is now able to shun the mantle of pipehood in the name of a new game of nonidentity whose nature may be ironic or mocking or sententious and serious but whose suggestive power relies on our understanding of a prior visual legend.

NOTES

This essay was sketched out while I was Ailsa Bruce Melon Senior Fellow at the Center for Advanced Study in the Visual Arts at the National Gallery of Art, Washington, DC. I wish to express my gratitude to the center and to its director, Henry Millon, for providing such a congenial setting for these ruminations.

[1] The calligram "aspires playfully to efface the oldest oppositions of our alphabetical civilization: to show and to name; to shape and to say; to reproduce and to articulate; to imitate and to signify; to look and to read" (Foucault, *This Is* 21).

[2] Foucault made the connection between Magritte and Roussel in a letter, to which Magritte replied: "I am pleased that you recognize a resemblance between Roussel and whatever is worthwhile in my own thought. What he imagines evokes nothing imaginary, it evokes the reality of the world that experience and reason treat in a confused manner" (qtd. in Foucault, *This Is* 58). Foucault was the author of *Raymond Roussel*.

[3] Among the many studies of Magritte's career, see Meuris; Torczyner; Sylvester, *Magritte*.

[4] On questions of dating see Sylvester, *Oil*; Blavier.

[5] Multiple pipes projecting out of the body of one person are a frequent motif in Magritte's work, for instance, in his *The Cripple* (*Le stropiat*) series. A malodorous freak with a bulbous plaid nose, the cripple smokes so many pipes that he appears as a literal *tête de pipe* (or "dickhead"). Analogous female images abound, but they rarely smoke. Rather, depicted nude with pipes issuing from their bodies, they loom as objects of desire. In either case pipes provide relays to zones of particular sensual intensity—mouth, lips, eyes, underarms, breasts, genitals—with the result that the multiplication of pipes figures an excessive, even monstrous, carnality. Nowhere are pipes simply or unproblematically penile.

[6]Far subtler overlay paintings like *The Thunderbolt* (*La foudre*), in which a pipe hovers mysteriously over a woman's naked body, seem to rely upon the same figurative nose-to-penis-to-pipe-to-mouth circuit exposed in *The Philosophical Lamp*, as hinted by the homonymic doubling between *la foudre* and *la foutre* ("to fuck her").

[7]On the overall development of this series, the most exhaustive study is Blavier's.

[8]Magritte's photographs are reproduced in Paquet.

[9]"The discovery of the ideal pipe material, the so-called briar-root, was quite accidental, as such discoveries often are. It was incidental to the revival of the cult of Napoleon in the second decade following his death in 1821, when the disasters of 1814 were forgotten. Those who wished to honor their late Emperor were not content to visit the tomb at Les Invalides, whither his ashes had been brought from St. Helena, but made a pilgrimage also to the birthplace of the Little Corporal in Corsica. Among these pilgrims was a French pipe-maker, who during his stay had the misfortune to break or lose his meerschaum pipe" (Dunhill, *Pipe* 193). On the production process of briar pipes, see Alfred Dunhill, *The Gentle Art of Smoking* (93–112); and on the pipe's history and place in Western image making, see Alexis Liebaert and Alain Maya, *Le grand livre des pipes*. Vulcanite was invented in 1878 and quickly superseded horn and amber.

[10]Balzac observes, "Since few Turks are wealthy enough to own one of those famous seraglios where they can waste away their youth, it follows that their early loss of generative powers may chiefly be attributed to the effects of three other stimulating agents—tobacco, opium, and coffee—the consumption of which renders a thirty-year-old Turk equal to a fifty-year-old European" (57; my trans.).

[11]For a mature example of the smoker iconography employed by Manet, see *The Beer Server* (*La serveuse de bocks*; 1879). Another prolific pipe smoker and pipe painter, Vincent van Gogh, was similarly interested in reworking elements from seventeenth-century Dutch genre painting.

[12]Many other Léger images come to mind, such as his 1920 oil painting *The Three Comrades*, in Amsterdam's Municipal Museum collection.

[13]Courbet's public image was so closely connected with his pipe smoking that contemporary cartoons always represented him in the act of smoking.

[14]The connection between Magritte's *The Betrayal of Images* and Le Corbusier's final image was noted long ago by Patrick Hughes, as indicated by Blavier (11).

[15]The full passage from the neoplasticist manifesto reads: "Man will choose or create his own material environment. He will not regret the absence of natural appearance, that aspect of nature which most people still regret even as they are forced against their will to abandon it. The truly evolved human will no longer attempt to bring beauty, health, or shelter to the city's streets and parks by means of trees and flowers. *He will build healthy and beautiful cities by opposing buildings and empty spaces in an equilibrated way.* Then the outdoors will satisfy him as much as the interior. [. . .] Through the intensified but variable rhythm of relationships in an almost mathematically pure plastic means, this art can come close to the 'superhuman' and certainly the universal. That is possible, even today, because art anticipates life. Neo-Plastic art loses something of the superhuman as it becomes realized in life in the form of material environment, yet retains it enough for the individual no longer to feel his petty personality but to be uplifted through beauty toward universal life." The title of the manifesto is "Neo-Plasticism: The Home—the Street—the City."

[16]The work was written with his friend and fellow painter Victor Servrankx. It was never published. On this episode, see Sylvester, *Magritte* 36.

WORKS CITED

Ambrosini, Lynne. "Edouard Manet's *Smoker*: Making Old Genres Modern." *Porticus* 17–19 (1994–96). 33–37.

Balzac, Honoré de. *Traité des excitants modernes*. Paris: Castor Astral, 1992.

Blavier, André. *Ceci n'est pas une pipe: Contribution furtive à l'étude d'un tableau de René Magritte*. Opinions et Documents 1. Verviers: Temps Mêlés, 1973.

Corbusier, Le. *Towards a New Architecture*. Trans. Frederick Etchells. London: Rodker, 1931.

Dunhill, Alfred. *The Gentle Art of Smoking*. New York: Putnam, 1954.

——. *The Pipe Book*. London: Baker, n.d.

Egbers, Henk. *Tabak in de Kunst*. Weert: Van Nelle, 1987.

Foucault, Michel. *Raymond Roussel*. Paris: Gallimard, 1963.

——. *This Is Not a Pipe*. Trans. James Harkness. Berkeley: U of California P, 1982.

Liebaert, Alexis, and Alain Maya. *Le grand livre des pipes*. Paris: Flammarion, 1993.

Meuris, Jacques. *Magritte*. Trans. J. A. Underwood. New York: Artabras, 1988.

Paquet, Marcel. *Photographies de Magritte*. Paris: Contrejour, 1982.

Postma, Frans, and Cees Boekraad. *26, rue du Départ: Mondrian's Studio in Paris, 1921–1936*. Berlin: Ernst, 1995.

Sylvester, David. *Magritte: The Silence of the World*. New York: Abrams, 1992.

——. *Oil Paintings, 1916–1930*. London: Wilson, 1992. Vol. 1 of *René Magritte: Catalogue raisonné*. Menil Foundation. 5 vols.

Torczyner, Harry. *Magritte: Ideas and Images*. Trans. Richard Miller. New York: Abrams, 1977.

Toussaint, Hélène. *Gustave Courbet, 1819–1877*. Paris: Editions des Musées Nationaux, 1977.

Renunciation Is a P[ei]rcing Virtue

SUSAN HOWE

> *Renunciation — is a piercing*
> *Virtue —*
> *the letting go*
>
> —Emily Dickinson

The slides I ordinarily show during my panel talk on Charles Sanders Peirce are all taken from his original manuscripts. They are *not* shot from microfilm copies or photocopies. A good number are from two small manuscript notebooks dating between 1905 and 1910, so this is work produced when he was between sixty-six and seventy-one years old. Others are from separate pages organized and grouped together by later scholars, philosophers, and editors; so the chronology is mixed. One of the manuscript books contains existential graphs. The other consists of definitions and number calculations for an analysis of time. During *this* twenty minute time period, putting thought in motion to define art in a way that includes science, these manuscripts are free to be drawings even poems. Perhaps the Word, giving rise to all pictures and graphs, is at the center of Peirce's philosophy.

I include here three short poems from a recent series I titled "Arisbe," and then read from one or two of the slides because there always was and always will be a secret affinity between symbolic logic and poetry.

The author is a poet and Professor of English at the State University of New York, Buffalo.

1908: CHARLES SANDERS PEIRCE

4 given Rays
can be crossed by how many rays?

———————

The design is to trace the analysis of this
problem back to its
first foundations

It is necessary to consider continuity
and I think the primitive and simple
continuity has the form of that of time
& therefore begin by considering time.
"Analysis of Time" (MS 138)

NAME IN FULL: Charles S. Peirce ("I am variously listed in print as Charles Santiago Peirce, Charles Saunders Peirce, and Charles Sanders Peirce. Under the circumstances a noncommital S. suits me best" [MS 1611]). PIERCE *v*; to run into or through as an instrument or pointed weapon does. PURSE *n*; a small bag closed with a drawstring and used to carry money. Even if he trained himself to be ambidextrous and could amaze his undergraduate classmates at Harvard by writing a question on the blackboard with one hand while simultaneously answering it with the other, P<u>eer</u>/se pronounced P<u>urr</u>/se blamed most of his problems on his own left-handedness.

1893: JOHN JAY CHAPMAN to MRS. HENRY WHITMAN: Charles Peirce wrote the definition of University in the Century Dictionary. He called it an institution for purposes of study. They wrote to him that their notion had been that a university was an institution for instruction. He wrote back that if they had any such notion they were grievously mistaken, that a university had not and never had had anything to do with instruction and that until we got over this idea we should not have any university in this country. He commended Johns Hopkins.

The abrupt dismissal of Charles Sanders Peirce by the trustees of the Johns Hopkins University from his position there as part-time lecturer in logic and literature (1879–84), for reasons never fully explained, might be termed a form of banishment. In spite of clear knowledge that he was a profoundly original thinker, an effective, often charismatic, teacher, in spite of the efforts of William James, who consistently recommended him for academic positions at Harvard University, the University of Chicago, and elsewhere, after 1884 Peirce was never again offered another teaching appointment. Scattered rumors and slanders (many of them continue to this day) variously represent America's great logician, the founder of pragmatism and one of the founders of mathematic, or symbolic, logic, as a decadent aesthete, a lecher, a liar, a libertine, queer, a wife beater, an alcoholic, a drug addict, a plagiarist, a wannabe robber baron, an unpractical pragmatist with suspect metaphysics.

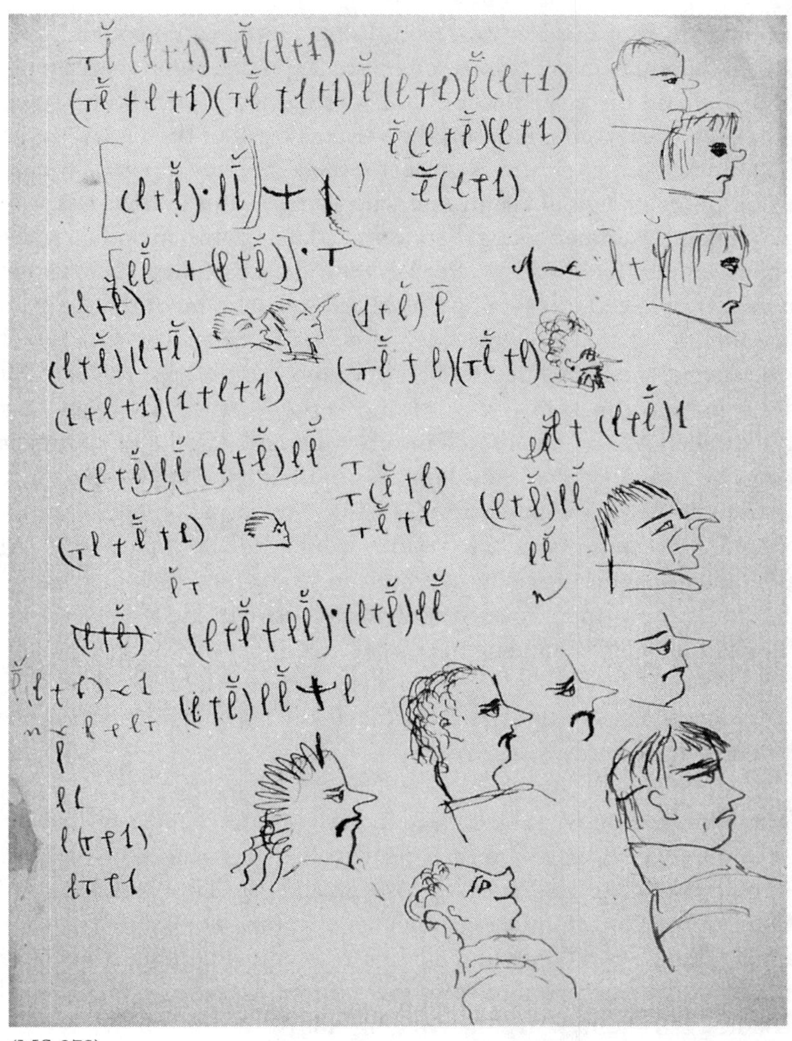

(MS 278)

In 1891 Peirce, the first meteorologist to use a wavelength of light as a unit of measure and the inventor of the quincuncial projection of two spheres, was forced to resign from the United States Coast and Geodetic Survey, where, among other things, he had been in charge of gravity and pendulum research for twenty years. According to Beverly S. Kent's *Charles S. Peirce: Logic and the Classification of the Sciences*, the United States Coast and Geodetic Survey's international reputation as America's premier scientific institution was largely indebted to Peirce's genuis.

Four years after his dismissal from Johns Hopkins, Peirce and his second wife Juliette Annette Froissy or Pourtalai pooled some recently inherited money and for one thousand dollars they acquired Thomas Quick's hundred-and-forty-acre farm on the western bank of the Delaware River ("the wildest county of the Northern States"). They covered the outer walls of Quick's original farmhouse with shingles in the then fashionable New England "summer cottage" style and added rooms, including a library for his large book collection. Perhaps the Peirces called their property "Arisbe" after the ancient colony of Miletus, the home of the first Greek philosophers, Thales, Anaximander, and Anaximenes, who first searched for the Arche, the Principle, the first of things. Or perhaps it was in reference to book 6, lines 13–19, in Homer's *Iliad* (strong-founded Arisbe, where dwelled Axylos, a man rich in substance and a friend to all humanity since in his house by the wayside he entertained all comers). An undated draft entry in Peirce's handwriting (MS 1611) for the *Biographical Dictionary of Notable Americans* reads: "He resides at his wife's country seat 'Arisbe,' near Milford, Pa., where he has a free school of philosophy, furnishing remunerative employment to such students as desire it. He also exercises the professions of chemist and engineer."

The school never materialized. Recklessly they acquired more land, apple and nut orchards, a slate quarry—

Forced to live on what he could earn by temporary means, Peirce produced a variety of book reviews and essays (often anonymously) for a variety of journals including the *Nation*, the *Monist*, and *Popular Science Monthly*. He gave occasional lectures, tutored students privately, worked on translations from the French and German, collaborated on various encyclopedias and dictionaries (he composed most of the definitions on logic, mathematics, mechanics, astronomy, astrology, weights, measures, and all words relating to universities for W. D. Whitney's *Century Dictionary* and most of the articles on logic for J. M. Baldwin's the *Dictionary of Philosophy and Psychology*), served as a consulting chemical engineer for the St. Lawrence Power Company, gave lessons in elocution to Episcopal ministers, developed an invention for electrolytic bleaching, concocted a "Genuine Imitation/Cologne Water," joined well-heeled fellow members of the Century Club in New York in a venture to produce cheap domestic lighting from acetylene gas with a generator he invented and patented. But the national economic collapse during the 1890s left him bankrupt. Even the Century Club expelled him around 1898. After 1900 Peirce gave up trying to earn his living either by teaching or by science pure and applied and became the first American to list his profession as that of logician—a "bucolic logician," as he put it.

During the summer of 1997 I spent many hours in New Haven in the bowels of Sterling Library because that's where the microform room is, almost underground, next to preservation. In an adjoining, more cryptlike corridor, behind some discarded, hopelessly outdated computer terminals and microfilm viewers (nothing from the outside will ever be seen on *them* again), the thirty-eight-reel *Microfilm Edition of the Charles S. Peirce Papers in the Houghton Library of Harvard University (1964; with supplemental reels issued in 1971)* is packed inside two drawers of a slate-gray metal file cabinet. No one stays for long in this passage or chamber because it's freezing and the noise from air-conditioning generators the university recently installed in a basement immediately underneath resembles roaring or loud sobbing.

> Suppose a man is locked in a
> room and does not want to go
> out his staying is voluntary
> is he at liberty no necessity
> What shall we finally say if
> Members of the Department of
> Philosophy Harvard University
> undertake the task of sorting
> his papers now in the custody
> of Harvard's Houghton Library

The microform room at Sterling has several new microfilm readers with Xerox copiers attached. At the left of each viewing screen there is a thin slot for a copy card. Above each slot five singular electric letters spell H E L L O in red as if to confide affection

in all their minute and terrible detail these five little icons could be teeth.

A microphotograph is a type of photography nearly as old as photography itself in which an original document is reproduced in a size too small to be read by the naked eye so here the human mind can understand far from it. Film in the form of a strip of 16 or 35 millimeters wide bearing a photographic record on a reduced scale of printed or other graphic matter for storage or transmission in a small space is enlarged to be read on a reading machine combining a light source and screen together in compact cabinet. The original remains perfect by being perfectly what it is because you can't touch it.

Upstairs at the circulation desk, an employee has put a nondescript signal on the horizontal black strip that bisects the verso oblong surface of my white plastic YALE UNIVERSITY LIBRARIES (Lux et Veritas) copy card so the space the cut encloses now represents five dollars. As if invisibilty is the only reality on the rapid highway of mechanical invention HELLO draws card number 156186 inside itself with a hiss.

It is strange how the dead appear in dreams where another space provides our living space as well. Another language another way of speaking so quietly always there in the shape of memories, thoughts, feelings, which are extramarginal outside of primary consciousness, yet must be classed as some sort of unawakened finite infinite articulation. Documents resemble people talking in sleep. To exist is one thing to be perceived another. I can spread historical information words and words we can never touch hovering around subconscious life where enunciation is born in distinction from what it enunciates when nothing rests in air when what is knowledge?

A person throws a stone
as fact through air not
face but appearance of
fact floating in vacua
Blind existential being
may possibly not occur
at all we know nothing
with absolute certainty
of existent things not even
the single "word" <u>the</u>

Lewis Mumford noted in *The Brown Decades: A Study of the Arts in America, 1865–1895* (1931) that the publication of Peirce's manuscripts had lagged for lack of a few thousand dollars to guarantee the initial expenses of his collected works and compared the situation to the concealment of Emily Dickinson's manuscripts by overzealous guardians. Martin Gardner wondered in *Logical Machines and Diagrams* (1982) if Peirce harbored unconscious compulsions toward cloudy writing that would enable him to complain later of his critics' inability to understand him. In "Communication, Semiotic Continuity, and the Margins of the Peircian Text" (1997), Mary Keeler and Christian Kloesel tell us the secondary literature on Peirce demonstrates only the hardiest scholars have made use of his manuscripts and even then only by way of photocopies, that his work is unpublishable in print form. I wonder why manuscripts are so underestimated in all academic disciplines even in science, linguistics, semiology. It's almost 1999.

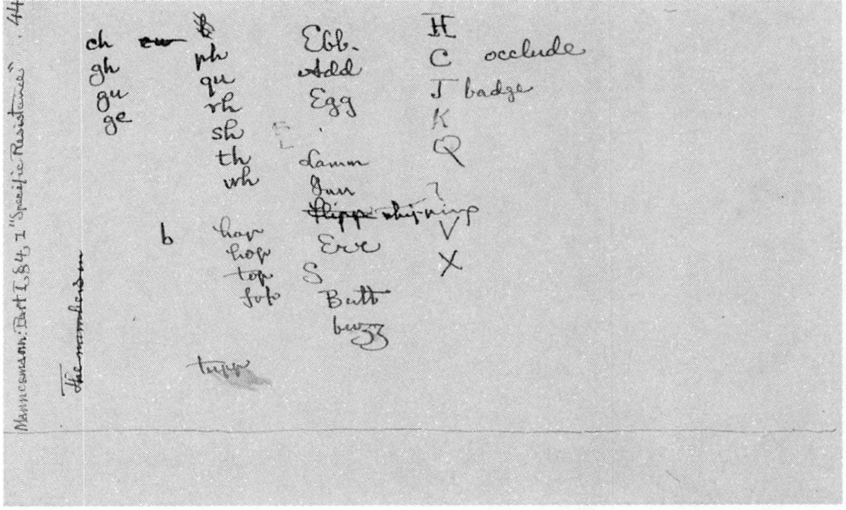

(MS 278)

While outlining the pragmatic principle in the *North American Review* (Oct. 1871) Peirce first coined the term PRAGMATISM, but his idea went unrecognized or unacknowledged until William James publicly used the word in a lecture at Berkeley in 1898 titled "Philosophical Conceptions and Practical Results." James said he was presenting "the principle of Peirce, the principle of pragmatism." Their ideas on the term and the principle were never the same. In 1903, after attending Peirce's Lowell lectures, James referred to the current ideas of his friend as "—flashes of light relieved against Cimmerian darkness." In 1905 Peirce invented the term *pragmaticism* because it was "ugly enough to keep it safe from kidnappers."

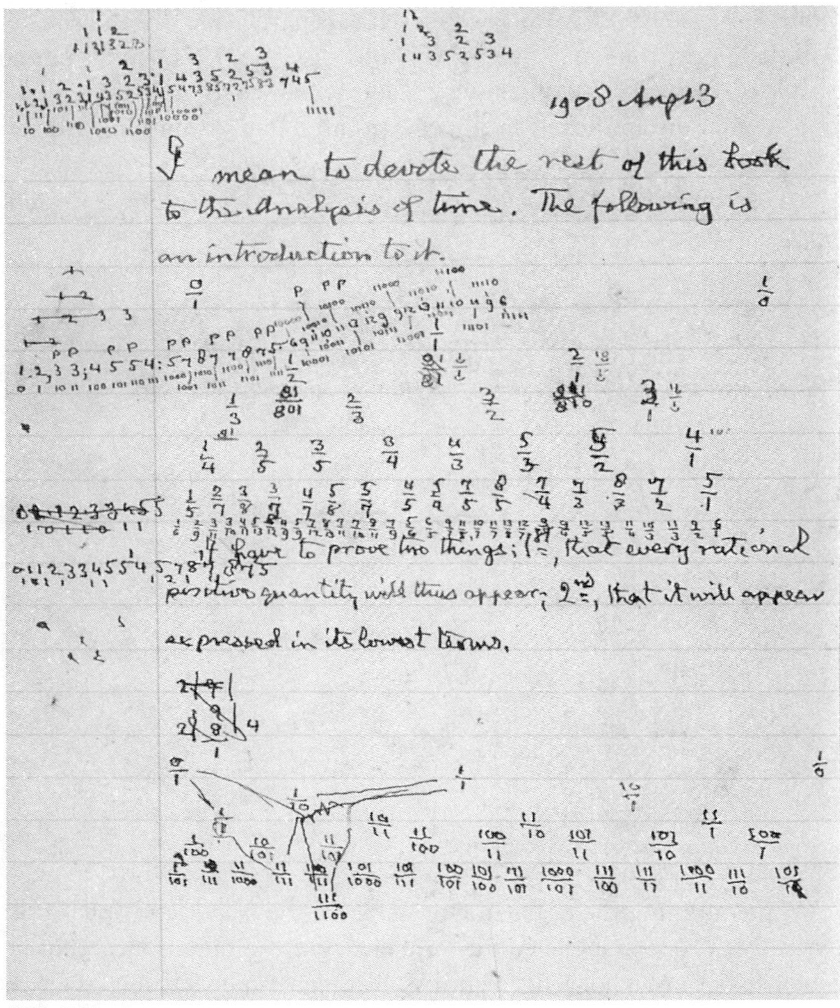

(MS 138)

C.O. Milford Pa. 1904
The way bleak north
presents itself here
as Heraclitean error
driving and driving
thought and austerity
nearer to lyricism
Often as black ice

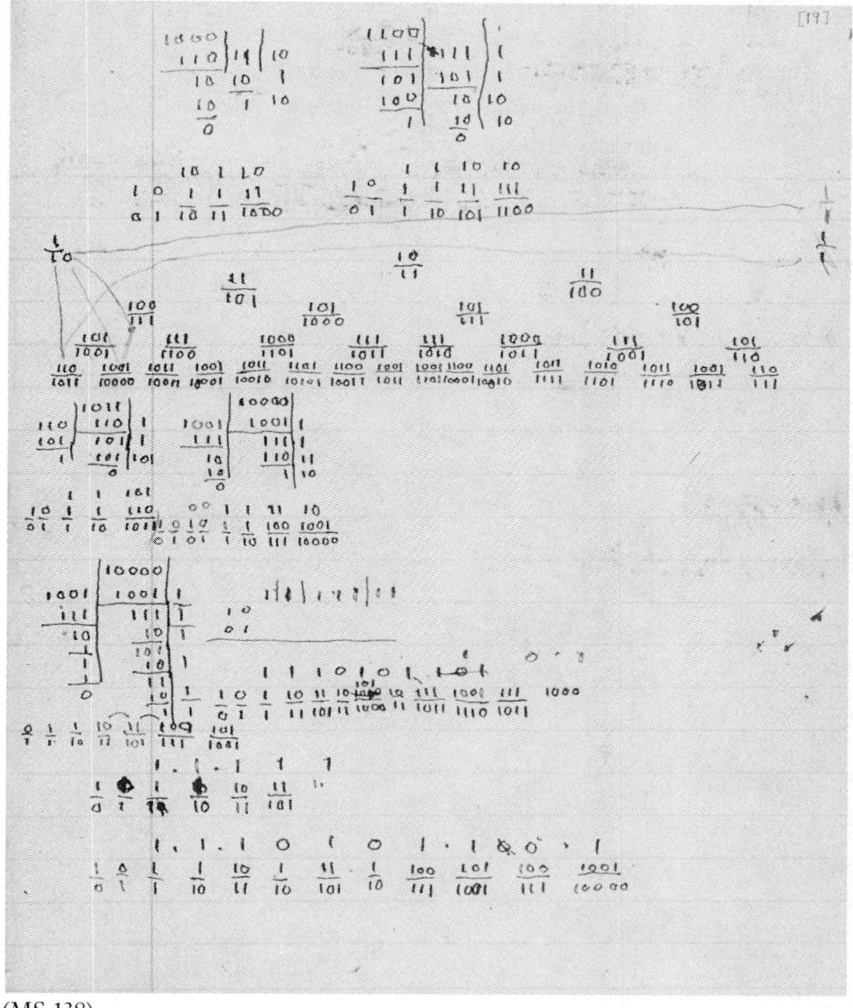

(MS 138)

For the latter third of his life this philosopher's philosopher who once yearned to be hired as a professor *somewhere* wrote over 2,000 words, diagrams, algebraic formulas, and or existential graphs a day. His unpublished writings (including his correspondence) come to more than 100,000 pages. Perhaps Peirce banished himself for logic's sake.

1907 October 6
The First Chapter of Logic.

O Creator out of blank nothing of this
Universe whose immense reality, sublimity,
and beauty so little thrills me as it should,
inspire me with the earnest desire to make
this chapter useful to my brethren!

"The Prescott Book" (MS 277)

(MS 865)

SOURCES

Chapman, John Jay. *John Jay Chapman and His Letters*. Ed. M. A. DeWolfe Howe. Boston: Houghton, 1937.

Dickinson, Emily. *The Manuscript Books of Emily Dickinson*. Ed. Ralph Franklin. Cambridge: Belknap–Harvard UP, 1981.

Gardner, Martin. *Logical Machines and Diagrams*. Chicago: U of Chicago P, 1982.

Homer. The Iliad *of Homer*. Trans. Richmond Lattimore. Chicago: U of Chicago P, 1951.

Howe, Susan. "Ether, Either." *Close Listening: Poetry and the Performed Word*. Ed. Charles Bernstein. New York: Oxford UP, 1998. 111–27.

———. From "Arisbe." *Chicago Review* 43.4 (1997): 23–27.

James, William. "The Pragmatic Method." *The Works of William James: Essays in Philosophy*. Frederick Burkhardt, gen. ed. Cambridge: Harvard UP, 1978. 123–39.

Keeler, Mary, and Christian Kloesel. "Communication, Semiotic Continuity, and the Margins of the Peircian Text." *The Margins of the Text*. Ed. D. C. Greetham. Ann Arbor: U of Michigan P, 1997.

Kent, Beverly S. *Charles S. Peirce: Logic and the Classification of the Sciences*. Kingston: McGill-Queen's UP, 1987.

Mumford, Lewis. *The Brown Decades: A Study of the Arts in America, 1865–1895*. New York: Harcourt, 1931.

Peirce, Charles Sanders. Manuscript collection. Houghton Library, Harvard Univ.

———. "What Pragmatism Is." *Monist* 15 (1905): 161–81.

The Tense Situation of Slavic:
Past, Present, Future

HENRY R. COOPER, JR.

For those who might be misled (or seduced) by my title to expect a discussion of, say, Russian verbal morphology or the clash of aspect and tense in Contemporary Standard Slovene, I've got three words from Dante, "Lasciate ogni speranza"—Forget about it! I'm not a Slavic linguist, so I'll leave it to others better versed in these matters to discourse on them. No, the "tense" of my title derives from *tensus* 'tension' rather than from *tempus* 'time,' and what I'd like to discuss here involves the challenges and difficulties of being in a field that is notoriously cyclical; alas, currently at the bottom of one of its cycles; and yet full of hope for the future.

Slavic got going seriously in the United States in the 1940s, which is about a hundred years after it became an academic discipline in Europe and Russia.[1] The impetus here of course was World War II and its aftermath, first because we were an ally of the Russians and the Poles and the Yugoslavs and then because we were their mortal enemy. At Indiana University the military organized the first courses in Russian and East European languages, and in 1947 (we celebrated our fiftieth anniversary last September) the university founded a program in Slavic studies, now known formally as the Department of Slavic Languages and Literatures. From the department there developed, first, the Summer Workshop in Slavic and East European Languages (1950), which in 1997 offered instruction in

The author is Professor of Slavic Literature and Chair of the Department of Slavic Languages and Literatures at Indiana University, Bloomington. A version of this article appeared in the Winter 1998 issue of the ADFL Bulletin.

twelve Slavic, East European, Central Asian, and Caucasian languages, and, second, the Russian and East European Institute (1958), a federally funded Title VI National Resource Center. After the initial novelty, however, enthusiasm and funding dried up and the realities of studying that "riddle wrapped in an enigma," as Churchill famously called Russia, set in. My retired colleague and the former chair of the Slavic department, William B. Edgerton, who remembers the 1950s well, still speaks of the frustrations of studying a country that at the time he could never hope to visit. Then too there were the sensitivities about studying anything that sniffed of Communism. Suffice it to say that after the heady 1940s, the 1950s saw the first of the pronounced, prolonged cyclical downturns in Slavic.

In October 1957, the Soviets sent into space that little beeping grapefruit-sized thing called *Sputnik*, and Slavic studies in the United States skyrocketed with it. Millions were spent in the name of national defense (the first two letters of the NDEA and NDFL, which so generously funded many Slavicists' educations in the 1960s, including my own), new programs and departments blossomed, and Russian (alone among the Slavic languages) even penetrated into high schools, at least for a time. Thanks to Public Law 480, many libraries became recipients of massive amounts of Slavic and East European books, and impressive national collections were established in some unlikely places, like Champaign-Urbana. In those heady days, Slavic languages, especially Russian, were the envy of the other foreign languages. The field was on steroids. For Slavicists it seemed that the sky was the limit. And that, it turned out, was literally true: even before we landed someone on the moon and "won" the space race, once again the harsh realities set in. When I reported to my army unit in Germany in 1969, I discovered to my dismay (and no little panic) that Russian "linguists" (as the army styles Russian speakers) were so numerous that they were loading sacks in the mailroom (if not worse; some were using their language expertise—I speak ironically, of course—in Vietnam). Another downswing in the Slavic sine curve had set in.

In Soviet history the 1970s marked the beginning of the aptly called period of stagnation of Leonid Brezhnev and company. To some degree the same was true of Slavic studies here and abroad. It was hard for us newly minted PhDs to find a job in the 1970s (too many degrees chasing too few openings), and many a Slavicist became an academic gypsy or didn't get tenure (ask me about it) or simply abandoned the field for greener pastures. I cite some statistics from the Winter 1997 *ADFL Bulletin* (Brod and Huber). If Russian enrollments were negligible before 1957, by 1960 they had risen to the point where Russian, with some 30,000 students, was in fourth place in the United States after the big three—French, Spanish, and

German. By the end of the decade Russian enrollments had swelled to 36,000, an 18% increase and still fourth place. But between 1970 and 1980 they fell by a full third (33.7%), to about 24,000, well below Italian and not much ahead of Hebrew, suffering about twice the loss of all foreign language study in the United States in that dreary period. I suspect Russian did not disappear altogether from the academic scene at this time not because administrators were planning ahead for better days but simply because of academic inertia and the fact that a number of Slavicists had managed to get tenure between 1960 and 1980. And there was always the "spy game," that is, the unspectacular but steady supply of jobs for Slavicists available through the CIA, the NSA, and the foreign service.

And then what happened? The new pope in 1978 did wonders for Polish enrollments: for the first time in Indiana University's history we had two sections of elementary Polish (never to be repeated, I'm sorry to say). And then Gorbachev, glasnost, perestroika: Russian enrollments went through the roof, up 86% in the 1980s to their highest level ever, almost 45,000 by 1990. Other Slavic languages, like Czech (for good reasons) and Serbo-Croatian (for tragic ones), also saw appreciable increases as the cold war ended and the East Bloc opened up. But this upswing was different from the earlier ones: it was not fueled by fear and ignorance of the Soviet Union, nor was it undergirded by massive infusions of government money (higher education had just lived through the "Reagan revolution," you will remember). Its cause seemed to be genuine interest in and enthusiasm for the changes going on in Russia and Eastern Europe. In my view Slavic in this country had for the first time found a natural market: students with Russian-language skills might actually aspire to a job with something other than the foreign service or the CIA. And the heritage students, that is, those with a Slavic background, who became a factor in our field after the emigrations from the Soviet Union beginning in the 1970s, added to our enrollments. (I might note that they added to our difficulties: for the first time we were confronted with significant numbers of students who could speak Slavic languages far better than they could read or write them.)

The universities did not respond to this upsurge in Slavic interest as they had before, with tenure lines and new or expanded departments. In many places graduate students, ABDs, adjuncts, and untenured PhDs carried the burdens of the new courses for as long as they lasted (administrators may not be good at predicting the future, but they are adept at learning from the past). When the enthusiasm faded, as it had to when it became apparent just how long and difficult a process democratizing and marketizing Eastern Europe and Russia was going to be, the field shrank rapidly: 1995 enrollments were again 24,000, precisely what they had been at the end of the 1970s. But the news is not all bad, in my opinion.

To make a simple-minded summation of all this history, the even-numbered decades—the 1940s, 1960s, 1980s—have been very good to Slavic: the odd-numbered ones—the 1950s, 1970s, 1990s—have been less kind. So where do we stand as we enter the last quarter of the 1990s and wait with eager longing the coming of the next even-numbered decade, the 20-aught-aughts? Let me tell you my hope.

At the moment we are in stasis, bottomed out, poised for rebound (pick the one you like best).

- Attempts to kill or severely reduce the larger Slavic programs in the country have failed, though all Slavic programs have been trimmed (at Indiana University we have managed to get about one line for every two retirements). But, then, most other academic departments are being pared these days, at least in the humanities.[2]
- We'll probably see some further reductions in the graduate components of Slavic programs, especially as fellowship money and job opportunities dry up and we scramble to find both alternative ways to support graduate study and alternative careers for students pursuing advanced degrees. Here, too, we are not much different from programs in English, French, German, and even Spanish, which are also scaling back.
- Russian undergraduate enrollments (the locomotive, I would suggest, that pulls all our trains) are probably falling no faster now than are United States foreign language enrollments in general (I have some reason to believe that this decline has now ended). And in the Slavic languages other than Russian—principally Polish and Czech, Serbo-Croatian, and Ukrainian and to a lesser extent Bulgarian—we see some solid (we also hope permanent) gains.[3]
- Stand-alone Russian programs below the PhD level and Russian programs that are components of departments of foreign languages are doubtless at the greatest risk of being phased out. In the overall climate of declining interest in foreign languages (French and German themselves are not exempt from this), Russian has been hit the hardest and will probably continue to be a target of opportunity for administrative budget-cutters for some time to come. My only hope here is that the present generation of Russian teachers will do what two of my friends did in the 1970s when confronted with a similar predicament: one, in Colorado, learned to teach Spanish; the other, in Massachusetts, organized overseas tours for his school. But they have kept Russian alive at their institutions, and they offer courses in it whenever there is a

demand. Even some of my colleagues at Indiana University have agreed to become Gastarbeiter in the linguistics department until our Slavic enrollments improve. This is not of course an ideal situation, but it does allow Russian to stay on the books, and Russian-teaching faculty members to stay on the payroll, as we wait for a better day.

What I am suggesting is that things in Slavic are not as bad as they seem at first glance. I suspect our current malaise is more an understandable queasiness about the rollercoaster ride Slavic has been on from 1980 (way down) to 1990 (way up) to 1995 (back down again); I don't think the field is suffering from anything fatal. If nothing else, I hope this opinion serves as an encouragement for colleagues in languages that have not experienced such wild fluctuations. We are living through a phase at the moment and not standing at the end of time.

And lest we lose sight of the fact, in at least one area we in Slavic have seen an absolute and terribly important improvement in the early 1990s. I think back to my colleague Bill Edgerton, who in the 1950s could not even dream of visiting the Soviet Union. Now, like our colleagues in virtually every other language, we can freely visit the countries that we study, work in their libraries and archives, talk openly with their citizens, collaborate on projects with those citizens (all without the assistance of the KGB or, for that matter, the FBI), sell them our books and tapes and disks, and enthusiastically buy theirs. We can prepare students for careers in Slavic that are neither exclusively academic (though we should not stop doing that) nor exclusively cold-war oriented. In a word, I believe we are rapidly becoming a normal field. The transformation is painful, but in the long run it is healthy.

Slavic as part of the national academic scene in this country is about fifty years old. That is not very old. Our early years were marred somewhat by feast and famine, but lately, as the wretched excesses of adolescence fade into the background, I would like to think we have become full-fledged, responsible, actively engaged members of the foreign language family. Just as Russia has transformed the G-7 into the Summit of the Eight, so we hope to convert the "big three" into the "frequently taught four." And I firmly believe that the future, indeed even current, importance of Russia and the Slavic world fully justifies our efforts and will enable us to reach our goal some time in the next millennium (but please don't press me for a precise year).

NOTES

[1]For a detailed history of Slavic studies in the United States that focuses on literature but that also has information on linguistics, see Edgerton. For an addendum to Edgerton on linguistics and administration, see Lunt. And for a survey that focuses on Slavic area studies, see Byrnes. As a scholarly discipline, before it became a university subject, Slavic is about two hundred years old, having been inaugurated by Enlightenment figures in the Austrian and Russian empires. The first teaching of Russian in the United States took place in 1896, by Leo Wiener, at Harvard.

[2]In August-September 1997 I conducted an informal telephone poll of some of the thirty-six (possibly thirty-seven) Slavic PhD-granting programs in the United States and Canada that were listed in the *AAASS Guide to Slavic Programs, 1993–95*, whose information was collected in 1992. Since then, at least eight have either been closed or in some way curtailed (e.g., several have put a moratorium on admitting new graduate students). It is possible that programs I was not able to reach are also in this situation.

[3]Also from my survey I learned that the programs that are still up and running report a slight overall increase in Russian enrollments for the 1997–98 academic year, often (oddly enough) at the upper levels. And where they are being offered, Polish and Czech in particular are enrolling better, sometimes much better, than in the past.

WORKS CITED

Brod, Richard, and Bettina J. Huber. "Foreign Language Enrollments in United States Institutions of Higher Education, Fall 1995." *ADFL Bulletin* 28.2 (1997): 55–61.

Byrnes, Robert F. *A History of Russian and East European Studies in the United States: Selected Essays*. Lanham: UP of America, 1994.

Edgerton, William B. "The History of Slavistic Scholarship in the United States." *Beiträge zur Geschichte der Slawistik in nichtslawischen Ländern*. Ed. Josef Hamm and Günther Wytrzens. Schriften der Balkankommission, Linguistische Abteilung, 30. Vienna: Österreichischen Akademie der Wissenschaften, 1985. 491–528.

Lunt, Horace G. "On the History of Slavic Studies in the United States." *Slavic Review* 46 (1987): 294–301.

French Studies: Back to the Future

NELLY FURMAN

As the new Europe becomes a reality, it will in time erase the memory of the once-autonomous countries—France, Germany, Italy, Spain, and the United Kingdom, to name a few—that historically were fierce enemies before becoming allies. In the forthcoming European federation, the countries of the old Europe, with their societies unified by specific languages, defined by precise geographical borders, and structured by distinctive histories, will little by little, like the Normans of yesteryear or the formerly independent realm of Burgundy, simply become events of the past relevant to scholars of history. National entities were made possible by the development of a formidable technology: the industrialization of print. As Benedict Anderson has shown, print culture enabled the sharing of information and allowed decrees and promulgations of a centralized government to reach every hamlet and outpost, thereby uniting people in "imagined communities" called nations (6). Print culture molded individuals into a collectivity with people they actually did not know but with whom they were sharing information at a distance, people who were presumably engaging in activities similar to their own. According to Anderson, imagining such things was made possible by the reading process itself. It was not simply that many people could share the same information but that newspapers made readers aware of the haphazard happening of events on a given day: "the arbitrariness of their inclusion and juxtaposition [. . .] shows that the linkage between them is imagined" (33). Moreover, novels formed omniscient

The author is Professor of French at Cornell University.

readers used to seeing characters who, unbeknownst to one another, performed within the same time frame different tasks in different venues. Representing actions and communities beyond the reach and experience of the readers themselves, the novel participated in the construct of nationhood. Thus in Anderson's view "the novel and the newspaper [. . .] provided the technical means for 're-presenting' the *kind* of imagined community that is the nation" (25). Furthermore, print culture, with its charts and maps, in addition to its written orders and dispatched reports, made it possible for national governments to launch into a century of colonial expansion.

Today we are on the eve of a new political order where large markets are to replace old countries, and we also stand at the dawn of a new technological age when electronic communication is about to eclipse print. It is not surprising that traditional disciplines in the humanities and the social sciences established a century ago in the age of nationhood and print culture seem of little interest to entering college students who flock to new curricula and new majors. Departments organized along national boundaries (France, Italy, Germany)—or language families (Romance, Slavic, etc.)—are representative of the past and willy-nilly will need to adapt to the new world order. Statistical evidence tells the story: enrollments in Russian, French, and German language and literature courses, as well as in English, were "noticeably lower in 1995 than they were in 1990" (Brod and Huber 56). But while students shun English courses and European languages—Spanish being the notable exception—they are enrolling in great numbers in communication studies and opting for newer interdisciplinary areas of study. In 1970, there were 10,324 majors in communications; in 1994, 51,164. During the same period (1970–94), interdisciplinary programs also posted a large increase: the number of majors went from 6,286 to 25,167 (Moebius 244).

A relatively new field in the academy, communications, whose focus of interest is the study of the media in their present forms, generally found its institutional home not in colleges of arts and sciences but in technological schools. Besides courses that examine market forces or teach the use of specific technologies, communications also offers courses in media analyses from rhetoric to film studies, and these are most often being taught by faculty members with doctorates from traditional departments of English, theater arts, or comparative literature.

Since the 1970s, traditional departments have had to share the jurisdiction and distribution of knowledge with theme-oriented interdisciplinary programs such as Africana studies, cultural studies, Jewish studies, lesbian and gay studies, Latino studies, Native American studies, peace studies, women's studies, and so on. Thus topical issues, such as those offered by interdisciplinary and area studies programs, as well as the study of the media and their market forces, are clearly the main poles of students' interests at this turn of the century.

In view of these changes, to continue to be fully engaged in the intellectual life of a changed society and to be perceived as relevant by incoming college students, departments teaching European languages and literatures need to rethink their goals, their disciplinary boundaries, and their course offerings. Students today live in the chaotic cultures of a cybernetic age controlled by global market forces in a world facing both exacerbated displays of nationalism and intensified claims for recognition of discrete ethnic identities. What follows is an attempt to formulate a feasible model for a French studies undergraduate program that might answer the needs of those students.

French, as the lingua franca that unites diverse societies and cultures, is the symbolic and real capital of a French studies program, the living memorial and active repository of the language's many histories. French studies cannot simply be concerned with the study of France's national cultural past; it must account as well for the francophone cultures it spawned during its colonialist expansion. While many departments of French language and literature count today among their faculty members at least one specialist in francophone literature, it may be time to forcefully expand curricular offerings in these fields by turning to other departments or programs—Africana studies, Asian studies, Near Eastern studies—to help shore up the study of francophone cultures. After all, nearly 300 million people outside France use French as a means of communication, and this diversity needs to be acknowledged and reflected in the curriculum. French studies could provide the academic venue, the organizational site that would link francophone communities. If the Web is to change our present educational landscape, which was built in the age of print culture, then our course offerings as well as our pedagogical emphases need to adjust to and exploit this new technology. The Internet pundit Esther Dyson points out that "the Net belongs to no particular country or group. The Net is not a global village, but an environment in which a profusion of different villages will flourish" (6). A French studies program could provide an environment for those studying any aspect of the many francophone communities throughout the world. In the academic marketplace of knowledge, French studies could serve as an interconnecting link to a plethora of transnational courses across disciplines within and between colleges.

With the end of nationalism comes the end of a print culture that we have taken for granted. Not that print will altogether disappear, but clearly print will no longer be the premier means of communication. Books, like other printed artifacts, may become curious objets d'art, valued for their appearance, loved or dismissed for their messages, admired for the beauty of their language, or cherished for the quality of their illustrations. But in the future, learning will not necessarily entail opening a book, and books will no longer be the main path to knowledge. Book burning as an act of political censorship or a gesture of political defiance may need to be explained to electronic users able to access unrestricted materials or to generate their own without mentors, referees, publishers, or distribution networks. The history of print technology, the effects of copyright laws, changes in postal regulations, and the establishment of distribution networks, as well as the publishing industry's marketing ploys (literary prizes, advertisements, paperback editions, etc.), are information that future generations may need to know in order to understand the importance of books, their challenges, their influence, their perceived dangers. It is a curious feature of our profession that except for those teaching the early periods of French literature—the Middle Ages and the Renaissance—most faculty members teaching French literature pay little attention to the print medium of the text being studied. Yet the appearance, disappearance, and reappearance of particular books—certain literary genres, distinctive authors, or specific works—are the telling history and symptomatic evidence of a society's changing cultural perceptions and ideological stances. The history of print has been the scholarly domain of intellectual historians and sociologists for whom books, pamphlets, and journals are cultural products opposing, reflecting, or sustaining the social fabric of particular periods and the political order of specific regimes. Literary creativity and critical inquiry similarly partake in the social constructs of their time; thus the emergence of specific forms of literary creativity, as well as the issues raised by aesthetic and theoretical concerns, might equally benefit from retrospective insights into their support of, or challenge to, established cultural norms and political rule. Political and cultural analyses of intellectual and artistic endeavors made possible by past technological breakthroughs answering to and in turn creating specific market forces are the necessary companion to understanding the literary object within its own developmental trajectory or setting the codes of its own reading strategies. To be relevant to students interested in communication and media, literature must be showcased in all its constitutive materialities, shown to be, in its inception and in its reception, an object framed in time and space, encapsulated in print technology, produced by market forces, and encased in the substance of language.

Attention to details and appreciation of collective and individual differences, not to mention intellectual humility, are some of the things learning a foreign language teaches. Learning to be understood in a second language, however frustrating that may be, reveals communication to be something more than simply correct usage. Ionesco proved that point in 1950 in his play *La cantatrice chauve*, where characters utter perfectly correct sentences in a perfectly plausible setting, yet their dialogue—merely the simulacrum of a conversation—appears only as absurd nonsense revealing vacuous spaces between interlocutors bereft of the desire to interact, to let language be the transactional object, the intersubjective mediating link between them. Whatever the limits of linguistic understanding and exchange, attempting communication is the sine qua non of living in society. Within the realm of reason and sociability, it is the linguistic medium that sets the limits of cultural intersubjectivity. Between the "I" that speaks or writes and the "you" that hears or reads, between these nonidentical subjectivities, even within the space of a commonly shared language, understanding is always, at best, an occasional yet necessary illusion.

It has often been pointed out that merely translating the expression "the flag, motherhood, and apple pie" means nothing in a culture imbued with the patriotism of "Liberté, Egalité, Fraternité"; the reverse is equally true, of course. Traditionally the task of the French teacher has been to point out the unbridgeable cultural gaps between signifying systems that reveal shared ideas but not shared cultural experiences. Besides pointing out the untranslatable space between languages, one can also show the linguistic mediations and negotiations within a culture, among those putatively using the same language. The teacher of French can thus open a linguistic medium, its literatures and cultures, to the understanding of communication as the virtual site of exchanges, misunderstandings, disagreements, and resolutions of imagined perceptions both within a culture and cross-culturally. As Lawrence Kritzman suggests, "The professor of French culture should prepare students to become more culturally competent by drawing on various analytical models and critical conceptions" in order to make students "more attentive to how and why they read the signs of culture" (11–12).

When the study of literature entered the French university system in the middle of the nineteenth century, first with Charles-Augustin Sainte-Beuve, later with Ferdinand Brunetière, but most particularly with Gustave Lanson, the study of literature was essentially conceived as an extension of history. This fact was made clear by the name of its methodology—"literary history," with its focus on *l'homme et l'œuvre*—and its offshoots, including biographies of authors, generational affinities, the evolution of literary genres, and so on. It was only in the 1960s, with A. J. Greimas, Roland Barthes, Gérard Genette, Julia Kristeva, and the *Tel Quel* group, that narratology, rhetoric, semiotics, and textuality became objects of study at the university level. The famed reading exercise, the quintessentially French explication de texte, was a high school pedagogical tool.[1] Ferdinand de Saussure's linguistics, Claude Lévi-Strauss's structuralism, Jacques Lacan's rereading of Sigmund Freud, Luce Irigaray's feminist psychoanalysis, Michel Foucault's discourse analyses, and Jacques Derrida's deconstructive readings—all these (bluntly massed together here) postmodern French theoretical discourses have changed the landscape of the humanities and the social sciences. Now that the writings of these authors are available in translation, "French theory" is no longer the reserve of French departments; rather, it now seems to be the bread and butter of departments of English and comparative literature. Yet what are generally not duplicated by faculty members in English or comparative literature are the deliberately slow, scrupulous, and laborious close readings of these theoreticians, that is to say, their working with, within, and through the linguistic medium; in short, what is not being taught "in translation" is the textual dimension, the linguistic presupposition, the inherently cultural component that informs postmodern theoretical positions. For one common denominator of all theoreticians of the postmodern is their understanding of the unavoidable materiality of language and the crisis in communication that this material barrier entails between subjects intrinsically different from one another but also at any given time nonidentical to themselves. In the age of electronic communication, language—both an oral and a written medium— plays a major role. Thus the close reading practices taught in French courses, whether these are conceived as explications de texte, semiotic exercises, textual readings (anthropological, psychoanalytical, etc.), or deconstructive processes, hone interpretative skills and the art of writing.

Students facing unfiltered electronic information may find it useful to learn to read with critical acumen, and in a world where good communication skills are a necessity, they might appreciate learning verbal dexterity and the art of linguistic seduction. In literature courses conceived as workshops in communication skills, students would learn to recognize narrative strategies and rhetorical devices and become skilled at setting up signifying chains, adept at defining semiotic parameters, and sensitized to textual repetitions, ruptures, and deviations. These reading and communication workshops could provide a forum for learning the enactment of a theoretical stance and provide the space and means to actualize theoretical phraseology into a critical praxis. The written component of these workshops could be teaching the structure, presentation, and thought processes of that other quintessentially formalized French exercise, the *dissertation*. It is not necessary for American students to wait to take classes in France during their junior year abroad to discover that French students do not think or argue like Americans. Writing *dissertations*, as opposed to "papers," would teach students a different form of argumentation and gathering of evidentiary materials. In a cybernetic world constructed in large part by the deployment of associative reasoning, learning to think according to other argumentative systems, or according to other epistemological parameters, may be an indispensable skill. Thus, rather than make coverage its major pedagogical goal, French studies could stress the development of analytical skills and thought processes. The final report of the MLA Committee on Professional Employment, published in December 1997, underscores that the mission of the university is not simply to provide students with a body of knowledge but more significantly to provide them with enduring analytical tools: "the object of institutions of higher education is to acquire and to disseminate knowledge as well as, most important, to develop in students the sophisticated intellectual strategies they will use for the rest of their lives, in and out of the workplace" (Gilbert 4). It is also the concern of Esther Dyson, who argues that

> you have to *think* to absorb words and transform them into ideas and arguments. You have to change the model with which you view the world, rather than just add some images to a large store of pictures, factoids, emotional resonances, and sound bites that don't support any structure. But if all you do is watch, you'll have a hard time formulating what you learned when it's over.
> (92)

In an article published in 1995, Robert Barr and John Tagg argue that a paradigm shift is taking place in American higher education: colleges that earlier existed to provide instruction now have to produce learning.

Textual approaches and formal aesthetics characterize the epistemological break of contemporary literary studies from literary history and nineteenth-century representational realism; in French historiography, the shift from nineteenth-century positivism to *la nouvelle histoire* with its focus on social and cultural history started between the two wars under the pressure of the school of *les Annales*. The reconfigurations of disciplinary interests within and between these allied academic fields are best exemplified by two major publications, both collections of articles, that appeared in the 1980s on the two sides of the Atlantic. In 1984, the historian Pierre Nora published the first volume of his monumental seven-volume *Les lieux de mémoire*; five years later, on this side of the Atlantic, Denis Hollier put out his hefty (1,158-page) *New History of French Literature*. Both works have now been translated.

For Nora, the passing of France's nationhood marks the end of an era as well as an epistemological rupture. Thus for him, history can no longer be conceived as it once was, that is to say, steeped in the ideology of the Enlightenment, where the past was looked at from the teleological axis of progress, interpreted through universal assertions, and explained according to causal and scientific models. Instead of a traditional history of events, Nora, who coined the phrase "lieux de mémoire," proposes a history of collectively shared sites of memory:

> Le lieu de mémoire suppose d'entrée de jeu, l'enfourchement de deux ordres de réalités: une réalité tangible, et saisissable, parfois matérielle, parfois moins, inscrite dans l'espace, le temps, le langage, la tradition, et une réalité purement symbolique, porteuse d'une histoire. La notion est faite pour englober à la fois des objets physiques et des objets symboliques, sur la base qu'ils ont "quelque chose" en commun.
>
> (3.1: 20; "Comment écrire l'histoire de France?")

> A site of the memory presupposes from the start the coupling of two realms of reality: one, tangible, graspable, sometimes material, sometimes less, inscribed in space, time, language, and tradition; the other, a purely symbolic one, is the bearer of a story or history. A site of memory is a concept created to include both physical and symbolic objects based on the notion that they share "something" in common.
>
> (My trans.)

Nora's "sites of memory" can be material or symbolic, inscribed in time and/or place, and they can be real or virtual: hence, events, monuments, generational experiences, cultural happenings, and ritualized activities can be construed as sites of memory, closely resembling yet distinct from historical reconstruction. In this respect, *la dissertation* like *l'explication de texte* can be considered *des lieux de mémoire* of a French education. A *lieu de mémoire* is history, but it is history as transmitted by the agency and volition of a community. The French *lieu de mémoire* recalls the expression *lieu commun*, a banality or commonplace expression. Thus a *lieu de mémoire* could be conceived as the banalization of an event through a collective recognition, a shared moment in time or space, a past *ayant eu lieu* becoming a present *ayant lieu*, recalled, recorded, and assessed by postmodern historiography:

> Lieu de mémoire, donc: toute unité significative, d'ordre matériel ou idéel, dont la volonté des hommes ou le travail du temps a fait un élément symbolique du patrimoine mémoriel d'une quelconque communauté. "Comment écrire l'histoire de France?"
>
> (3.1: 20; "Comment écrire l'histoire de France?")

> Site of memory: any significant entity, whether material or non-material in nature, which by dint of human will or the work of time has become a symbolic element of the memorial heritage of any community.
>
> (Nora, *Realms* xvii)

For Nora, then, shared memories, as opposed to a unified history, mean that historical research is set to pursue new objects of study, particularly the social and cultural events that cement group identity: "Identité, mémoire et patrimoine: les trois mots clés de la conscience contemporaine, les trois faces du nouveau continent Culture" 'Identity, memory, and patrimony: the three key words of contemporary consciousness . . .' (3.3: 1009; "L'ère de la commémoration"; my trans.). In 1882, Ernest Renan in his famed conference "Qu'est-ce qu'une Nation?" described the nation as a spiritual community of people from a variety of backgrounds, places, and languages, willing to forget their individualized pasts and their acrimonies, willing to be united in the present and forge a common future for themselves through shared sacrifices. And Renan foresaw the end of nationhood and the making of a European community: "Les nations ne sont pas quelque chose d'éternel. Elles ont commencé, elles finiront. La confédération européenne, probablement, les remplacera" 'Nations are not eternal. They had a beginning; they will have an end. They will probably be replaced by the European confederation' (242; my trans.). At the dawn of the new Europe, Nora reverses Renan's argument for the building of nations, to underscore that, in a postnational moment, it is remembering, remembering collective experiences, that cements communities and gives their members a cultural identity.

A cursory glance at the tables of contents of Nora's edited volumes reveals numerous articles on subjects once considered to belong more properly to literary history: to wit, "Les centenaires de Voltaire et de Rousseau," "Les funérailles de Victor Hugo," "Proverbes, contes et chansons," "*A la recherche du temps perdu* de Marcel Proust," and "La visite au grand écrivain."

Whereas Nora's title, *Les lieux de mémoire*, obliquely calls attention to a new historiographical focus, Hollier's *New History of French Literature* lets it immediately be known that the book does not follow a traditional approach. Hence in Hollier's book French literature is not presented "as a simple inventory of authors or titles, but rather as a historical and cultural field viewed from a wide array of contemporary critical perspectives" (xix). Each entry in Hollier's book is attached to a specific date, and the dates follow an axiological pattern from AD 778, which marks the death of Roland at Roncevaux, to 1989, the bicentennial of the French Revolution. In addition, attached at the end of the volume is a chronology of the major events of French history, as well as a map of metropolitan France today. But these dates and gestures toward a traditional historical presentation of literature framed by national borders are perversely ironic, for they no longer correspond to the traditional usage of dates as markers of "historical" events. Hollier explains:

> Each date is followed by a "headline," evoking an event, which specifies not so much the essay's content as its chronological point of departure. Usually the event is literary—typically the publication of an original work, of a journal, or of a translation; the first performance of a play; the death of an author. But some events are literary only in terms of their repercussions, and some of those repercussions are far removed from their origins in time and place. The juxtaposition of these events is designed to produce an effect of heterogeneity and to disrupt the traditional orderliness of most histories of literature: essays devoted to a genre coexist with essays devoted to one book, institutions are presented alongside literary movements, large surveys next to detailed analysis of specific landmarks [. . .]. (xix)

In Hollier's *New History of French Literature*, one finds essays entitled "Evangelism," "Civil Rights and the Wrongs of Women," "Seventeen Eighty-Nine," "Haute Couture and Haute Culture," "The Dreyfus Affair," and "On Schools, Churches, and Museums." In short, one finds essays on topics once considered the domain of historical studies. Moreover, the map of modern France notwithstanding, there is an acknowledgment, albeit a brief one, of francophone literatures. Some of the essays one finds in Nora's and Hollier's books testify, then, to the reorientation of the vectors of scholarly interests within and between the fields of history and literature. As both Nora's *Lieux de mémoire* and Hollier's *New History of French Literature* demonstrate, the boundaries between history and literature are now more permeable than ever, occasioned in part by the internal reconfigurations of the disciplines themselves. This is not to say that historians and literary scholars, although they may be interested in the same events or documents, have similar aims and analogous methodologies. History and literature are today separate disciplines of scholarly inquiry differently plowing the same cultural fields. This is more than merely a metaphor, for the word *culture*, which in Latin refers to a cultivated piece of land (*agri*), took on by metaphoric displacement and metonymic extension the meaning of being educated in or knowledgeable about a specific domain, "la culture des arts et des lettres" (Hollier xx). Thus *culture* covers a semantic network that includes at one and the same time a material medium (such as the earth, or language, or documents) and an intellectual activity resulting in human creativity. In our new world order, cultures and communities are set to replace national histories and interests, and as a consequence it is their specificities and ethnological features that beckon the research interests of both historical and literary studies. For Hollier, as for Nora, "history" cannot be understood as it once was. Thus, although the table of contents of Hollier's volume may at first glance seem to present itself as a traditional "history of," its concept of a historical scheme is not causal or developmental but rather that of pivotal moments, or sites:

> Rather than following the usual periodization schemes by centuries, as often as possible we have favored much briefer time spans and focused on nodal points, coincidences, returns, resurgences. (xx)

Literature has a double function: understood simply as a representational form of art, literature depicts events, describes social phenomena, evokes cultural moments; literature is here conceived as a historical artifact. But when understood as a literary project, literature cannot be disassociated from its linguistic medium; as for any art form, in the literary object, form and content, inside and outside are inseparable; the linguistic medium is the space of literature qua literature. As Roland Barthes demonstrates in his essay "Histoire ou littérature," literature is a paradoxical object: as a cultural artifact it may be shown, as critics have done, to belong to a certain time and place or to be influenced by a certain network of forces, but as an artistic creation it exceeds all historical, social, cultural, and psychological explanations and exceeds as well all the rhetorical devices and signifying sequences readers may have discovered over time. For Hollier, literature needs to be viewed in this double perspective: as a cultural artifact and as an artistic endeavor. Consequently for him "the possibility of a history of literature is thus dependent on both literature's resistance to history and literature's resistance to literature" (xxv).

On the cover of Hollier's *New History of French Literature*, we are reminded that the book presents "a panorama of literature in its cultural context—music, painting, politics, and monument public and private." As today's academic offerings in general cultural courses show, other artistic endeavors (art, film, architecture, oral literature, etc.) may displace and substitute themselves for the study of literature, and these associative sites of cultural production are today the hallmark of cultural studies per se.

What Nora's *Lieux de mémoire* and Hollier's *New History of French Literature* teach us is to think of culture as a network of sites, as one would find on the Web. These sites are outside any preordered path, outside any *theoria*, outside the diachronic linearity of time and are reachable in a variety of ways, haphazardly or by association or by any other routing mechanism. Some of these sites could turn into courses that address literary issues, cultural events, or social phenomena across time and place. French studies could thus offer, to students who have attained a certain level of language competence and successfully completed gateway prerequisites, a multiplicity of courses: reading and communication workshops to learn critical approaches and textual processes; traditional courses in literary history that focus on periods, literary genres, authors, or specific texts; topical cultural issues (*la querelle des femmes, l'intellectuel, les discours scientifiques,* etc.) or events (Saint-Barthélemy, the Dreyfus Affair, 1968, the turn of the century, etc.) and their repercussions in the early modern or modern period. To a large degree, these types of courses are already offered in many colleges.

While in its international reach the language of the Net is English, many of its constitutive communities will continue, for the foreseeable future, to speak in their own language or languages, and the educated communities of the world will probably be bilingual. A French studies program might well exemplify this bilingualism. After all, there are far more undergraduates enrolled in French classes than there are French majors. Students in agriculture, anthropology, film, history, art history, hotel schools, international studies, and other disciplines may be attracted by courses relevant to their educational major, taught in French or in English. Thus, in addition to a French language and literature major, a French studies program could provide majors in French or francophone area studies with cross-listed courses from other departments, team-taught interdisciplinary courses, or tandem courses offered by faculty members in different fields on a given topic or theme to mark its cross-disciplinary relevance (the Revolution and its traumas; the colonial exhibitions; mapping the world; the discourses of love in painting, music, literature; etc.). Such curricular offerings are already listed in the catalogs of many colleges; we need to assess whether there can be a consensus among us to revitalize our programs according to a few shared educational necessities and goals.

A cybernetic world is not bound by geographical borders or time zones, and it is without center or periphery, but it is regulated by market forces and populated by virtual communities linked by mutual interests. The marketplace of knowledge is no different. The challenge then is to create a French studies program that is attractive to students with pluridisciplinary interests, across national borders and historical time zones, answering the needs of today's society.

NOTES

My thanks to Abby Zanger for her thoughtful comments on this paper.

[1]On the history of literary criticism within the French university system, see Compagnon.

WORKS CITED

Anderson, Benedict. *Imagined Communities: Reflections on the Origin and Spread of Nationalism*. London: Verso, 1983.

Barr, Robert, and John Tagg. "From Teaching to Learning—A New Paradigm for Undergraduate Education." *Change* Nov.-Dec. 1995: 13–25.

Barthes, Roland. "Histoire ou littérature." *Sur Racine*. Paris: Seuil, 1963.

Brod, Richard, and Bettina J. Huber. "Foreign Language Enrollments in United States Institutions of Higher Education, Fall 1995." *ADFL Bulletin* 28.2 (1997): 55–61.

Compagnon, Antoine. *La troisième république des lettres, de Flaubert à Proust*. Paris: Seuil, 1983.

Dyson, Esther. *Release 2.0: A Design for Living in the Digital Age*. New York: Broadway, 1997.

Gilbert, Sandra M. *Final Report, MLA Committee on Professional Employment*. New York: MLA, 1997.

Hollier, Denis, ed. *A New History of French Literature*. Cambridge: Harvard UP, 1989. Trans. as *De la littérature française*. Ed. François Rigolot. Paris: Bordas, 1993.

Kritzman, Lawrence. "Identity Crises: France, Culture and the Idea of the Nation." *Substance* 24.1–2 (1995): 5–20.

Moebius, William. "Lines in the Sand: Comparative Literature and the National Literature Departments." *Comparative Literature* 49.3 (1997): 243–58.

Nora, Pierre. *Les lieux de mémoire*. 7 vols. Paris: Gallimard, 1984–92. Selections trans. as *Realms of Memory*. Trans. Nora. 2 vols. New York: Columbia UP, 1996–98.

Renan, Ernest. *Qu'est-ce qu'une nation? et autres écrits politiques*. Présentation Raoul Girardet. Paris: Imprimerie nationale, 1996.

The Fate of German Studies after the End of the Cold War

PETER UWE HOHENDAHL

Fifty years ago—shortly after World War II—modern language professors gathered for the first time, at the University of Kentucky, to examine the major task that lay ahead of them—namely, to restore intellectual contacts with colleagues in this country and abroad, to rethink the goals of foreign language programs after the turmoil of a global war, and, in the German case, to reconsider the values and possible use of German culture after the experience of National Socialism. For the United States it was certainly a moment of historical optimism: after the defeat of Germany and Japan, the country was ready to accept the challenge of global leadership that was bestowed on it when the European powers were clearly no longer in a position to resume traditional roles of domination. The organizers of the first Kentucky conference, whether they fully understood the global historical shift of those years or not, must have grasped the unexpected opportunities for foreign language departments that came with the new global mission of the United States, opportunities that were soon channeled into the rigid mold of the cold war, in which every phenomenon, whether political or cultural, was looked at and defined in terms of its function in the struggle between democracy and totalitarianism.

Clearly, language and literature programs had to be strengthened so that they could participate in the larger rebuilding and expansion of the American university, which for the first time made a serious attempt to

The author is Professor of German and Comparative Literature at Cornell University. A version of this article appeared in the Winter 1998 issue of the ADFL Bulletin.

open its doors to those who had not been born into a social class in which college training was taken for granted. That the Kentucky conference has been successful for the last five decades, that it embraced the challenges of the 1970s, when all of a sudden the traditional structure of foreign language departments was seriously jeopardized by the abolition of the language requirement, and that the conference accepted and participated in the changes of the 1980s, when, once more, familiar definitions of our roles were undercut by new theoretical outlooks—these accomplishments speak for the strength of the Kentucky Foreign Language Conference.

It is in this spirit of innovation and questioning that I want to raise a number of issues that most of us are aware of, although we do not always like to be reminded of them. Today's mood is much more somber than the atmosphere of the immediate postwar years. American universities and colleges find themselves in a state of siege that has left its traces in our professional lives. Its most obvious symptom is the spirit of cost cutting, an unprecedented tendency among university administrators to reduce expenditures and to streamline structures—and therefore to look critically at programs that have relatively high infrastructure costs, such as small language departments. The more the business corporation becomes the model for the American university, the less we can take the preservation of traditional institutions and programs for granted. Another symptom is the significant decline in language enrollment since 1991 that the staff of the MLA has recently documented. While French departments have lost almost 25% of their previous enrollments, in the case of German the loss is even higher: we have 27.8% fewer students enrolled in German language classes today than six years ago. The consequences for faculty development are more than obvious. By traditional standards, universities and colleges need fewer German and French teachers, or at least fewer regular tenured faculty members. As we know all too well, universities have responded increasingly to this crisis by hiring part-time teachers, thereby maintaining maximum financial flexibility.

The present situation in the job market seems to bear this assumption out. In the last three years we have reached a low that reminds us of the 1970s, when, for the first time after a decade of expansion, the academic labor market seemed to collapse. Of course, we have to remind ourselves that the trend toward downsizing is not limited to language and literature departments; it has reached physics and chemistry as well, disciplines that have prospered for decades because they could count on external funding. Scientists are told to think small, an order they find much harder to swallow than the humanists do, where there never was a lot of money.

This reminder is important because it will help us to read the larger picture before we draw hasty conclusions and embark on a course of action that might do more harm than good. But how does it all hang together? Is there a connection between the decline in language enrollment in French, German, and Russian (but not in Spanish), on the one hand, and the budget crisis at American universities, on the other? Is there a link between the fate of the German program and the physics department? I suspect that there is a tie, but not a direct one or a connection that can be explained in immediate causal terms. I believe that the end of the cold war, which some fifty years ago began to shape foreign language departments, has had a greater impact on American postsecondary education than we realize.

This is fairly obvious in the case of the sciences. The model of fundamental political confrontation, in which at any moment each side had to be ready for global warfare, encouraged large government expenditures. Universities received money for basic research that could be translated into defense technology. To a much smaller extent, even language departments took part in this boost. Older faculty members, now mostly retired, will remember the so-called *Sputnik* effect of the late 1950s, when languages were suddenly seen as a critical tool in the ongoing confrontation. The end of the cold war has made these expenditures superfluous. Moreover, the end of the cold war, it seems to me, has directly and indirectly affected the mission and function of American postsecondary education. It is possible, I believe, that the American research university (state or private), which for forty years was the engine of technological and economic progress and therefore crucial for social change, is losing its pivotal role. If there is indeed a process of marginalization at work (which conservatives would certainly welcome, because they do not trust the university), the smaller liberal arts college would also be affected, since it has served as a kind of *Zubringer*, or feeder, for the large research university.

Clearly today, American universities and colleges are on their own; neither the federal government nor the states feel strongly committed to provide the funding necessary for the ambitious teaching and research programs that were developed during the 1970s and 1980s. From the point of view of the political and economic leaders of this country, there is no longer an urgent need to support these programs, since they have no apparent function in the post–cold war economy. Furthermore, the publicly acclaimed drive toward privatization of public tasks leaves the university and the college in the cold.

This is our situation: we are faced with a rapid metamorphosis of higher education, as part of a larger structural transformation in the political and social sphere, that begins to touch our professional lives, mostly in negative terms. Under these circumstances we may lose our confidence to do what we do best—to teach our students the intricacies of a foreign language and the use and value of a foreign culture. What is to be done?

First of all, we have to understand that the traditional structure of the college and the university could survive after World War II because of an unspoken special agreement with society at large. Colleges and universities were considered exempt from the law of the market. The corporate model of the business world was not rigorously applied to higher education, which was seen as part of the public sphere. This policy gave us in the humanities space to produce and transmit knowledge that was not judged in terms of immediate social applicability. The standard of technological applicability was enforced mainly in the natural sciences and to some extent in the social sciences. But the primary enforcer was the state, not private business. The knowledge produced in the humanities, and especially in literature departments, had a unique function: it served as a kind of counterweight to the dominance of instrumental reason in the scientific community. In the public eye, learning languages and reading literature for their own sake balanced the utility of education in the sciences. The postwar triumph of the New Criticism articulated precisely this understanding of the humanities as a sheltered form of autonomy. As long as this balance of knowledge worked, the relative autonomy of the university was not radically questioned. The university was allowed to preserve its older structure as a community of teachers, scholars, and students. In a certain way, it was the cold war, the feeling of a permanent threat to our political and economic system, that preserved the university.

I fear that with the end of the cold war, this arrangement has come to an end. The strong state as a protector of the relative independence of the university is being dismantled. The lines between the public and the private sphere are being redrawn, with an increasing emphasis on the private. For the university this means that now the corporate model of the business sector is offered as the new standard to measure performance. This is the climate in which we will have to work in the near future, whether we are at a state or a private institution.

I believe that the application of the corporate model to the university is a fundamental mistake, because it assumes a market orientation that is ultimately counterproductive. We will have to persuade our administrations that they should not automatically cave in to the demands of their boards and regents, who frequently ask for accountability primarily in financial terms. But I realize that, at most places, the input of the faculty and the students is not strong enough to resist the present trend. In addition, in the long run mere resistance and maintenance of familiar structures cannot be successful, since these structures were historically determined and the historical parameters have definitely changed. New and fresh responses are needed, but workable patterns have not yet emerged. This makes it very difficult for us to get our bearings right.

Still, we have to make decisions about our professional future. Therefore we have to think about our discipline in a rapidly changing context. Can the corporate model be our friend? The concept of friendship would probably be misplaced, but we can ask the more pragmatic question: Can we use this model to our advantage? Although there are risks involved, the model has its own rewards. On the positive side, it favors competition, mobility, diversity, and, within the limits of cost efficiency, innovation. On the negative side, it disregards tradition (and with it continuity) and loyalty of the institution to the faculty (and vice versa). There is no place for strong and lasting attachments to the academic institution and its educational mission. (In this model, by the way, tenure is not a necessity, perhaps not even a desirable feature.) The corporate model of the 1990s, unlike that of the 1950s, tends to be decentralized; emphasis is placed on the mobility and efficiency of the individual unit.

Here lie the opportunities for the enterprising department that wants to experiment by trying out new curricula and different forms of organization, preferably, of course, without asking the dean for additional funds. This orientation applies both to language instruction and to literature and cultural programs. By and large, today's colleges and universities feel less threatened by new and potentially radical ideas than a generation ago, because—in the world of the global market—ideas are products like any other consumer good and have to be tried and tested before they can be sold to the general public. For this reason, ideological interference is less likely than fifty years ago, when the state in its role as protector also expected the political loyalty of the faculty in the war against communism. Ideological interference has become more a local matter. (A Baptist college, for instance, defines its mission in terms of specific religious ideas and norms and expects its faculty to accept these ideas and norms as a frame of reference.)

Of course, the call for innovation and experiments does not come unexpectedly or strike us as out of the ordinary. During the late 1980s, for example, Germanists in this country began to ask questions about the fate of the discipline. Their project started as a movement to bring the study of German literature and culture closer to the American home ground by redefining the parameters of the field. The so-called Americanization of Germanics challenged the assumed leadership role of German *Germanistik* and called for a specifically American agenda. The recent intensive debate about cultural studies has clearly helped us revitalize the discipline, precisely because the participants in the exchange did not simply call for a new methodology but suggested, rather, the possibility of multiple interdisciplinary approaches that would redesign the field and provide connections with other disciplines in the humanities and in the social sciences. At this point there is no need to rehash this comprehensive debate, which is still fresh in our minds. Instead, I want to draw some conclusions that were not yet available when we began to question the traditional mission of the German department a decade ago.

When we started to examine the status of Germanics in the 1980s, we were motivated primarily by internal problems: first, a perceived isolation of Germanics vis-à-vis the rest of the humanities and, second, a growing sense that our theoretical and methodological framework was less suited to deal with contemporary cultural problems. The traditional emphasis on the German literary canon seemed especially inadequate. Our search for a new theoretical model, aided by a series of conferences and symposia (the so-called *Wüstenkonferenzen*, organized by the German Academic Exchange), initially proceeded without our being much aware of the structural transformation that occurred in the American university more or less at the same time. Looking back at the recent developments from the present vantage point, we can recognize the structural link. The cultural studies movement anticipated and responded to the emerging dominance of the corporate model.

The notion of a response is, of course, ambiguous. It can mean a form of adaptation that ensures survival; it can also encompass a critical reaction that calls into question the undeniably affirmative character of the new university. Much recent work (in teaching as well as research)—for example, feminism, colonial and postcolonial studies, and scholarship in minority literatures—has offered a critical perspective that cannot be harmonized with the notion of academic efficiency. For the most part, though, universities and colleges have tolerated, if not actively supported, these innovative programs, sometimes to the dismay of conservative intellectuals who had the ear of the public and therefore could stir up controversial debates in the public sphere. I am talking about the culture wars of the late 1980s and early 1990s. It seems, however, that ultimately universities are actually less interested in and threatened by these debates than one might expect, as long as these controversial academic programs attract student interest. In the entrepreneurial climate of the 1990s, innovation seems more important than a dogmatic defense of older paradigms in the humanities that conservative intellectuals have embraced as the supposed expression of the national welfare.

There is a curious irony at work: it used to be the intellectual outside the university whose critical interventions questioned the status quo, whereas academic teachers typically functioned as agents of the reproduction of knowledge. Today, the critical stance has moved inside the university, while public intellectuals have taken up the defense of tradition. Hence the moment of critique has attached itself to the teacher in the classroom.

It is the double aspect of teacher and intellectual that makes our work more interesting and more significant. But what does it mean to be an intellectual in the classroom? In the 1990s, this role implies flexible strength rather than dogmatic opposition—for instance, the willingness to accept and make use of the opportunities given by the corporate model. This cannot be done without a moment of *Umfunktionierung* ("refunctioning"), to quote an old Brechtian term. While the conservative critics of the university want the faculty to return to the traditional role of reproducing and disseminating accepted forms of knowledge through familiar disciplinary channels, we have to recognize that the new decentralized university, with its increasing breakdown of established organizational structures and boundaries, encourages different modes of producing and disseminating knowledge. To give an example: our language programs will have to respond to the needs of the business school and the engineering division, whose faculty members are increasingly aware of the multilingual, international environment of their agendas. Yet this does not mean that we have to define courses that serve these needs in strictly functional terms. As Claire Kramsch has repeatedly argued in recent publications, the process of learning a language consists of more than acquiring competence. The cultural experience that is part of the process can well correct the one-dimensional understanding of specialized language acquisition. To put it differently, the transfer of specialized knowledge and the conception of a critical perspective do not logically exclude each other. In the same way, the typical introductory course in German literature, the traditional workhorse of most German departments, is not a priori doomed because of its old-fashioned content. Everything depends on the arrangement and the presentation of the literary texts. If the instructor acts as an intellectual rather than as a mere mouthpiece of conventional wisdom, the old intro course could effectively reorganize the ideas of the students of the class.

Please do not understand the last example as a dogmatic defense of a pure literature program on my part. I do not believe that such an orientation would provide a successful strategy for the next century. Instead, we will have to examine the institutional context in which we operate. Therefore I would like to make a few suggestions. If I were asked by an incoming chair of a German department what to do to strengthen the German program, I would make three recommendations. First, do not isolate your department from the rest of the college or university. Do not encourage the perception, on the part of the dean or the chairs of the English and the history departments, that the German department is simply pursuing its separate agenda, an agenda that is of no relevance to other units. It is vital to the survival of the German program that the administration as well as neighboring departments perceive the program as part of a larger educational mission. Only through continued contacts with other programs and a clear articulation of a readiness to conceive of its program as part of the larger mission can the German faculty preserve its place in the new university. At the same time, it is important for the German program to demonstrate its special contributions to the larger mission. A mere duplication of trends and approaches from other fields is inadequate. In my opinion, it would be almost suicidal for a German program, for example, to ignore the great philosophical tradition from Kant to the Frankfurt school and hand it over to other programs.

The second point I would make when talking to an incoming chair is closely related to the first: the department always has to be prepared for change. It would be dangerous to rely on a specific curriculum as the solution to our problems. We all know that curriculum reform is a difficult and time-consuming process. Since we have many obligations in our professional lives, we do not want to go through such a difficult process all the time. But it is essential, I feel, to be vigilant at every moment. Solutions that were successful five years ago may not suffice in the future. The shift to cultural studies, for instance—which has rightly preoccupied many departments in the recent past—will have to be reviewed as well. Given the swiftness of the changes in postsecondary education, it would be imprudent to rely on a notion of programmatic stability.

My third point is more specific. It concerns the language program. As much as I would emphasize the teaching of the German language as a vital part of the German department, my advice would be not to rely exclusively on the traditional structure in which language instruction serves as the basis for all other departmental activities. I believe that we have to reconceptualize the relation between language instruction and the teaching of culture. In view of the recent enrollment losses that I mentioned, it might be judicious to develop a program that does not depend entirely on the use of the German language as a medium.

As I pointed out, I do not believe that the corporate model is ultimately well suited for the college and the university, and I hope that administrators will come to a similar conclusion in the near future. But for the time being, we have to live with it and have to be prepared for its demands and expectations.

Some Implications
of Curricular Change at the
University of Houston

DAVID MAZELLA

When the English department at the University of Houston first considered changing its undergraduate major, we felt the biggest problem with our program was one of staffing. And so it was: our existing faculty could no longer cover the conventional sequence of historical periods in British and American literature. After some investigation, however, we realized that our growing problems with period coverage had seriously weakened the pedagogical rationale of the entire undergraduate curriculum, and in ways that could not be easily remedied. Though we might slowly begin to replace vacant positions one at a time, we would not be able to recoup our long-term losses in the near future, especially when we were teaching ever-increasing numbers of students. While we fought to regain faculty lines lost or vacated in previous years, we would still need to create a curriculum that could function with our current level of faculty. If indeed the university had effectively abandoned the coverage model in its policies on replacing faculty lines, then the department's commitment to this model would have to be reexamined. Our only option, therefore, was to initiate our own discussions of the major, to see if we could come up with a new and more workable program of studies, a program shaped by the department's pedagogical goals and responsibilities and not by the vagaries of university funding and faculty retirements.

The author is Assistant Professor of English at the University of Houston.

These preliminary discussions about the curriculum, first in committee, then in the department as a whole, were as important in their way as the proposal that was ultimately approved and put into place. A number of interesting consequences unfolded from them. First of all, the discussions forced us to examine more concretely what current policies were accomplishing or not accomplishing for our students. Second, they gave us an opportunity to reflect on the department's role within the university and on whether we wished our curriculum to reinforce or counter those external forces. Third, the debates over the English major led us to look again at the pedagogical goals of student research in literature classes generally and at how student work should or should not reflect the current state of graduate and advanced research in the humanities. The debates were complicated by the fact that as a department within a large, urban, public research university, we typically teach students who at the advanced level are still acquiring skills or knowledge that beginning students at elite schools are expected to have. (This is not to say that students at those schools are perfectly prepared or that ours are not; it is only to say that the question of gaps in students' preparation formed an explicit, if not obsessive, part of our curricular discussion in ways that it does not at other kinds of schools.) If research equals advanced work, as is assumed at most of the graduate programs where we trained, then how could the majority of our students, with their diverse backgrounds and uneven academic preparation, ever proceed to that stage, having escaped the usual battery of survey courses, textbooks, and standardized tests typically found at the initial level of instruction? To put the problem another way, can we as a faculty accept the assumption, usually left unstated, that institutions like ours are essentially dedicated to remedial training, so that most of our students will never be expected to conduct serious intellectual inquiry? Is there such a thing as a remedial university still worthy of the name *university*? How can we ratify such an arrangement for our students without its seriously affecting our work as their teachers?

Yet even if we do contest the relegation of our students to a lower level of educational expectation, we are still left with the problem of understanding our particular educational niche and with the more practical concerns of conducting and directing research in a setting such as ours. Much of what I propose here will hardly seem revolutionary to colleagues at institutions with a long history of research. Such a history gives faculty members at those institutions powerful arguments for tenure, faculty development leaves, an intimate teaching environment, and a regularly changing undergraduate curriculum. The situation, however, is far more uncertain at institutions that acquired their research missions more recently. As a public institution in the nation's fourth-largest city, our university is continually asked why it should bother to maintain a full-scale tenured and tenure-track research faculty, especially when it takes most of its students from the local community. Since this community mission has helped drive the university's expansion for the past twenty years, the discussion about the English major forced us to ask ourselves as a faculty, What are the consequences of this mission at the curricular level, and what kinds of intellectual inquiry should we expect from our students and ourselves? One of the more interesting discoveries we made was that the curricular debate quickly opened up a related debate about faculty research, one that suggested finally that we should demand from students what we demand from ourselves, no more and no less. This means that teaching even at the introductory levels should remain current and be informed by our research activities and that students should be expected to conduct genuine intellectual inquiry—in other words, research—in courses where they are also acquiring certain skills. As I argue at the end of this essay, the future of research (and of the research faculty) at the large public university is at stake when administrators mull over such questions as the relation of research to teaching, and literature departments need to be able to provide convincing answers to those questions if they wish to continue in anything like their present form.

I have watched this extended process of curricular change from a number of vantage points since joining the English department in 1995: originally I was a member of the committee that initiated the revisions to the English major, and I was part of the group that helped formulate the guidelines for the new required gateway course called Introduction to Literary Studies. Subsequently I designed and taught my version of this course, Swift and Literary Studies. What follows is my account of the discussions leading up to the changes in the major and of how those changes have played out, in the department and in the classroom, since the proposal was approved. So far I have been encouraged by the results, though I have learned the difficulties of managing a curriculum when two of the most important factors, student needs and university support, lie outside the department's control.

BACKGROUND

The University of Houston is a Carnegie research II university and serves about thirty-one thousand students from the Houston metropolitan area. It is a commuter school, with a student population that reflects the ethnic diversity of the city (56% white, 14% Asian or Pacific Islander, 14% Hispanic, 9% African American, and 7% international). The English department, which now employs roughly forty full-time tenured and tenure-track faculty members, teaches students from every segment of the university: in the lower division, we (meaning faculty members, TAs, and lecturers) teach about thirteen thousand students annually in our core curriculum's first- and second-year required composition and introductory literature courses; in the upper division, which is taught chiefly by tenured and tenure-track faculty members, we maintain between six hundred and seven hundred majors, plus nine hundred or so from other majors or colleges taking our advanced courses; at the graduate level, we have about two hundred students in our literature, creative writing, and linguistics programs, working on degrees ranging from the MA through the PhD. Most of our students are older and employed while they earn their degrees, and on average they take five to six years to graduate.

Like many other departments, we have seen our tenured faculty numbers shrink and our workloads increase since the 1970s. As I mentioned earlier, this trend made it increasingly difficult to offer the entire repertoire of required courses in any given year, particularly in the wake of research and medical leaves, retirements, and so on. Economic pressures were leaving their mark on other aspects of the curriculum: class sizes steadily crept up (lower-division classes, including composition, are now capped at twenty-seven; upper-division literature and linguistics at thirty; upper-division composition and creative writing at twenty), while the courses grew increasingly standardized in their approach and choice of subject matter. The result was a curriculum consisting largely of historical surveys. No matter what their topic, these surveys usually conformed to a general model in which professors introduced students to the literature of a particular period by having them study the works of a succession of canonical figures. Many excellent courses were being taught with this structure, but the problems caused by our overreliance on it were becoming apparent. Many on the faculty had noticed that it was difficult to vary the authors taught from year to year or to discuss literary theory or even literary criticism in any extensive way. These introductory survey courses were also rarely complemented by the appropriate advanced courses that would feature more intensive reading and analysis of the same material. It was the multiplying difficulties of maintaining such a curriculum that forced the Upper Division Curriculum Committee to reconsider the major in 1995.

From the faculty point of view, professors under the old system generally taught the same required survey courses year after year, in classes that were generally filled to capacity. Advanced or elective courses constituted only a fraction of our offerings and even then sometimes closed for lack of students. Our desire for a curriculum that ran smoothly and chronologically from beginning to end, with students working through progressively advanced topics, was effectively undone by the contingencies of student schedules and departmental staffing. Students spent so much time and energy fulfilling their period requirements—out of order and often at random— that the putative goal of our curriculum, an advanced understanding of at least some portion of American or British literature, was attained rarely and only when students resisted the atomizing force of the requirements. At the same time, the two most important professional trends of the 1970s and 1980s in English studies, the incorporation of literary theory into the curriculum and the recovery of a host of noncanonical writers, could be followed only intermittently and in ways that left the official curriculum unaffected. This increasing gap between the movement of the profession and the demands of teaching left many faculty members and students dissatisfied. The faculty, then, had plenty of good reasons to return to the question of our curriculum, to discover whether we could make it work better.

From the student point of view, the system that had developed since the last round of curricular changes, in the 1970s, could be frustrating. Required courses quickly filled up whenever offered, and uncertainty about the scheduling of some hard-to-find classes made students take those first rather than pursue electives or even a particular interest in a period. Work schedules or conflicts with other classes often prevented students from taking the required courses anyway, so that the department received large numbers of petitions for substitutions of requirements. The department's inability to offer the required courses in a regular rotation and its unwillingness to lengthen the already extended graduation times of a predominantly part-time student body made such petitions hard to refuse, even as they subverted the purpose of the requirements. Hence the rationale underlying the old system—the notion of complete coverage of the field of literature—had effectively been undermined from within and without. The existing requirements, we learned, were actually discouraging students from more intensive study in specific fields. To make matters worse, the chronic problems with the gaps in our course offerings were particularly damaging to the majors most in need of direction from the department, those wishing to pursue English at the graduate level. These students wondered whether the new theories and authors they were hearing about in other contexts would ever make it into our curriculum.

THE PROPOSAL: INTRODUCTION TO LITERARY STUDIES

The Upper Division Curriculum Committee, after a long series of discussions directed by the committee chair, Pat Yongue, recommended that the department change the requirements for its literary studies major, moving from a strict chronological sequence of surveys to a more open system of elective and nonelective courses. Yet simply increasing the number of electives would not address the need for a correspondingly revised structure, for some principle beyond period coverage to organize a new curriculum for teachers and students alike. The committee's solution was a new required course, Introduction to Literary Studies, which would help students enter the contemporary discussion of literature at the college level. In a memorandum to Yongue, I described the proposed course in the following way:

> The Intro to Lit Study course should be pragmatic, emphasizing methods of critical reading and critical writing. Topics might include exploiting the library's resources, incorporating other critical voices into one's own research project, working between literature and other contexts such as history or the visual arts, studying the impact of various new approaches (feminism, ethnic studies, queer theory, etc.) on literary criticism. The specific goals of the course should be provided by the individual instructor. The general goal should be to promote reflection upon and discussion of the practices of critical reading and critical writing.

As it turned out, a key element of the proposal's success in the committee was leaving the specific design of the course to the discretion of individual teachers, who were to be encouraged to use their own research specialties and interests in its design. Not only would that feature give interested faculty members another opportunity to design new courses closely connected with their research; it also meant that the already divided committee would not have to decide for itself, or dictate to the rest of the department, precisely what should be taught in such a course. This deliberately pluralist feature of the proposal permitted those who could agree at least on the need for the course to design their own versions of it. After all, even the course's proponents were not quite sure what shape it would finally take or how it would play out over a number of semesters. The proposal therefore was passed by the committee and brought to the department as a whole for a vote.

At the departmental meeting to vote on the proposal, discussion focused on the potential problems of removing the coverage model as a requirement and on whether our students would abandon British literature, or pre–twentieth-century writing altogether, in their rush to the electives. Some faculty members in British studies wondered whether in the absence of the traditional requirements students would still take courses in Shakespeare, Milton, or Chaucer. Would we be cheating our students if we permitted them, especially those interested in graduate school, to ignore canonical British authors and instead read exclusively in such new fields as minority literature and women's studies? At the same time, we could not pretend that the local high schools had introduced our students to much literature at all, let alone British or pre–twentieth-century literature, so student preferences, such as they were, had been shaped without any real exposure to literary history. The committee's answer to these objections was two-part: first, we had left in a distribution requirement for pre–nineteenth-century British and American literature and, second, prospective graduate school applicants would be closely advised to ensure that they maintained a reasonable balance of traditional and untraditional fields in their undergraduate education. The committee did not foresee, and certainly did not intend, the disappearance of Shakespeare, Milton, and Chaucer (the names most frequently mentioned) from the curriculum.

The prominent role of theory in the new course disturbed some other faculty members, because of its elevation of theory within the literature curriculum as a whole. Would introducing theory to students at this stage of their education divert them from the study of literature? Some asked, Why address theoretical issues in a new introductory course instead of in the advanced elective classes or seminars that were taught in the past? Interestingly, objections like this were not so much against theory as against specialization. Many professors uncomfortable with the proposal were themselves currently teaching and writing about theory; they feared that most of our students had read too little literature to be ready for theory's more specialized concerns. The members of the committee responded by noting that theory was only one component of the course, alongside the writing and research segments; that some exposure to theory even at the beginning stage of studies would enhance students' reading; and that teaching the introductory course in this way would make possible more interesting teaching and discussion later on. Though the discussion was heated, the proposal finally passed. Shortly thereafter, a member of our department, María González, volunteered to teach an experimental section of the course in the spring of 1997, while we waited for the proposal to take effect. Students were enthusiastic about the opportunity to take such a course, which they felt was long overdue, and so Introduction to Literary Studies officially entered our roster in the fall of 1997 as the only required course for our new literary studies option within the major.

Swift and Literary Studies

When it was my turn to design an introduction course for the fall of 1997 (one of five sections given annually), I wanted my version to have several features that would sharply distinguish it from other courses in our roster. These features included:

- a concentration on a single literary author or work, using the divergences within the existing body of criticism to talk both about the work's critical history and about current critical approaches
- exploration of a limited group of theoretical texts, selected for their usefulness in relation to the chosen author
- extensive discussion of library research methods in a variety of media, including CD-ROM and the Internet, and of how these forms of research could be incorporated into one's writing process. The emphasis would be less on the technical process of searches than on developing the powers of discrimination necessary for making the best use of the library and its electronic resources in a limited span of time.

To reduce these different activities to a manageable program, I began with a group of concepts that I considered indispensable for the practice of academic literary criticism. These concepts included "author," "work," "criticism," and "archive," which would serve as ongoing topics of investigation throughout the semester.

To give a concrete instance of author and work, I organized the entire course around Jonathan Swift's *Gulliver's Travels*; this single text became the vehicle for our discussions of authorship, literature, and interpretation during the term. *Gulliver's Travels* also offered a number of ways for the class to think about the historically changing practices of literary criticism and interpretation, most obviously because of Swift's continual satire on willful or blind commentators. In addition, the work has provoked a rich and contradictory critical history that continues to the present, as in recent postcolonial debates over Swift's status as an Irish or Anglo-Irish intellectual. In my plan, I would first teach *Gulliver's Travels* in its entirety, then move through a sequence of theorists whose work informs four critical contexts (structuralism, poststructuralism, gender studies, and postcolonialism) that have particularly affected Swift studies in the twentieth century. In this deliberately recursive structure, the class would return to Swift's writing after reading a particular group of theorists, so that *Gulliver's Travels* would remain at the beginning and end, if not the center, of our activities. In effect, I would treat both Swift and the theorists as primary texts, worthy of historical contextualization, accurate recapitulation, and careful critical interpretation and discussion. The semester would culminate in a research paper on Swift that drew on all the kinds of work done by students since the beginning of the semester.

Since this was a new and still-evolving course, I experimented with the format for student participation, to see whether I could improve students' level of engagement with some very difficult material. To encourage more of a collaborative, studio setting for their classwork, I had students supplement their individual essay assignments by working together for the whole semester as members of three-person research teams. In this manner, they learned much of the historical, contextual, or background materials as part of a group, visiting special collections, generating annotated bibliographies, and making their theoretical presentations collectively to the rest of the class. To ensure that these research activities were seen not simply as busywork but as part of a process leading to a concrete end, I also photocopied and placed on reserve each group's annotated bibliographies and presentation handouts for the general use of the class in their final research papers. At the end of the semester, each group submitted a portfolio containing its collected work. The group grade it received was factored into each student's essay grades. Moreover, I tried to encourage participation in an ungraded electronic discussion group, which offered yet another forum for discussion outside class.

This set of goals should help explain what might seem the most puzzling feature of Swift and Literary Studies: its dual historical focus (see app.). The course functioned as an advanced study of *Gulliver's Travels* even while it introduced students to current issues in literary theory, criticism, and scholarship. I placed my discussion of Swift and contemporary literary criticism within the historical and conceptual framework of the Enlightenment—a framework that could mediate between these two areas. In keeping with this structure, I would have students read *Gulliver's Travels* from beginning to end for the first four weeks, interpreting it in the historical contexts of Enlightenment travel literature (pt. 1), political thought (pt. 2), science (pt. 3), and psychology (pt. 4). For the next twelve weeks they would work through four "digressions": on structuralism (Marx, Freud, Saussure, Lévi-Strauss), on poststructuralism (Derrida, Foucault), on gender theory (Irigaray, Lacan, Butler), and on postcolonialism (Said, Spivak). The theorists would generally be represented by complete essays or book chapters, though students would read all of Michel Foucault's *History of Sexuality: An Introduction* and Sigmund Freud's *Jokes and Their Relation to the Unconscious*. During the segments on individual theorists, each of these figures or approaches would be read as a specific response to certain aspects of implications of Enlightenment thought. After each long critical digression, students would return to selected passages of *Gulliver's Travels* for an open discussion class. In these meetings, they would be asked how their readings of, say, Judith Butler or Foucault affected their interpretations of Swift. Essay assignments, annotated bibliographies, and presentations would all be designed to force students to consolidate and extend their knowledge; I would ask them to confront the various theorists in their response essays and group presentations for each segment, and to cap off the process with a brief research paper on Swift.

When I was finished drawing up this plan, I felt a bit like Swift's professor at the Grand Academy of Lagado, who employed forty student assistants to create and record new combinations of words. Looking over the elaborate schedule and list of topics covered, I asked myself, How would my students perform in a course this demanding? Would my teaching, like the word machine we would undoubtedly discuss during the poststructuralism segment, produce only a travesty of scholarship? Swift's description of this "Project for improving speculative Knowledge by practical and mechanical Operations" was not encouraging: "[T]he Professor shewed me several Volumes in large Folio already collected, of broken Sentences, which he intended to piece together; and out of those rich Materials to give the World a compleat Body of all Arts and Sciences" (173–75). This was not the kind of result I was looking for.

Teaching the Course

Nonetheless, I began the semester with some readings from Immanuel Kant's "What Is Enlightenment?" and John Bender's "A New History of the Enlightenment?" to give students a general sense of what the concept "Enlightenment" meant in the period between Swift and Kant and how Swift as an Anglo-Irish writer could participate in, yet still criticize, the aspects of the Enlightenment embodied by my ambitious counterpart in experimental, speculative, and combinatorial knowledges, the professor at the Grand Academy of Lagado. For the next four weeks, we read through *Gulliver's Travels* slowly enough for the students to feel confident about their ability to understand and interpret the text from beginning to end. During this time, the research teams began assembling their first annotated bibliographies on selected topics in Swift criticism, to be handed in at the end of the fourth week. The real challenges appeared after the fifth week, when students began doing presentations and response essays on the theoretical texts. With each passing week, the students felt that they, like Gulliver, were sailing farther and farther away from home, with little hope of finding themselves or their starting point the same as when they set out. The open days I had scheduled, which were intended for discussing Swift, were used instead for clarifying the theorists we had just read, though everyone tried to steer the open discussions back to Swift whenever possible. It was at this point that the research groups' presentations grew in importance; the presentations began to sustain class discussion at the moments when I was finding it difficult to move things along. The group reports regularly obliged at least three students to take some responsibility for the class, while the presentations themselves, which were generally of a very high quality, became a natural platform for further in-class discussion. Despite the difficulties, most students improved their writing over the course of the semester, and even those who had never before been exposed to Swift or critical theory began to write about both topics with increasing sophistication. When I graded the group portfolios and final papers at the semester's end, I was particularly struck by the consistency and intellectual substance of the work submitted. The course's intensive focus on Swift and its accumulation of collective bibliographies, histories, and outlines on Swift, Swift criticism, and literary theorists and approaches had yielded an impressive group of papers. The randomness or padding I had sometimes found in even the best student research papers was gone. This batch of undergraduate writing excelled anything I had ever received before at the University of Houston.

The students' response throughout the semester and in the final written evaluations was generally positive, even as students acknowledged the heavy demands of the course. I discovered that many were pleased to be taking a separate class designed to introduce them to the authors and concepts that they would use throughout their advanced work in the major, a class, moreover, where basic questions could be raised and addressed without embarrassment. I also learned that in the absence of such a course, many had long been disturbed by the way our curriculum failed to maintain the distinction between beginning and advanced work. Students had long complained of the random groupings the old curriculum created in every class, and rarely felt that they had mastered any particular area before moving on. Students often commented about the unaccustomed pleasure, disappointment, or relief they found in directly reading the works of authors like Foucault or Luce Irigaray, who had been only names conjured up or alluded to in other courses. Some students were surprised that literary studies could encompass so many kinds of methods, materials, and questions. This sense of surprise took positive and negative turns. Some felt that the sheer range of the material covered betrayed a lack of focus; they complained about the amount of reading assigned and the stylistic density of most of the theorists. As one student wrote, "I felt a very high level of frustration all semester—the thinkers we read were incredibly difficult, and I felt disoriented, although I attended class every meeting." Yet most of the class felt that the challenges of the course, though significant, had brought them into contact with intellectual problems and questions that they never would have sought out otherwise. As another student commented, "I originally took [the course] to fulfill a requirement, but I found the material interesting and new (for me). In fact, I can say that I learned more new ideas and ways of thinking in this class than any other I've taken yet."

In general, students were either stimulated or put off by the course's open design, because it demanded that they participate in and ultimately contribute to a collective research project. Every member of the class had to help define the topics we investigated and the methods appropriate for investigating them. In effect, the course was not just about Swift; it was also about Swift read within a number of contexts, for specific interpretive purposes. I believe that the cumulative effect of the different types of inquiry conducted by the class (library and electronic research, response essays, group presentations, etc.) permitted students to begin conceptualizing Swift in a way they had never before attempted. The novelty disconcerted some and intrigued others. In this course, research was treated not just as an empirical task of collecting facts about a particular author or text but also as the far more demanding work of conceptualizing a particular problem within a literary field, investigating it, and trying to answer the questions it raised. When conceived in this way, research becomes a distinctive part of a university (read: postsecondary) education, no matter where that university is located and no matter what kind of student the university is attempting to educate. As professionals dedicated to both research and teaching, we owe our students no less.

Since our decision to restructure the major, assessing the new major's impact (like every other step in this process) has been more complicated than we first expected. For one thing, our budgeting and enrollments have not been stable enough to allow us to discern any real trends in the responses to the changes. Anecdotally, we know that most faculty members enjoy teaching the class and most students enjoy taking it despite the heavy demands it places on both; at the very least, we have not thus far experienced any serious challenge to the new system. We also know that different faculty members have taken on the gateway course every semester it has been offered, so that by next spring a total of eight department members will have tried their versions. Most who have taught the course plan to teach it again. Our students seem equally satisfied with the new arrangement, partly because those graduating under the current plan have exchanged a host of required courses for just one. The new major simplifies and speeds up the process for those interested in graduating quickly, while it offers students at the beginning of advanced course work more opportunities to develop special interests and pursue specific subjects in greater depth. In the coming year, we will be monitoring enrollment figures, graduation rates, GRE scores, and graduate and professional school admissions to see whether we can discern any improvement in those areas. But these kinds of data are often too indirect, ambiguous, or delayed to tell us what is currently happening with students. A look at graduation rates leads us to factors that seem inseparable from the nature of our particular student body; for example, the geographical dispersion of students or their need to work while taking classes. These factors make it difficult to gauge whether a dip in enrollment is caused by our policies or by the job market that keeps pulling our students out of our classrooms.

We do know, however, that the shift to a more elective structure for the major has not dramatically affected the overall balance in our curriculum between traditional and untraditional fields. Interest in canonical, British, or pre–nineteenth-century literature and authors has remained robust, even while we offer new courses in fields such as Mexican American literature. Admittedly, the policy changes have made it harder to predict which courses from our newly expanded roster of electives are needed and which will attract sufficient numbers of students in a given semester. Despite this new complication for scheduling, the Upper Division Curriculum Committee is now attempting to build into the curriculum more slots for advanced classes and seminars. A tier of interesting introductory courses suggests the pedagogical need for a corresponding set of advanced courses, though this perceived need returns us to one of the fundamental questions we began with: Just how committed is the university administration to an interesting and regularly changing undergraduate curriculum? I doubt that such a curriculum can ever emerge if administration and faculty do not share such a goal, and a key role of a tenured research university faculty is to remind administrators of the pedagogical and curricular implications of their decisions. The faculty in a public university like ours should therefore use the issue of curriculum—specifically, the creation and maintenance of an up-to-date, stimulating curriculum for all undergraduates regardless of background—as a way to argue that a full-time, tenured faculty's commitment to research is not merely a matter of personal ambition and professional duty but also a way to maintain a high-quality educational environment that benefits students.

NOTE

I would like to thank my UH colleagues Pat Yongue, María González, and Jay Kastely for their comments, encouragement, and patience over the past three years.

APPENDIX
Syllabus for English 3301, Fall 1997

Week	Tuesday	Thursday
1	Swift, *Gulliver's Travels*, pt. 1. Travel literature.	*GT*, pt. 1. Travel literature.
2	*GT*, pt. 2. Political thought. Form research groups, sign up for bibliography and presentation topics.	*GT*, pt. 2. Political thought. Meeting in rare-book room. Groups will gather information from Swift materials there for their bibliographies.
3	*GT*, pt. 3. Science. Groups continue work on bibliographies.	*GT*, pt. 3. Science. Groups continue work on bibliographies.
4	*GT*, pt. 4. Psychology. Groups continue work on bibliographies.	*GT*, pt. 4. Psychology. Research groups hand in Swift bibliographies, which I will photocopy and distribute to rest of class.
5	**Structuralism and Its Precursors.** Ideology critique: Marx, selections from *German Ideology*. Presentation A.	Psychoanalysis: Freud, *Jokes and Their Relation to the Unconscious*. Presentation B.
6	Linguistics: Saussure, selections from *Course*. Presentation C.	Structuralist anthropology: Lévi-Strauss, "The Structural Study of Myth."
7	Lévi-Strauss, "Four Winnebago Myths." Presentation D.	Open discussion day: Swift, myth, language.
8	Open discussion day. Paper 1 due: on Marx, Freud, Saussure, or Lévi-Strauss. Groups A–D hand in presentations.	**Poststructuralism.** Derrida, "Structure, Sign, and Play." Presentation E.
9	Derrida, "Structure, Sign, and Play."	Foucault, "What Is an Author?" and "Nietzsche, Genealogy, History." Presentation F.
10	Foucault, *History of Sexuality*.	Foucault, *History of Sexuality*.
11	Open discussion day: Swift, science, criticism.	Open discussion day. Paper 2 due: on Derrida or Foucault. Groups E and F hand in presentations.
12	**Gender Theory.** Lacan, "The Meaning of the Phallus." Presentation G.	Irigaray, "Women on the Market." Presentation H.
13	Butler, *Gender Trouble*. Presentation I.	Butler, *Gender Trouble*.
14	Open discussion day: Swift and the feminine. Paper 3 due: on Irigaray, Lacan, or Butler. Groups G–I hand in presentations.	Thanksgiving break.
15	**Postcolonialism.** Said, "Orientalism." Presentation J.	Spivak, "Can the Subaltern Speak?" Presentation K.

Final Grade Breakdown

- Response essays: 40%. You will hand in two brief (2–3 pp.) papers, each 20% of the final grade. These are in response to one of the questions I will distribute for each theorist.
- Research groups: 20%. You will work as part of a three-person team all semester and as part of that group produce two annotated bibliographies (one critical, one theoretical) to be presented to the class, then handed in for a provisional grade. At the end of the semester, each team will hand in its complete portfolio (containing bibliographies, questions, classwork, etc.) to show its collective accomplishments during the semester.
- Participation: 10%. This includes contributions to in-class discussions, research teams, and the electronic discussion group devoted to the class.
- Final research paper: 30%. A final, 7- to 8-page paper, which can be developed from an earlier response essay or presentation, on some aspect of Swift.

READING LIST

Bender, John. "A New History of the Enlightenment?" *The Profession of Eighteenth-Century Literature*. Ed. Leo Damrosch. Madison: U of Wisconsin P, 1992. 62–83.

Butler, Judith. *Gender Trouble: Feminism and the Subversion of Identity*. New York: Routledge, 1990.

De George, Richard T., and Fernande M. De George, eds. *The Structuralists: From Marx to Lévi-Strauss*. Garden City: Anchor, 1972.

Derrida, Jacques. "Structure, Sign, and Play in the Discourse of the Human Sciences." Trans. Alan Bass. *Writing and Difference*. Chicago: U of Chicago P, 1978. 278–93.

Foucault, Michel. *The History of Sexuality*. Vol. 1. Trans. Robert Hurley. New York: Vintage, 1980.

———. "Nietzsche, Genealogy, History." Trans. Donald F. Bouchard and Sherry Simon. *The Foucault Reader*. Ed. Paul Rabinow. New York: Pantheon, 1984. 76–100.

———. "What Is an Author?" Trans. Josué V. Harari. Foucault, *Reader* 101–20.

Freud, Sigmund. *Jokes and Their Relation to the Unconscious*. Trans. James Strachey. New York: Norton, 1960.

Irigaray, Luce. "Women on the Market." *This Sex Which Is Not One*. Ithaca: Cornell UP, 1985. 170–91.

Kant, Immanuel. "What Is Enlightenment?" Trans. and ed. Lewis White Beck. *Kant on History*. New York: Macmillan, 1963. 3–10.

Lacan, Jacques. "The Meaning of the Phallus." Trans. Jacqueline Rose. *Feminine Sexuality: Jacques Lacan and the Ecole Freudienne*. Ed. Juliet Mitchell and Jacqueline Rose. New York: Norton, 1985. 74–85.

Lévi-Strauss, Claude. "Four Winnebago Myths." De George and De George 195–208.

———. "The Structural Study of Myth." De George and De George 169–94.

Marx, Karl. "The German Ideology: Part I." Trans. S. Ryazanskaya. *The Marx-Engels Reader*. Ed. Robert C. Tucker. New York: Norton, 1978. 146–202.

Said, Edward W. *Orientalism*. New York: Vintage, 1979.

———. "Swift as Intellectual." Said, *World* 72–89.

———. "Swift's Tory Anarchy." Said, *World* 54–71.

———. *The World, the Text, and the Critic*. Cambridge: Harvard UP, 1983.

Saussure, Ferdinand de. "Course in General Linguistics." De George and De George 58–79.

Spivak, Gayatri Chakravorty. "Can the Subaltern Speak?" *Marxism and the Interpretation of Culture*. Ed. Cary Nelson and Lawrence Grossberg. Urbana: U of Illinois P, 1988. 271–313.

Swift, Jonathan. *Gulliver's Travels*. Ed. Christopher Fox. Boston: Bedford, 1995.

Collegiality, Crisis, and Cultural Studies

LAUREN BERLANT

Humility is not conventionally associated with the project of cultural studies. This is because, despite constant assertions that their knowledge is historically contingent and politically specific and will not always be true, the scholars who engage in this work seem to want to change the world through criticism: they risk grandiosity of the intellect in believing that their critical acts and pedagogical practices will have concrete effects that, collectively repeated over long duration, might help to bring into being a better understanding of cultural struggles and create a less unjust world. They seem always to know whether a cultural event is a positive, a negative, or an ambivalent thing; they are often accused of having no patience for reading or research or for appreciating beauty; they are said to take too much rhetorical pleasure in studying political pain; they appear greedily to critique professional protocols while also seeking their protections and rewards.

As if these evidences of grandiosity were not enough, there is also the question of what kinds of knowledge cultural studies seeks to produce. Even the theorists and anthologists find defining cultural studies an impossible task, since it has no proper methodology, object of study, or home discipline. Yet reading through the anthologies one can still identify a set of recognizable engagements that are of a scale so immense that it is hard to see how any practitioner of cultural studies can ever put pen to paper

The author is Professor of English and of the Humanities in the Department of English at the University of Chicago. A version of this article appeared in the Fall 1997 issue of the ADE Bulletin.

(Baker, Best, and Lindeborg; During; Franklin, Lury, and Stacey; Grossberg, Nelson, and Treichler; Hall, "Legacies" and "Paradigms"; McRobbie). Dedicated to engaging with and writing the history of the present, cultural studies seeks to address and explicate the geopolitical specificity of cultural forms and practices; to describe not only the hierarchical mechanisms that produce identities of all kinds but also the contexts for agential practice, resistance, and experience articulated around those mechanisms; to track in particular peoples' ordinary lives the effects of discursive and institutional practices of domination, subordination, and hegemony; to appraise technologies of intimacy, longing, aversion, and ecstasy; and to historicize political spaces and forms like bodies, schools, cities, nations, and transnational corporations. While some of these domains and interests can be found in traditional humanistic work (e.g., work whose central concern is not the contemporary pressures and struggles to which it responds), cultural studies is also engaged in an experiment with the organization of knowledge around the objects, spaces, and events it entextualizes. In much cultural studies work the object or event does not organize the meaning and value of criticism. Instead, new sites of knowledge are brought into being through the textual performance (thus the *MLA Bibliography* has a terrible time classifying cultural studies essays, for frequently there is in them no known, obvious, or central object of value, interpretation, theoretical speculation, or culture). Perhaps this is why I prefer the definition Fredric Jameson offers in an essay that begins, "The desire called Cultural Studies . . . " (251).

At the time of this writing, a backlash against cultural studies is emerging in the humanities and the humanistic social sciences. This resistance expresses important concerns about the risks of cultural or historical anachronism and comparison; about the status of scholarship that seems at times to be motivated by an unself-conscious presentism or a smug moralism; about the analytic status of various forms of generic syncretism, especially autobiographical critical writing; about nonrigorous engagements with a mass culture that is all too available for reading; and about the apparent desire to create confusion regarding the kinds of behaviors, knowledges, and practices that should constitute professionalism, both among colleagues and between faculty members and students. Many scholars who politicize their work, such as Gayatri Spivak, agree with those who are typically their antagonists that work on culture and power should be held to exacting notions of evidence, argument, research, tone, and theoretical and historical rigor (116).

But it is hasty and frequently in bad faith to identify cultural studies in general as anecdotal, posturing, and easy to do. It is merely defensive to assume that cultural studies' sites of challenge and critical experimentality inherently or even usually preclude the production of consequential knowledge and the consideration of serious concepts. Those of us who work with theory are all familiar with the use of humiliating ad hominem anecdotes to generalize about strange or threatening kinds of thinking; we have all heard colleagues distort or amplify weak sentences or underdeveloped terms in particular cases to make a general point—for example, "It's just bad sociology about trivial objects." There are many reasons why this kind of cheap shot, as well as more subtle ones, must be countered.

The backlash against cultural studies is often a displaced expression of discomfort with work on contemporary culture. Attacking cultural studies is frequently a way of expressing a kind of fatigue with issues of "race, class, and gender." (Even cultural studies types often use the word *mantra* to express their alienation from this phrase and their fear that it reflects a shallow habit of thought rather than a truly risky engagement.) It is sometimes a way of talking about the fear of losing what little standing intellectual work in the humanities has gained through its studied irrelevance (or superiority) to capitalist culture. It can express an aversion to popular culture or to popularized criticism. It can signal a faculty member's fear of becoming irrelevant to graduate students and to the changing profession. At the same time it can express antielitism—against the star system or in defense of a commonsense definition of proper intellectual objects and postures (Shumway; Guillory, "Preprofessionalism"). On the left it frequently expresses a fear that critical metatheory will lose its standing as the ground of politics and serious thought.

I am not saying that work in cultural studies is always what I wish it were or that these anxieties are without foundation. But since attacks on cultural studies cloak many kinds of worthy and unworthy suspicion and ambivalence, it behooves us to try to say what these hidden feelings are and to disaggregate them from one another.[1] There are, of course, substantive intellectual issues that stem from what I call "the problem of tinny knowledge" and "the problem of sexy knowledge." But there are also less conspicuous issues of institutional culture that should be addressed as contexts of what we are calling "the crisis."[2] One ground of my argument concerns an area of professional life for which virtually no faculty member is trained: collegiality. I mean by this term a cluster of issues relevant to the public management of professional life: the inevitable vulnerability that comes from having ideas and doing work in public; the strangeness of negotiating the odd intimacy of institutional association with colleagues we know well yet barely know; the hierarchies of professorship that mediate, though it's never clear how, the personal relationships among faculty members; the interpersonal effort involved in the daily grind of professorship; the strain of optimistic institution building in this difficult context. But because "professionals" are trained to do skill-based tasks but not to participate in institutional life and because humanities scholars in particular are trained to focus on their individual intellectual pursuits rather than their public status, little explicit pedagogy about the contradictions and complexities of institutional life ever takes place when students become colleagues. We learn to be professionals as assistant professors, when we are institutionally at our weakest; we figure out institutional cultures and imitate those whom we like or who we think have institutional savvy; we follow our survival instincts; we figure out how not to feel constantly threatened by the possible disrespect of colleagues and students and how to read the meaning of their respect; we brood about the demons that chase us and the ones that we chase, or we don't brood about them and instead just act and react. Our dignity often seems to be on the line, but no one ever talks about institutional life as a debilitating collective nightmare, which it so often is.

These issues of vulnerability, dignity, and respect are so sotto voce, so tacit and hidden in the institutional culture of the academy that they tend to be expressed and visible only when an institutional transformation seems to be emerging. At moments of change, we are terrible at keeping distinct the different feelings this cluster of issues inspires. Thus when new knowledge projects come along, especially ones that challenge established aesthetic or academic contexts and concerns, they charge these issues, bringing them to voice, but in a way that displaces and distorts what is extremely personal and structural about questions of power and value in the practice of institutional culture. In short, we improvise around our old anxieties, and the new thing—here, cultural studies—gives shape to issues that its eradication would not eradicate from our lives.

In other words, whatever concerns we have about the challenge cultural studies presents to traditional or disciplinary literary study, we must be attentive to how the trepidation around that issue displaces or allegorizes other questions of power and legitimacy in the academy, which used to operate, so I hear, as a genteel and gentlemanly place where people could assume that they recognized the same objects as objects of knowledge and where intelligence and goodwill would be enough, somehow, to ensure the making of collegial intellectual worlds. At stake in this discussion, then, is the value of certain kinds of thinking. But I also consider the need for an explicitness about collegiality and professional life that is direct without being brutal: specifically, an explicitness about how to handle the critical, pedagogical, and personal differences that get especially animated when we are managing departmental curricula, hiring, promotion, and tenure; teaching (especially teaching graduate students); and making intellectual public spheres. Keeping these two axes of practice in mind, I try to address more specifically some ways of recasting the emanations from the so-called crisis of critical culture.

I begin with some anecdotal evidence, for as we all know, that's what cultural studies people do. I have just finished a book on sex and citizenship called *The Queen of America Goes to Washington City*. In contrast to my first book, which is organized almost entirely around one canonical novel, and my third (in process), which is mainly organized around popular non-canonical novels about women and their "classic" filmic incarnations, there is barely any "literature" in this book—though there is, of course, a lot of reading. As I traveled around giving papers from this project, I was startled at the frequency with which well-meaning people said aggressive and defensive things to me about loving my thinking but hating my archive or about their need for me to say in print what I must be thinking—that the popular texts on which I write are bad art and as such cannot sustain interest "on their own." (For nonhearsay evidence of the disciplinary discomfort this project has raised, see Nelson and Gaonkar 15–18.) These events made me curious and turned into a kind of metacontext for my own methodological self-understanding, on which I report briefly in the introduction to *The Queen of America*. Were these questions expressions of disciplinary anxiety? Were they suggestions that these texts aren't hard enough for someone with my professional training and skills? Should there be some mimesis between the kind of mind one has and the kind of text one reads? Is it necessary to balance out the perceived lack of aesthetic value of the texts I work on with the cultural capital of critical metatheory?

I didn't feel particularly defensive about these interrogations, but the anxiety they evidenced did surprise me. My sense is that everything needs to be read: the materials that most strongly define any present moment are as likely to become historical ephemera as they are to become apparent master texts. The very ephemerality of an archive makes it worth reading. Its very popularity or its effects on everyday life or its expression of emblematic knowledge makes it important. Its very ordinariness requires reflecting on what is merely undramatically explicit. (Of course, in saying this, I might as well be a scholar of some premodern period. But perhaps because the objects of much work in cultural studies are not in rare book rooms, interest in contemporary popular works is rarely given the same respect as interest in older materials, a respect that might make questions about what makes an archive more vital and central in pedagogy in the field.)

This experience helped me clarify the professional juncture at which I and others in United States cultural studies stand: because humanists traditionally accrue value by being intimate with the classics (literary and theoretical), those who think through popular materials and contextualize them through atypical kinds of rhetoric threaten to degrade the value of intellectual life in general and of the humanities in particular. That is to say, it is not the popularity or the contemporaneity of the materials that makes this work feel precarious but the sense that the stories told about the materials aren't hard enough, that they require too little overcoming of temporal, cultural, or linguistic alterity. Many of my interlocutors would have been happier if I had spoken more metatheoretically, so nervous are they about the lack of value emanating from popular culture. For some, arcane archives and theories provide the necessary ballast for criticism of contemporary ephemera, for they affirm the distance between the knower and the known that makes thinking an enterprise of courage and merit.

I won't comment further on my own work in this regard, apart from noting that thinking is never easy and archives never obvious, but my experiences do raise serious questions about how authors committed to writing contemporary culture understand the exacting demands of thinking historically in the making of a present. Carolyn Steedman calls these demands "the transference of the past" in cultural studies: historicizing critical questions means understanding the inevitable activity of anachronism in keeping histories signifying, open, vital, and productive. Sometimes this involves working through the prehistory of issues that compel us in the present. But when scholars study the present how can anyone know whether they know anything that counts, that matters, that should survive its utterance? What is the status of an anecdote, of an example, of the case and the argument it bolsters? And what is the value of knowledge read off of a simple or banal or unskillfully crafted text? In literary and media terms, these questions represent a desire for critics to understand things about meaning everyone used to have to know: that genres have material and semiotic histories, that political questions have traditions, that identities and capitalism are always in crisis, that clichés might be tropes with complex genealogies. To me the questions seem to indicate not the weakness of cultural studies but the vitality and critical promise of its engagements.

When evaluating students and one another, surely we must constantly monitor the impulse to assume that knowledges we would not want to have or to save are not worth having, saving, or disseminating. So much depends on whether the thinker can think originally and strongly with his or her examples; so much depends on whether disparate texts can be made to seem like sufficient grounds for an archive whose implications for knowledge are TBA: but these arguments are banalities. Yet how often, in departmental meetings or editorial contexts, does one have to argue that there is nothing inevitable about the value an object carries, even a canonical object? And if an essay seems heartless and tinny, empty and brainless, or lacking courage but full of bluster, the reason may not be that the wizard is not a wizard, just an ordinary person who writes cultural studies. Perhaps the text has a wisdom it takes time to decipher. Or maybe the author doesn't even know his or her own argument. Or maybe the reader finds the logic hard or doesn't want to be surprised by a context for knowledge. But if cultural studies constantly raises the question of shallowness or incomplete thinking—because its texts are so available and because its claims are so strangely both populist and avant-garde—these two questions are not that different from those we constantly raise about the relations among archives, cases, concepts, and arguments that use more obviously alien and historicized texts. It is true that cultural studies students often assume that the present exists and assume that they are already competent to understand it: these assumptions are both theoretically false and usually ethnocentric. Working against the presumption that the present is transparent requires strenuous teaching and self-monitoring about how modernities are generated, become facts scholars think they know about the political and rhetorical contexts of people's lives. But is it worthwhile to have competence in the present? It must be, and in this regard cultural studies critics share a project with traditional historians who study how texts, institutions, and persons have generated a sense of their own present and consider periodicity in general.

Of course, these questions of presentism do not take place in an institutional vacuum, and so I want to move from the internal question of the easy archive to the more complicated question of sexy knowledge and to the anxieties cultural studies work raises, that issues not about selves and bodies and pain and power will no longer be studied by anyone. Those who worry about cultural studies see that identity politics is a popular ground of criticism, yet to some it seems too easy a ground or seems too protected by the aura of authenticity that gives the writer authority prior to and in excess of what his or her ideas might merit. What is the point of intellectual work that can't be argued with, except from within the identity form, if then? Skeptics also see how much fun cultural studies people have in overreading, moralizing about, and radically recontextualizing commodities and mass-culture texts; perhaps skeptics believe that the university, Casaubon-like, makes knowledge valuable by associating it with seriousness, pain, and death so that few would want to seek it and thus preserves knowledge as the valuable property of elites. Maybe so. But it is also true, as John Guillory (*Cultural Capital*) and Dave Hickey write, that much work in literature—work on genre, on beauty, on poetry, on narrative—seems almost impossible to imagine undefensively now without the legitimating context of power-knowledge studies. And if a concern with how power makes meaning makes knowledge sexy, those who have other interests or other ways of writing tend to feel resentful that certain styles of trendy professional gloss protected by what feels like proleptic moralizing are widely published, while other work that makes less grandiose claims about meaning and power can barely find audiences. We all have fine students suffering on the market because they don't sound like the putative cutting edge. At the same time, many of us have fine cultural studies students on the market who don't get seriously considered because they do sound cutting-edge. A colleague tells me that this phenomenon has been called "the revenge of the disrespected."

But who has cultivated conversations across these intellectual and theoretical fields to see whether disrespect is what reigns or alienation, confusion, and mutual defensiveness? To the extent that this phenomenon is generational, why are those on the bottom (the assistant professors and lecturers and graduate students) so often made to seem like the cause of the discomfort, made to feel responsible for building bridges to the tenured, when they have virtually nothing to stand on, much worse prospects for professional life than anyone else ever had? (And why are these same populations being blamed for the star system?) In some departments, I know, this breach is not lived generationally: rather, a sense that lifestyles go along with modes of thought makes some people think that if their work occupies a distinct professional habitus, they have no interests, inclinations, or commitments in common with their colleagues who are associated with other intellectual practices. I think the "crisis" of cultural studies requires more attention to these overimplicit domains of personal and professional value. As universities downsize and every hire comes to seem like a victory for a certain group's desire for the department's future, faculty members feel, unnecessarily, I think, that to survive they must take sides in what is almost always a no-win situation.

This point brings me to the third circle of hell, the political economy of the contemporary academy, and to the questions of graduate education raised not only by the specter of a generation trained to do sexy but tinny intellectual work but also by the ways cultural studies' emergence might play out structural changes in the United States university and in the economy in general, as a virtual industry of metaprofessional texts has been arguing (Berlant, "Feminism"; Guillory, "Preprofessionalism"; Martin; Nelson). The question of graduate education comes in two parts, it seems to me: the first might be called "the tragedy of early professionalization" and the second "academia postutopia."

Another way to track the questions I've been raising about the institutional contexts for suspicion about cultural studies is to note how it plays out as a concern about graduate teaching, one of the most direct means of disciplinary reproduction and change. What vague answer do we give when a graduate student asks, "What do I have to do to get a job?" Students try to read their prospects by looking at their teachers: Who among us represents a horizon of possibility? Who can help students survive (in) the profession? The ideal faculty member might have what looks from the outside like a "good" career but might also be someone with a different kind of profile or no one at all. Survival seems random, virtually magical. But after attending the MLA convention, area and regional conferences, and the cluster of graduate student conferences that proliferate yearly, students come more and more to see their task in graduate school as achieving a critical position, a finished look, the aura of authorship, and the mastery of an original archive; less and less do they seem to have the privilege of being students, by which I mean nostalgically to remember the time when there was time enough to do a lot of research that panned out in nothing but knowledge—no dissertation, no publication, no conference paper. The early professionalization of graduate students isn't all bad—it's deinfantilizing. But the sense that time is a vise imminently around the necks of students who cannot afford either to be in or out of graduate school has to be one condition for the proliferation of cultural studies. Remember, I am not saying that cultural studies is easy to do—nothing is easy to do well. I am saying that the problem of selling oneself on a virtually imaginary market has made many graduate students feel threatened and impatient and has mixed up questions about inclination and talent with the desire to be in a critical discussion and thus to be desirable to someone—in a peer group, on a hiring committee, or on an editorial board. Partly, this situation is a result of the star system; surely it is evidence of how grim graduate students' lives have become.

One further reason that certain forms of cultural studies have gained so much energy now is the pressure on graduate students to be original, to publish, and to go on the market with a finished dissertation that is as close to a book as imaginable. Most graduate students are already stretched to the limit with student loans, and many teach virtually full-time as TAs: given what we know about the conditions under which even the privileged are now being trained in graduate school, the requirement that incoming faculty members look like tenured professors once did seems cruel and bizarre. Why is this situation the norm? Cary Nelson argues that "what underwrites the fragile ethics of this whole enterprise is the logic of apprenticeship—graduate students are in training to become higher-paid professors. But if there are no jobs [since the profession has massively overproduced PhDs,] the whole logic collapses and graduate student teachers become exploited labor. . . . [And] the injustices generate rage and self-loathing, contained by the ideology of professionalism" (131–32). At the University of Illinois, Urbana, many graduate students teach the same course loads as assistant professors do, make substantially less money, and get no benefits. If these students are politically engaged and want their work to be integrated with their struggle for living or if they see media studies and cultural studies as instrumental knowledge contexts, who can blame them?

Why have these incongruities and contradictions in the conditions and expectations of professional production not become a central topic in discussions about the political economy of knowledge, about pedagogy, or about hiring in the university? Why haven't they been joined by discussions of the ways industrial speed-up has affected already hired faculty members, who are suffering under burgeoning teaching and advising responsibilities while performing voluntary labor in transdisciplinary areas we care about and the university needs, like cultural studies, queer and feminist studies, ethnicity- and race-based departments, media studies, centers for global culture, and so on? It might be that the exhaustion and overproduction have become so normal for so many faculty members that the situation sounds like normal academic life when graduate students experience it. But again, I think that the farther from tenure scholars are, the more time they should have to develop their relation to thinking and working. This is not the general view of the academy.

Sometimes students complete great dissertations, and some assistant professors write more essays and books than their seniors did. But what happens to new PhDs when they compete with five hundred others for a broadly defined job? What happens when young faculty members come up for promotion or try for fellowships? I'd like to close by addressing one more aspect of the crisis in institutional culture that has been stimulated but not created by the emergence of cultural studies in the United States. It has to do with something rarely spoken of in public but central to many academic contexts: peer review and field expertise in professional evaluations. As I have said, an environment of distrust characterizes many literature departments (and departments in other fields), and this distrust has to do with largely unworked-through differences over the relative value of archival, theoretical, and rhetorical mastery—anxieties that the often strange and estranging work broadly defined as cultural studies intensifies. Anyone who has ever run a hiring meeting or sat on admissions committees or participated in tenure and promotion decisions knows how much euphemized language is spoken at these meetings. It often takes a wizard or a hardened cynic to figure out what the real discussion is about, and too often the public discussion reeks of the pro forma. Sometimes it is hard to find anyone who comes into a meeting not knowing how they're going to vote. It's as though discussion means nothing, is a performance of professionality that is not about persuasion or building collective intellectual or pedagogical contexts. Moreover, because few not already intimate colleagues trust one another and no one trusts promises of confidentiality, it is also hard to know how to interpret the evaluations we encounter. Here we should be giving our attention to developing mechanisms for collectively considering the political and ethical conundrums of local institutional life. We should be building strategies for naming and delineating the differences between concerns about intellectual value and the inevitable personal (dis)comforts that can make our inevitable collegial antagonisms into sites of panicky improvisation. We should be seriously reconsidering how peer review works. Of course, in advocating these considerations, I have strayed from the topic of crisis and cultural studies. But I would rather talk about the problems of ethics, value, trust, hierarchy, and labor in academic life than use cultural studies as an alibi, one more time, for the urgency of responding to the institutional pressures of the present that have rendered so many of us bitter or angry or tired or cynical or perhaps simply confused about what to do in this moment of intellectual expansion and economical downsizing in the United States academy.

NOTES

[1] The preceding three paragraphs revise material from my book *The Queen of America Goes to Washington City*.

[2] I wrote this essay in response to a request to meditate on the following hypothesis: that cultural studies destabilizes the institutional standing of English departments, both because it challenges the value of the study of literature and because it creates personal and intellectual disaffection among colleagues. I was asked to do this as someone who "does" cultural studies.

WORKS CITED

Baker, Houston A., Jr., Stephen Best, and Ruth H. Lindeborg. "Representing Blackness / Representing Britain: Cultural Studies and the Politics of Knowledge." *Black British Cultural Studies*. Ed. Baker, Manthia Diawara, and Lindeborg. Chicago: U of Chicago P, 1996. 1–15.

Berlant, Lauren. "Feminism and the Institutions of Intimacy." *The Politics of Research*. Ed. E. Ann Kaplan and George Levine. New Brunswick: Rutgers UP, 1997.

———. *The Queen of America Goes to Washington City: Essays on Sex and Citizenship*. Durham: Duke UP, 1997.

During, Simon. Introduction. *The Cultural Studies Reader*. New York: Routlege, 1993. 1–25.

Franklin, Sarah, Celia Lury, and Jackie Stacey. "Feminism and Cultural Studies: Pasts, Presents, Futures." *Off-Centre: Feminism and Cultural Studies*. Ed. Franklin, Lury, and Stacey. New York: Harper, 1991. 1–19.

Grossberg, Lawrence, Cary Nelson, and Paula Treichler, eds. *Cultural Studies*. New York: Routledge, 1992.

———. "Cultural Studies: An Introduction." Grossberg, Nelson, and Treichler, *Cultural Studies* 1–22.

Guillory, John. *Cultural Capital: The Problem of Literary Canon Formation*. Chicago: U of Chicago P, 1993.

———. "Preprofessionalism: What Graduate Students Want." *Profession 1996*. New York: MLA, 1996. 91–99.

Hall, Stuart. "Cultural Studies and Its Theoretical Legacies." Grossberg, Nelson, and Treichler, *Cultural Studies* 277–94.

———. "Cultural Studies: Two Paradigms." *Culture/Power/History: A Reader in Contemporary Social Theory*. Ed. Nicholas B. Dirks, Geoffrey H. Eley, and Sherry B. Ortner. 1980. Princeton: Princeton UP, 1994. 520–38.

Hickey, Dave. *The Invisible Dragon: Four Essays on Beauty*. Los Angeles: Art Issues, 1993.

Jameson, Fredric. "On *Cultural Studies*." *The Identity in Question*. Ed. John Rajchman. New York: Routledge, 1995. 251–95.

Martin, Biddy. "Teaching Literature, Changing Cultures." *PMLA* 112 (1997): 7–25.

McRobbie, Angela. *Postmodernism and Popular Culture*. New York: Routledge, 1994.

Nelson, Cary. "Lessons from the Job Wars: Late Capitalism Arrives on Campus." *Social Text* 44 (1995): 119–34.

Nelson, Cary, and Dilip Parameshwar Gaonkar. "Cultural Studies and the Politics of Disciplinarity." *Disciplinarity and Dissent in Cultural Studies*. Ed. Nelson and Gaonkar. New York: Routledge, 1996. 1–19.

Spivak, Gayatri Chakravorty. "Time and Timing." *Chronotypes: The Construction of Time*. Ed. John Bender and David Wellbery. Stanford: Stanford UP, 1991. 99–117, 235–41.

Shumway, David. "The Star System in Literary Studies." *PMLA* 112 (1997): 85–100.

Steedman, Carolyn. "Culture, Cultural Studies, and the Historians." Grossberg, Nelson, and Treichler, *Cultural Studies* 613–21.

Is Teaching the Literature of Western Culture Inconsistent with Valuing Diversity?

LORI SCHROEDER HASLEM

DIVERSITY, THE CORE, AND THE LITERARY "CANON"

I have often recalled two particular comments that for me open up key pedagogical issues in my own discipline—literature, especially English literature—and that continue to spur my thinking about the meaning and goals of curricular diversity. One of these comments came from a fellow faculty member concerned about the performance of incoming freshmen in his classes and frustrated that there was not a common body of literary knowledge that he could expect from them. "It used to be," he said, "that we could count on their having read at least certain authors—such as Hemingway—in high school." He then wanted to know which works he could at least count on their reading in any section of our college's freshman writing course. I did not explain to my colleague—someone very much involved in issues of diversity—that Hemingway is these days hardly the darling of literature professors committed to issues of diversity, but I did talk with him about the enormous difficulty of having it both ways, that is, of urging our students to value diverse literatures while simultaneously expecting them to share a given body of literary knowledge.

Such difficulty is especially pronounced with regard to diversifying any kind of core curriculum. After all, *core* by definition refers to something central throughout a student's four years of college, and as things currently

---

The author is Assistant Professor of English at Knox College.

---

stand at the college where I teach and probably at many other colleges and universities, even two sections of the same core course may share not even a single offering.[1] From one point of view, this may be a strength (the core offers diverse literary selections), but from another, it may be a decided weakness (core courses cannot be well integrated with one another from year to year because there is so little common content). There is likewise a trade-off when we strive to assign works in common across the core, as my colleague seemed to wish we would. For the more we do so, the more we convey that there is an entrenched "canon"—a group of literary works most worth study—and thereby limit the diversity of literature we can offer.

My colleague's question, therefore, reopened for me what are perplexing questions about the ideological and pedagogical bases of a diversified curriculum. Must we sacrifice core diversity to gain core solidity or, conversely, sacrifice core solidity to gain core diversity? Can we build a solid, cohesive, four-year core without requiring students to read and study at least some of the same works or authors? If not, how do we (and *can* we even) decide which works or authors should be canonized as core essentials? Should the diversity of authors' ethnic and gendered identities, for instance, be the principle on which we base most or all selections? And must we assume that teaching the previously canonized literature of Western culture is now inconsistent with the goals of curricular diversity? These are not unanswerable questions, in my judgment, but they are ones that must be faced honestly.

A couple of summers ago, I looked forward to facing such questions honestly by participating in a summer institute on values and diversity at my college. But even after the institute we were no closer to resolving them than we were when we started. Determined to achieve some kind of practical and documentable results, we devoted ourselves to working on improving diversity in individual course offerings. Our facilitator gave faculty participants the aim of revamping one of our courses as though it were to be taught to a poor female student of color. We were not asked to consider the assumption that surely underpinned this directive, namely, that our courses (as previously taught) were presumably aimed at many or all students *except* the poor female student of color. Also, we were not asked to consider how each course could help our hypothetical student to build on or further explore diversity issues introduced in her previous courses, in the core or otherwise. So most of us did what was probably expected: we sought ways to bring in authors not usually taught in our courses or to introduce class exercises not previously conducted.

Perhaps what we accomplished was of some merit. But I think now that our approach fell short in the way that projects in diversifying the curriculum seem to me so often to fall short: we focused on how to supplement or to reconfigure the content of individual courses and said little about how we could articulate and communicate to students our shared reasons—across and among the many individual courses we revamped—for highlighting "difference" and "diversity." Perhaps without speaking of it we were basing our collective efforts on the broad (I daresay on the old-fashioned and humanistic) assumption that exposing students to "difference" is inherently good for their intellectual health[2]—an assumption that I generally share but whose terms I find at times maddeningly slippery. Or perhaps many in the group felt, as I did, that we ought not to raise the issue of unifying our thinking on goals and purposes; after all, this was an institute on diversity, not unity. But this last possibility also leaves me wondering now whether we do not, ironically, weaken the project of valuing diversity by too often treating unity and diversity as mutually exclusive principles when of course they are not. Such binary thinking can, I think, pose a particular danger for a core curriculum.

The other comment that still stimulates my pedagogical thinking on diversity came from a student during that summer institute. We were asked to assemble in small groups to outline our utopian visions of the college in the year 2000. Some envisioned better wheelchair accessibility, increased scholarship dollars for students of color, or female administrators at the highest levels. But one young woman expressed her desire to cut Shakespeare from the core because he did not speak to her experience as a young Asian American woman.

In some ways I regret that I did not respond to this young woman's complaint. I did not respond partly because it was the first day, partly because we were instructed to indulge each other's utopias, partly because I was not altogether sure how comfortable the student participants would be with disagreement coming from the faculty and partly because I—as the only faculty member in attendance who specialized in Shakespeare—was afraid of sounding damnably partisan. Also, since I had heard many students make similar claims at the beginning of a course on Shakespeare only to retract them later, her opinion did not greatly surprise me. What did surprise me as the institute progressed, however, was that the young woman's sentiments about the irrelevance of the dead white European Shakespeare were shared in spirit by many of the other participants. That is, the tacit understanding seemed to be that the literature not only of Shakespeare but also of all Western culture was and is somehow a culprit literature inconsistent with the aims of diversity. It seemed to be a given that the single best way to achieve curricular diversity is to incorporate works and ideas by authors (especially non-Western authors) of diverse ethnic and gendered identities as much as possible.

Now, I agree that it is valuable to take this idea as one of the principles for diversifying the curriculum (though, of course, the phrase "as much as possible" in itself presents myriad problems of interpretation). The whole of the curriculum should not be the province of any single cultural outlook; even less should the literature of any culture be summarily revered rather than painstakingly studied and critiqued. But I also think that either to include or to exclude works from the curriculum on the basis of the authors' identities is dangerously limiting and perhaps even self-defeating if it becomes the sole or the primary principle for diversification. I say self-defeating because, as Ross Chambers observes, there is a basic irony involved in the project of eradicating Western authors and plugging in non-Western authors:

> The most crippling blindness that can afflict [...] a pedagogy is blindness to its own constitution and function within the system it works against, a blindness to its own systematicity.
>
> Our relation to the canon is a case in point [...]. We seek to oppose the canon by changing the titles of texts and the names of authors that figure there [...], not opposing the system of canonicity itself. Because exclusions from the canon have in the past been legitimated on absurd grounds having to do with social identities of authors, we now find ourselves forced into the inclusion of texts on the same grounds. (20)[3]

Compounding the irony, as Chambers further notes, is that canonizing certain authors while decanonizing others also positions us outside prevailing literary theory, which holds that literary meaning is an ever-shifting thing dependent on many factors: reader, text, author, historical conditions, cultural assumptions, and so on. Obviously, then, we cannot serve the goals of literary diversity simply by reconfiguring the authors of the canon (even if that were a "simple" enterprise).

Perhaps we first need to admit that because of the limits naturally imposed on us by the course-and-syllabus system, we teachers cannot escape doing a certain amount of canonizing whenever we include certain texts and exclude others from our courses. Students will inevitably regard those we include as somehow more worth study than those excluded. So when we exclude some texts and include others solely on the basis of who the authors are, we are not in any way dissolving the canon; we are simply canonizing a new group of texts. In my view we often fail to admit that such privileging of a new set of texts is not synonymous with achieving curricular diversity. For surely the project of diversifying the curriculum must involve a reappraisal of pedagogical approach as well as curricular content, a conclusion that seems obvious to me because it is so widely accepted—and practiced—in my field.[4]

But it was clearly not the obvious conclusion of the young woman who felt that a necessary first step in diversifying the core would be to toss out Shakespeare. And I wish I could now say to her what I would like to have said then: "If we read only texts that speak to our own unique identities, we isolate and limit ourselves. I wish someone had encouraged you to try reading—Shakespeare or anyone—not to find yourself faithfully replicated in and by the text but rather to explore otherness in it and, where necessary, to take issue with the portions of the text that misrepresent you as a woman, as someone of non-Western heritage, as a human being. For it is in the very nexus of your agreements and disagreements with the text that you can learn not only to read Shakespeare or any author but, most important, to read and to understand yourself as a unique person with unique values."

Since every bit of course and classroom content is value-laden and since all values are subjectively related and understood, it especially behooves us faculty members to make ourselves conscious of which values we espouse and communicate through our teaching and other interactions with students. Accordingly, I believe, course content—though a deeply important issue to curricular diversity—should actually figure less in our thinking on how to educate students than should the teachers' and students' handling of course content, their collective efforts to bring to the surface and to grapple with whichever values are being asserted and whichever are being overturned or tested. And where the study of literature is concerned, the effort of surfacing and grappling with values must first and crucially involve the not-so-easy business of trying to understand who is doing the asserting or overturning of these values: the author? the text? a character in the text? the teacher? the student(s)? To my thinking, it is precisely this "surfacing" of values that should be a primary—if not the primary—principle behind diversifying the literature curriculum. By teaching according to such a principle we can best educate our students on how to read for the diversity of values that is in and that surrounds any literature; otherwise, we communicate to them the idea that diverse values are the special territory of works by selected or previously underrepresented authors.

My own answer to the question I pose in this essay's title is a resounding no. Of course teaching the literature of Western culture is not inconsistent with valuing diversity. Courses either featuring or including Western literature (but especially English literature, on which I am best informed) can and do contribute as much to a curriculum devoted to valuing diversity as courses on ethnic and women's literature, provided that both kinds of courses are indeed taught and provided that both are taught with the main purpose of exploring the values and assumptions of students and authors.

VALUING "DEAD WHITE EUROPEAN MALES"

The kinds of English courses I have taught over the past ten years or so have necessarily affected my outlook on what it means to address issues of diversity in the classroom. The courses I now teach, some composition and some literature, belong to the core. Every year I also teach large sections of a survey course covering early English literature (roughly *Beowulf* through Milton). In choosing the literature to be studied in some of these classes, I have considerable latitude. But in the others, I am much more restricted by historical periods. And yet I feel, and this may strike some as odd, that I have had some of my greatest successes in helping students to address issues of diversity in the very courses that focus on writings by early modern Caucasian English men. I find myself alternately suspicious of and encouraged by these perceived successes—suspicious because I listen to and understand the criticism that Western literature's modes and representations are often exclusivist, encouraged because I like to think that this early literature is helping my students (as it has helped me) to distinguish carefully between the truths and the untruths about early English literary exclusivism. I suspect that many others in teaching positions similar to my own have experienced such vacillations.

If part of the goal is truly to educate students about the cultural exclusivism that is indeed reflected in and by much Western literature, it is crucial that they develop and hone the skills of analyzing and reacting to what is now often characterized by many outside the field as the evil empire of literature. These analytical skills are especially important, I would argue, for literature majors. No one seems to deny that the literature of Western culture has had extraordinary influence (sometimes desirable, sometimes not) on modern-day American culture. I want my students not to conclude simply that such influence should or should not have occurred but rather to consider how and why it has occurred and continues to occur. And I believe they cannot consider the hows and whys without studying a significant portion of that literature firsthand. My English majors, for instance, are often surprised and fascinated by how many current attitudes toward women they find seeded in such early works as *Beowulf*, where women are mainly the pawns of a patriarchal warrior culture; in Castiglione's *The Courtier*, where women are cast as vehicles for male salvation; or in Chaucer's Wife of Bath's Tale, where the title character takes on (with varied, often ironic, success) many of the misogynistic attitudes of her era. To be educated on feminist issues, these students find, means being educated on the literary history of feminist issues (though of course we do not read any of these works with the sole purpose of excavating feminist issues).

Moreover, it is only by reading works generated over the course of centuries that students can consider that the body of early literature is not static—in thought or in mode—but ever fresh with new challenges to previous social practices and to religious, philosophic, and political thought. Students can be encouraged to discover that the so-called canon of early literature, a term that implies constituents of sacred and unchallenged worth, has in fact always been about progression, change, and—yes—often even diversification.[5] Such a view rightly presents the early literary canon as the established basis for—rather than the bogeyman of—our current attempts to diversify the curriculum.

Equally at issue, too, must be the increasingly popular but ultimately quite incorrect view that all literature of earlier periods reflects a monolithic attitude toward women, races, and sexual orientations. This notion is widely accepted among the students themselves and, if left unchallenged, fosters the kind of shallow, "too bad they weren't as enlightened as we are" attitude that a curriculum dedicated to diversity and values ought especially to combat. For the pedagogy of such a curriculum should be based on the importance of challenging assumptions—*everyone's* assumptions.

With such goals in mind, I spend much time in my early English literature classes trying to get students to consider that even in works that on many levels uphold a given worldview (as *Beowulf* does with the early Anglo-Saxon warrior culture or *The Canterbury Tales* does with Christianity), there are also points in the text that call the assumptions of those worldviews clearly into question. Many students are surprised to realize that authors writing during a period when "people just thought that way" actually represent discrete and often unconventional outlooks. Indeed, they are surprised to find that any author—but especially a white European male author from centuries ago—would express (as today's students themselves often do) mixed feelings about the prevailing culture or politics of the day. When the diverse values of authors previously believed to represent a monolithic worldview emerge as something to be figured out rather than to be memorized for a test, students begin to participate in what I believe should be an overarching curricular goal: to recognize and question, and then to adjust or reaffirm, the many underpinnings and nuances of their own values and assumptions.

SURFACING VALUES: READING TO FIND SELF, READING TO FIND OTHER

There are in my experience two particularly valuable ways for successfully addressing diversity issues in the teaching of early English literature, both involving pedagogical approaches. One of these I have already broached: students must be encouraged to see authors of an earlier time period as possessing and representing unique values, even as students themselves do. It is this project—whereby students learn to recognize both authors and themselves as uniquely and complexly valued—that I earlier termed "surfacing." The second of these approaches (not really separable from the first) involves introducing, and helping students to weigh against one another, the many ways of reading these works. After all, both the literature itself and the literary theory by which meaning is formed are bound by historical circumstances and political viewpoints.

First, let's look at what I call the surfacing of values. Whenever I teach Shakespeare, I begin with the controversial play *The Taming of the Shrew*. Invariably, on the first or second day of our discussion students respond (almost universally and sometimes with boredom) to the misogyny Katherina faces as "just" a case of "how things were for women back then." I welcome this response as an opportunity to begin surfacing the values that students often attempt to dismiss, assuming that whatever happens in a Shakespearean play would have been fully condoned by both Shakespeare and his Elizabethan audiences. So the first step in surfacing values has to be helping students to look closely at what Shakespeare has written to see how he builds sympathy for Katherina by developing her as an emotionally and psychologically confused woman and those around her as, basically, jerks. It is also worthwhile to point out that sitting on the English throne at the time was Elizabeth I, probably the most strong-willed and politically astute woman ever to rule England.

The idea that Shakespeare may not fully (or at all) agree with the sexist treatment of such independent-minded women as Katherina (or Elizabeth) is one that the students are quick to pick up on, perhaps mainly because they see that this is what their teacher (for the time being anyway) wants them to think. But the work is far from finished there. Because *The Taming of the Shrew* is such a complicated play, especially its ending (on the meaning of which not even the most respected Shakespearean scholars can agree), students are forced to wonder whether Shakespeare is in the end espousing or disespousing male domination of the female. I try as deliberately and as objectively as possible to help them see the evidence on both sides of the argument: Kate and Petruchio seem to establish a private bond that transcends mundane concerns about who in public seems to have the upper hand; nevertheless, there is the perhaps disturbing final insistence that male dominance must be publicly upheld, no matter what occurs in the private realm.

When I lay it out this way and then remove myself from judging the final scene's meaning, I witness remarkable things. Students suddenly realize that they themselves are crucially involved in deciding which values are affirmed or dislodged with the play's close. The discussion is no longer about what "Shakespeare intended" so much as it is about the students' own values and how they find those values at stake in the play. Some discover, for instance, that they believe there really is nothing harmful in bowing to the patriarchal tradition so long as it is "only" a superficial hierarchical code, while others discover that they cannot abide that code even as a cover for an ostensibly more meaningful relationship. Best of all, students begin to realize that the classroom is itself multivalued. A good text—like *The Taming of the Shrew*—can help them to see and to appreciate that. Moreover, by honing this skill of surfacing assumptions (both one's own and the author's—as well as the author's culture's), students can, ideally, discover that producing sound scholarship and being committed to exploring values are remarkably similar enterprises. When, for instance, the first Shakespeare papers come due, students are often eager either to continue to articulate their thoughts on the ending of *The Taming of the Shrew* or to take up some other arguable interpretation of the values espoused by a play—such as whether Shakespeare himself exhibits racist attitudes toward Othello or Shylock or whether only Shakespeare's characters do.

As I have said, it behooves us faculty members to be conscious of the values that we ourselves communicate because everything we do in the classroom will be value-laden. When we discussed this assumption in the summer institute on a couple of separate occasions, it led unfailingly to the near-consensus conclusion that therefore faculty members might as well be upfront about their own political views and values. But I continue to think (as I did during the institute) that there is a decided danger in doing so.

Some might argue that it is impossible to remove myself, as I just claimed, from pronouncing a judgment on the meaning of *The Taming of the Shrew*'s ending, that I am being coercive while pretending not to be, that I misleadingly suggest to my students that it is possible to be a blank slate of values. But I believe that holding value judgments in check is not the same thing as pretending not to have them and that a great deal would be lost if I made my own views too clear to the class. Students' values and assumptions simply cannot and will not be surfaced if the teacher's are too obvious. So the single value I want to communicate foremost in the classroom is a tolerance of and even more an intellectual curiosity about—though of course not necessarily an agreement with—others' opinions and values.

Indeed, ensuring the kind of classroom tolerance that is necessary for surfacing values is a challenge, because one can be so easily drawn either into the seemingly hypocritical position of *enforcing* tolerance among the students or else into the position of seemingly legitimizing all opinions no matter how weakly supported. Such challenges arose for me in a senior core course (on literary utopias and dystopias), when one outspoken young man asserted, for several class periods in a row, opinions very bothersome to many of his classmates. During our discussions of works such as Plato's *Republic*, Thomas More's *Utopia*, and Margaret Atwood's *The Handmaid's Tale*, the young man openly and eagerly expressed his views on matters such as communism and capitalism, sexual lifestyles, and suitable social roles for women.

Students repeatedly chafed at their classmate's views. I could tell that many were looking to me to discredit his opinions. But I tried my hardest not to do so, first, because the student was offering in great detail and with obvious conviction his rationale for thinking what he thought (he was not thoughtlessly hurling insults) and, second, because I feel strongly that everyone's opinion should be given a fair hearing if the surfacing of values is to be realized.

What happened in my classroom was that the students took over—which is exactly what I believe should have happened. Those with a different political viewpoint took issue point by point with the opinions voiced by the young man, who continued to argue the logic of his own conclusions. What I, as their teacher, encouraged was not this or that opinion but rather the degree to which students displayed the courage and the thoughtfulness of their convictions. No one, I think, either completely won or lost these debates (which occurred on many occasions), but I truly believe that the classroom became a more openly valued forum than it would have been if I had planted myself firmly on either side of the debates. This does not mean, of course, that I sat back silently. Instead, I was in the midst of things, acting as both teacher and moderator. As I said, I often encouraged the thoughtfulness and courage of respondents. I also often helped students by restating in my own words what I heard them saying in unclear terms, and I occasionally pursued my own line of questioning on an unclear point (e.g., when one student claimed that poverty is a necessary element in a diverse society). But even when I did assert my own values, I tried to do so by getting the students to better explain or to consider how they reached the conclusions they had (e.g., in the above instance regarding poverty and diversity, just how was "diversity" being defined by this student?). I am not trying to say that I have all the answers for encouraging tolerance of opinions in the classroom—some of my students from this class, I know, thought I was too tolerant of what they viewed to be intolerant political views. What I am saying is that there is surely *something* to be gained by a conscious suppressing of the teacher's values in the service of allowing students to scrutinize their own.

What I am also saying is that my attempts to surface values in this way have been quite compatible with teaching works of early English literature. Indeed, in my opinion, professors of Western literature engage their students in surfacing and exploring the values surrounding the literature much more often than they are credited with doing by many outside the field. Those of us who teach the so-called classics (now a highly suspicious appellation) often come up against the prejudice that we are somehow old-fashioned or unenlightened. But in fact anyone who knows much about recent literary scholarship (that generated, say, over the last three decades) knows that scholarly approaches to the early literature are anything but old-fashioned and stodgy. Thus my other pedagogical approach to addressing diversity issues with the early literature is to introduce students to the myriad ways in which scholars themselves have approached, and continue to reapproach, this literature. And this is where the teacher's learning is brought to bear on the classroom discussion, which I believe—despite my trying to surface everyone's values—must never be allowed to degenerate simply into a my-reading-versus-your-reading stalemate.

My earlier claim that students can be encouraged to view the early literary canon as in a sense prefiguring our current attempts to diversify the curriculum is, I realize, a controversial one. But past, current, and ongoing scholarship on this early literature testifies to the fact that there is more than one creditable way to read Chaucer, More, or Christopher Marlowe. As students try to convince others of their own opinions that, for example, Chaucer's Wife of Bath prefigures modern feminists, that More's communist utopians must be more miserable than they seem, or that Marlowe's *Edward II* involves a gay relationship that is crucial to the plot, they must be urged to consider what scholars have said on such matters and thus to bolster their instinctive readings with learning.

In a more general way, too, students can be encouraged to see that the meaning of a literary work and thus the values it represents are always affected by the critical lens one wears while reading (and often students must first be persuaded that it is impossible to read without wearing some kind of critical lens). Of course the various critical approaches that scholars have applied to the early literature are too many and too theoretically intricate to recount here, but let me give just one brief example of how giving students even a somewhat watered-down version of critical theory can widen the discussion of literary values.

Let's take *Paradise Lost*, where Milton's version of the creation of Eve unfailingly both intrigues and rankles students. In Milton's version Eve remembers first waking up to herself, walking to a pool of water, and being so captivated by the image she sees reflected there that she is reluctant to leave it. When she is subsequently taken to Adam she is impressed, but she still believes the image in the water to be superior to what she now sees before her. After some gentle explanation and persuasion from on high, she recognizes that since she owes her very being to this creature before her, he is indeed her superior despite her first impressions to the contrary.

To give an overview of the various possible critical approaches to this episode is to summarize the spectrum of responses that students themselves instinctively have toward it. There are the ostensibly old-fashioned—but certainly not outmoded—approaches by which students consider the relation of Milton's myth to its sources (the Narcissus myth, the Genesis accounts); examine the structural features of the Eve creation myth alongside those of Adam, Lucifer, and other Miltonic characters; or recognize the place of this myth within the history of Judeo-Christian thought. There are also approaches more recently advanced, for example, the historicist approach that whenever Milton describes power structures in his epic—as with Eve and Adam, Adam and God, Satan and God—he is also addressing seventeenth-century historical and political issues surrounding England's monarchical power (often an abused power in Milton's eyes). Or there is the feminist reading that sees Eve's first experiences as epitomizing the way in which women were and are socially and psychologically indoctrinated to feel inferior to men.[6] Thus whether students see Milton as offering a charming and faithful retelling of Greek or Judeo-Christian myth or whether they see him as revealing political or sexist attitudes, they understand that there have been and are scholars with similar views, and students are accordingly encouraged to seek outside scholarly support for their conclusions. When Edmund Spenser's Red Crosse Knight is in a serious predicament with a nasty dragon, Una advises him to add faith unto his works. When I send students off to find scholarship to support their instinctive readings, I like to think of them as adding work (library work) unto their faith.

When carried out most successfully, these pedagogical approaches help to impress on students that Western literature from earlier periods need not be a "dead" thing, that it can be both appreciated as an expression of an earlier culture and reanimated by their own cultural views. The most successful case of such reanimation is, of course, Shakespeare. And I would argue—partly in response to the young woman who wanted to toss out Shakespeare—that much of this revived interest in his work is in fact due to the plays' relentless attention to diversity, to "otherness": how to read otherness, how to represent otherness, how to reconcile otherness to oneself, and so on. Much critical attention has been given to this aspect of Shakespeare's characters, who often put on roles that are "other," not "self," only to discover something of self *in* the other or something of other in the self. Moreover, those who keep up on Shakespeare performances around the world know that productions have been mounted worldwide to address diversity issues (e.g., *Romeo and Juliet* in Sarajevo, where the two lovers' families are split along Croatian and Serbian lines, and in Israel, where the two are torn by Israeli and Palestinian loyalties). The same is true in the United States, where both productions of the plays and experiments in the classroom abound.[7]

Thus when I think back to the directive from our facilitator at the institute—to refashion our courses with a poor female student of color in mind—I have to wonder what I could or should do with a Shakespeare course that already seems to be naturally geared toward diverse students. I can't but think, too, of Maya Angelou's famous observation that, to her mind, Shakespeare could not have been other than a black woman because it was impossible to imagine the human sufferings he explored to be any other than those a black woman would suffer.[8] When I teach not only Shakespeare but all the early literature as well, I hope for my students precisely this sort of true absorption, this making over, this reanimating and internalizing of—and, yes, sometimes the rejecting of—the diverse struggles and values found in a literature that I fear is being blithely marginalized in too many college and university curricula purportedly devoted to diversity.

NOTES

I wish to acknowledge and thank the Faculty Senate Research and Development Committee of Le Moyne College for supporting my writing of this essay.

[1]At the time that I wrote this essay I was an assistant professor at Le Moyne College, Syracuse, New York. I have recently left Le Moyne to take a similar position at Knox College, Galesburg, Illinois.

[2]Lawrence Lipking sums up the humanistic argument that education (and perhaps especially an American education) ought to be mainly concerned with encouraging students to see beyond themselves: "To entertain, and be entertained by, ideas that are not identical with yours is what teaching and learning are all about. The *pluribus* in our all-American motto counts just as much as the *unum*" (9).

[3]On the topic of reconfiguring the canon as a misdirected goal, see also Guillory.

[4]It is impossible to note here all the many essays written on pedagogical approaches to multicultural studies. In general, one might peruse almost any issue of *College English* or some of the MLA's many publications devoted to pedagogy.

[5]On the special problems and fallacious logic involved in viewing the literary canon as ever being closed in the first place, see Stewart 12–13; Suleri; and Chambers.

[6]For a wide variety of approaches to *Paradise Lost*, some of which I have mentioned here, see such seminal authors as Frye; Fish; Hill; and Froula.

[7]For documentation of successful experiments in addressing diversity issues by teaching Shakespeare (in both high school and college classrooms), see any issue of *Shakespeare and the Classroom*, published by Ohio Northern University, or the several special issues of *Shakespeare Quarterly* (the 1974, 1984, and 1990 summer issues) devoted to the topic.

[8]Angelou's observation also appears in Cheney 14.

WORKS CITED

Angelou, Maya. "Journey to the Heartland." Natl. Assembly of Local Arts Agencies. Cedar Rapids. 12 June 1985.

Chambers, Ross. "Irony and the Canon." *Profession 90*. New York: MLA, 1990. 18–24.

Cheney, Lynne V. *Humanities in America: A Report to the President, the Congress, and the American People*. Washington: NEH, 1988.

Fish, Stanley. *Surprised by Sin: The Reader in* Paradise Lost. Berkeley: U of California P, 1971.

Froula, Christine. "When Eve Reads Milton: Undoing the Canonical Economy." *Critical Inquiry* 10 (1983): 322–47.

Frye, Northrop. *The Return of Eden: Five Essays on Milton's Epics*. Toronto: U of Toronto P, 1965.

Guillory, John. *Cultural Capital: The Problem of Literary Canon Formation*. Chicago: U of Chicago P, 1993.

Hill, Christopher. *Milton and the English Revolution*. New York: Viking, 1977.

Lipking, Lawrence. "Teaching America." *Profession 90*. New York: MLA, 1990. 8–11.

Stewart, Susan. "The State of Cultural Theory and the Future of Literary Form." *Profession 93*. New York: MLA, 1993. 12–15.

Suleri, Sara. "Multiculturalism and Its Discontents." *Profession 93*. New York: MLA, 1993. 16–17.

The Way We Work Now

MARA HOLT AND LEON ANDERSON

The past decade has been marked by attacks in the press and in state legislatures on privileged academics—"tenured radicals" and "profscam" artists conning their students and the public, teaching little more than ten hours a week, if that, while other Americans are working harder and longer than ever. The gap between this discourse and our experiences as academics is immense. We see academics facing many of the same pressures and conflicts as other workers, as well as some particular to academic life. But overwork in the academy is only beginning to be discussed as a problem. More often academic overwork has been treated by faculty members with a bravado reminiscent of army enlistment advertisements: "the toughest job you'll ever love." So, for instance, Wayne Booth comments on the back cover of James Phelan's book *Beyond the Tenure Track*: "Nobody else has traced so [. . .] honestly the pressures, anxieties and joys of the scholar-teacher-parent-citizen: over-committed, over-extended, out on too many limbs—and loving it all the while." But not all academic readers of Phelan's book would share Booth's enthusiasm. The idea of reveling in the frustrations of our work strikes us as misguided—consistent with the perverse valorization of late-modern type A culture that links the overactive, high-achievement society with the overwhelmed individual.

While the literature on overwork in general has multiplied exponentially following the publication of Juliet Schor's *The Overworked American*, academics have been slow to critically examine their situations. But this is

Mara Holt is Associate Professor of English at Ohio University. Leon Anderson is Associate Professor of Sociology at Ohio University.

changing. The AAUP magazine, *Academe*, devoted its September-October 1996 issue to the topic "How We Spend Our Time." A roundtable at the 1997 Conference on College Composition and Communication convention featured papers titled "So What Do You Do with All Your Free Time?," by Dawn Formo, and "What about a Personal Life in the Academy?," by Anne Thorpe. And NCTE has taken an aggressive interest in working conditions, broadly defined, by holding working sessions on working conditions at NCTE and CCCC meetings and beginning a study-group program called Researching Practice: Working Conditions.

Still, with a few exceptions (e.g., Schell), most recent examinations of academic working conditions have focused primarily on the (certainly critical issue of) overwork and underpay of adjunct faculty members (see Abel; McConnel; Uchmanowicz) while largely ignoring the work lives of tenure-line faculty members, including faculty administrators such as chairs and writing program administrators. Yet an understanding of both tenure-line and adjunct academic work is essential. This article examines the working conditions of tenure-line faculty members and explicitly recognizes the connections between their situation and the situation of adjunct faculty members.

How Hard Do We Work?

The full-time faculty workload increased "from forty-four hours a week to fifty-two between 1977 and 1988," according to a report of the Washington-based State Higher Educational Executive Officers (qtd. in Aronowitz and DiFazio 235). The results of an informal survey we took at the 1995 College English Association of Ohio meeting, as well as the information available from our university's institutional research office and our own personal observations of colleagues from around the country, suggest that the fifty-hour-plus workload continues unabated. And yet, the call for an increase in faculty work time is commonly heard in the press and in legislatures. In 1994 the Ohio Board of Regents pressured Ohio universities to increase faculty workloads by ten percent, and elsewhere, state legislatures have called for faculty members to begin providing verifiable documentation that they are actually putting in a forty-hour week.

While most faculty members have a feeling that we work well beyond the standard forty-hour work week, few of us seem to have any firm sense of the number of hours we spend "on the job." Part of the reason for this uncertainty has to do with the times and places of our work. Most faculty members mix their weekday office work with evening and weekend work in a variety of places, including the library, research sites, coffee shops, and home, in addition to the office and the classroom. Because of this differently structured schedule and our interesting tendency to label research as our "own work," our work time can easily absorb more of our daily lives than we realize.

Furthermore, professional demands come from so many different quarters—within the university and the national (sometimes international) communities—that it is easy to stretch oneself too thin. Our time commitments extend absurdly into the future: we are asked to plan what we will teach fifteen months from now, to plan participation in conferences often a year or more in advance, and to promise funding agencies the next several years of our lives. We seldom have any realistic sense of what our circumstances will be in the long run; therefore, we typically underestimate how busy we will be, and our lives are regularly invaded by crisis and despair because of missed deadlines and work crunches.

Of course, academics have always had these problems, but the demands of academic life are proliferating. Virtually all the department chairs we have queried agree that the paperwork involved in administering departments has mushroomed in the past decade. The work within departments has increased as well. Faculty members advise more students, work to improve hiring practices, participate in training graduate TAs, mentor new faculty members, and participate in continuous assessment. Tenure letters must be written—and written carefully. As graduate application forms get more complicated, so do our roles as recommenders. Electronic communication, touted as a timesaver, has meant the development of new electronic journals, e-mail, the listserv, the World Wide Web, and the constant need to update one's computer skills, including computer-assisted instruction. Books, journals, and conferences abound, partly because everyone needs vita items. The books and journals require editorial boards, editors, and reviewers.

It is not only that academics have too much work. We also face the problem of simultaneous multiple roles: teacher, researcher, and administrator, to name a few. Shirley Fisher, in her book *Stress in Academic Life*, cites "role overload" as a major problem because of the frequency with which faculty members experience work interruptions and "role switching" (76). This overload increases stress and the risk of failure at specific tasks. The constant barrage of conflicting demands is captured by Kenneth Gergen in his book *The Saturated Self*. He details a morning's fragmented tasks after returning from a two-day conference, then notes: "The hours had been wholly consumed by the process of relating—face to face, electronically, and by letter. [. . .] And so keen was the competition for 'relational time' that virtually none of the interchanges seemed effective in the ways I wished" (1). Often by itself any given demand does not seem extraordinary, but cumulatively they can be overwhelming. UCLA and Stanford professors Shelley Taylor and Joanne Martin claim that "no one would ever try to combine a family and [an academic] career without a wife-equivalent, if he or she fully understood what it entailed" (55). Many of us carry around chronic guilt about failing to meet family and professional commitments and not being able to get our own work done.

These issues are exacerbated for women and other underrepresented groups. Women, especially African American women, have historically been cast in both physically and emotionally nurturing roles more than men have, and this imbalance has an effect on the work expected of women academics. Arlie Hochschild notes in her book *The Managed Heart* that when a woman instructor challenges her students, she is likely to be perceived as cold and controlling, even bitchy, while male faculty members who act similarly may be seen as "having high standards" (168). Furthermore, women often do invisible work. One male academic in Sally Barr-Ebest's study of writing program administrators unwittingly captured the problem of gender-biased responsibility in his academic experience when he said, "I personally don't see lack of status for women—in graduate school and in my current department, women seem to have as much if not more responsibility than male counterparts" (64). This view presents extra work as a career advantage for women, just as job listings for writing program administrators in the MLA *Job Information List* often "disguise the political dangers of administrating a writing program within the language of opportunity" (Janangelo 61). Typically the extra work is devalued, unrewarded, not even seen.

Why Do We Overwork?

We wish to discuss three specific forces that we believe have played a part in promoting academic overwork: the proletarianization of academic labor, technology under the sway of capitalism and bureaucracy, and competitive individualism. By "proletarianization" we refer to the erosion of worker autonomy described by Marx. The deterioration of faculty working conditions is evidenced in reduced faculty control over the educational process, calls for increased faculty teaching time, the "speeding up" of academic research, and the increase in temporary and part-time employment. The most obvious degradation of academic employment is the rise of part-time academic instructors—"freeway flyers," to use Frances McConnel's graphic term—who are frequently forced to teach at several institutions simultaneously. Since 1970 the number of full-time faculty members in the United

States has risen by approximately half, while the number of part-time faculty members has tripled. During this time the proportion of faculty members who were full-time dropped from nearly 80% to under 60% (United States 231). Similarly, the number of nontenured tenure-line faculty members declined by 10.3% between 1975 and 1993. Women in particular have been disadvantaged in the move to less secure academic employment, as indicated by their far heavier representation among non-tenure-line and part-time faculty members than among tenure-line appointments (Benjamin). Under the banner of financial exigency, this trend has continued unabated, as exemplified in efforts by the CUNY system's administration to replace a majority of retiring faculty members with adjunct instructors. And in a disturbing high-tech development, we see discussions about outsourcing of teaching through Internet education by scholars from poorer countries, such as India, where academic wages are low (Schoening).

The overwork of tenure-line faculty members and adjuncts is interdependent. For one thing, the increase in adjunct labor reduces the administrative and service labor pools, impeding self-governance and increasing the service load for full-time faculty members. At California State University, Hayward, for instance, where the number of adjunct lecturers surged from one-quarter to nearly half of the total faculty between 1992 and 1995, department chairs have voiced concern about the diminished number of faculty members available for service work (Leatherman). The overwork of tenure-line faculty members and adjuncts is also intertwined because part-timers end up being what Marx and Engels term a "reserve army of the poor," who can be called on to replace tenure-line faculty members in times of crisis and restructuring. As long as adjuncts exist as a significant disadvantaged workforce, the position of tenure-line faculty members will also be precarious.

Our universities have been following the lean and mean strategy popularized by 1980s United States business culture, calling for us to do more with less—creating harried working conditions for both part-time and full-time faculty members in the process. And yet, as Robert Horn and Robert Jerome note, the supposed increase in efficiency that has accompanied leveraged buyouts and hostile takeovers has damaged long-range productivity while redistributing wealth from workers to stockholders and, particularly, to late-twentieth-century robber barons—hardly an appropriate model for higher education. Horn and Jerome remark that "to be a viable source of information, creativity, and insight, the faculty member must maintain ownership of the educational process" (36). But we find ourselves caught in a vicious cycle described in broader terms by the Marxist Ernest Mandel, who observed that workers are incapable of setting their own goals and agendas unless they have sufficient time for decision making. Our overwork today feeds into our lack of time for self-governance, which results in yet further assaults on our working conditions.

The second force contributing to academic overwork is technology under the sway of capitalism and bureaucratization. The relation between electronic technologies and work time is complex. Certainly the computer revolution has opened new and exciting opportunities in education, but we must also acknowledge less sanguine aspects of the effect of computer technology on academic workloads. Aronowitz and DiFazio contend that "the effect of technological change—not only machines but also organization—on the professoriat has been to increase workload" (236). One reason is that the incorporation of computer technologies in universities has served as a rationale for the reduction of academic support staff at a time of enormous increases in bureaucratic paperwork. The dramatic increase in assessment activities, largely as a result of demands from accrediting organizations and state legislatures, provides a case in point. Computers have enabled the easy manipulation of quantitative information by offices of institutional research to provide data for a range of evaluative reports and as fodder for various new educational initiatives that are frequently plagued with difficulties, due in large part to rushed and haphazard top-down agenda setting and lack of recognition that faculty members need time to accomplish them.

Another reason that computer technology has not saved us the time we had hoped for is that the technology must be learned and relearned. In a highly competitive capitalistic system, technological obsolescence is profitable and change is omnipresent. We must always be learning new word-processing programs, e-mail systems, software, hardware. Glossy *MacZone* catalogs arrive as regularly now in faculty mailboxes as do flyers for new textbooks. While each new version of a word-processing program or advance in computer technology may potentially add some increment of time savings, the time loss from continuous tinkering and learning of new systems erodes the time savings we might have had. We face the myth of Sisyphus in a high-tech mutation, packing a computer upstairs to the office, only to throw it out the window as obsolete.

We must also acknowledge the perverse results of our own ambitions when they are channeled into competitive academic individualism. Competitive individualism is certainly connected to the "fear of falling" in the academy today, but it also reflects the "hope of climbing" mind-set typical of many adolescents looking at rock stars: "I'm going to grow up to be one too." The academic hierarchy is complete with its own superstars who serve as models of what we can become. But not everyone can be a superstar. Those who aspire to superstar status need such material conditions as minimal teaching loads, support in other parts of their lives (such as the traditional faculty spouse), and substantial freedom from collegial service. And yet the distribution of these academic perks is highly gendered and uneven across institutions.

The hyperdeveloped competitive system with its overemphasis on publication is flawed, notwithstanding Cary Nelson's recent market-economic defense of "superstars" and their salaries. Nelson presents a social Darwinist argument consistent with market-based calculation. Faculty superstars, he argues, enhance departmental reproductive success (and hence institutional prestige) since they are able to sell new PhDs (41). This is the approach that has created enormous superstar salaries and "superteams" in professional sports. Undoubtedly superteam owners (as well as some team members) profit enormously. But it may behoove us to take a broader view, looking not at the reproductive success of an individual department but at the vitality of our discipline more broadly, in terms of the intellectual opportunities for the majority of its members rather than only the merits of a few. Nelson may be right in arguing that academic superstars merit their salaries because of the prestige they can bring an institution, but he ignores the division of departmental labor on which their achievements are commonly based. Perhaps what is most significantly missed in Nelson's argument is the broader disciplinary and institutional effect of the superstar model of academic prestige. This competitive individualism ups the ante for everyone, creating what Gordon Fellman has called "an orgy of 'productivity'" (27) and longer CVs, at least for some (and a sense of failure for others), but not necessarily good scholarship or good workplaces. Indeed, as James Sosnoski has pointed out, such a narrow and competitive model of intellectual achievement serves as an administrative justification for higher workloads for those faculty members who fail to make the grade.

We are not arguing against the value of scholarship. Rather, we are asserting the value of a less driven and competitive academic culture that valorizes the need for unharried time for creative intellectual work, not only in publication but in teaching and administrative activities as well, as envisioned by Ernest Boyer in *Scholarship Reconsidered* and in the MLA Commission on Professional Service document "Making Faculty Work Visible." To limit our conception of scholarship to publication is to render invisible the intellectual work that many of us do, just as the domestic labor of women—so essential to maintaining economic life—was invisible to early Marxists. Furthermore, the gendered division of academic labor continues to relegate much of women's work to intellectually invisible—even if critically necessary—domains, devaluing the time spent in such activities.

Women then find themselves having less time to work on the kinds of scholarship that are recognized and rewarded and may often be judged as intellectual underachievers in their departments.

Taken together, these three trends (the proletarianization of academic labor, technology under the sway of bureaucracy and capitalism, and competitive academic individualism) have produced an academic milieu far afield from the leisured life of the mind captured in the Greek *schole*, from which the English words *scholar* and *school* derive. Our harried environment with its incessant demands erodes the quality of our lives more broadly as we sacrifice time and energy to do work that by virtue of its all-consuming nature loses some of its significance. The other sources of potential personal and collective meaning in our lives atrophy from lack of attention. As Anne Thorpe has described it, based on responses to her Internet survey of English faculty members, academic life has become characterized by a "climate of self-sacrifice" that leads many of us to question our career choices. Still, while many of us may feel a need for more time for reflection in our professional lives and for more of a life beyond our work, we may fear damaging our already precarious public image if we attempt to scale back on our workloads, or perhaps more directly, we may fear being perceived as slackers within our own departments and institutions. We have internalized what others expect of us.

A Defense of Leisure

While at first glance it might seem difficult at this historical juncture for tenure-line faculty members to advocate a more leisured pace to their work, we believe that it is possible to make a reasoned and compelling argument for an expansion of reflective leisure and time away from work, one that is consistent with significant currents in American society. Reflective leisure is central to intellectual work because it provides the mental space for free play essential for the cultivation of critical creativity. It provides an idiosyncratic personal space where the given is not yet reified and where perhaps even heretical ideas can be entertained. In the free space of reflective leisure, with one's guard down, the previously unthinkable can be conceived. Such a state of childlike wonder has been recognized as the portal to discovery and invention by creative thinkers across intellectual fields. As James D. Watson, the codiscoverer of the genetic code of DNA, has said, "It is necessary to be slightly underemployed if you are to do something significant" (qtd. in Griesman 47–48). Poetry is rich with praise for leisurely and playful inspiration, as in Whitman's memorable lines from "Song of Myself":

> I loafe and invite my soul,
> I lean and loafe at my ease observing a spear of summer grass.　　(61)

Various psychological, linguistic, and social explanations have been proposed for the connections between leisure and creative activity, all of which recognize in one way or another that much creative work cannot be done in a rigidly instrumental and straightforward manner. We need the freedom to jump the track, to follow unexpected leads—even potential dead ends. Such a perspective on reflective leisure undercuts the dichotomy of work and play. Furthermore, as John Dewey observed in *Democracy and Education*, the critical and creative skills necessary for intellectual life are the same kinds of skills required for meaningful democratic participation. The point is clear: it is imperative that we advocate the social and temporal space necessary to cultivate creativity and social responsibility in ourselves and in our students.

Consistent with our desire to reduce academic overwork while enriching academic life is the emergence in the past decade of a multifaceted popular critique of overwork in industrial societies. In the United States this movement rose to prominence in the wake of 1980s yuppie culture as many young professionals and other workers began to question the high personal and social costs of endless work. By the early 1990s twelve-step "workaholics" groups were forming around the country as many men and women sought a social base of support for reducing what they felt was the destructive prominence of work in their lives. Within this movement overwork has been conceptualized as "the cleanest of all addictions" (Fassel vii) and therefore one of the most pernicious. Several unexpectedly best-selling books have also explored the economics of overwork (Hunnicut; Schor) and lifestyle changes of "downshifting" (Saltzman) and voluntary simplicity (Elgin; St. James). Even books and workshops touting overwork themes to corporate professionals (e.g., Mackoff) have gained popularity. Meanwhile accolades about organizational work practices in Japan (long noted for its extreme work ethic) have been replaced by media attention to highly publicized cases of *karoshi*, or death by overwork, among Japanese line workers and executives (Lamont-Brown).

The overwork movement combines a variety of themes that reject work (especially remunerated employment) as the center of life and focuses on developing more balanced and multifaceted lives. The sociologist Anthony Giddens and others have argued that we are facing a paradigmatic shift away from an overemphasis on work that has plagued Western society since the Enlightenment and is evidenced in such diverse thinkers as Marx (despite his reliance on artistic creativity as the master trope for unalienated work) and Benjamin Franklin. Feminism, of course, has provided a major challenge to the valorization of work, especially as the participation of women in the United States remunerated labor market has increased dramatically during the past two decades. An overemphasis on work crushes a broader range of interrelated ethical concerns, such as commitment to familial and other social bonds and responsibility for political participation. As Robert Bellah and his colleagues observe in their book *The Good Society*, one of the most important resources for a working participatory democracy is the time to pursue it—a point that harks back to Athenian Greeks, for whom the major raison d'être for leisure was to provide the time for democratic governance (flawed as that democracy was). As a popular cultural trend, the overwork movement can certainly be critiqued from various angles as classist, racist, and sexist (e.g., Vanderbilt), but such critiques, we believe, have more to do with the existing cultural manifestations of the movement than with its broader potential. Up to this point, few academics have taken part in the discussion. Our participation as academics is crucial if we are to build connections to the movement and hope to influence it in emancipatory ways.

NO EASY ANSWERS

It is encouraging that disciplinary organizations have followed the lead of the AAUP in confronting working conditions, as exemplified by the CCCC's adoption of the Wyoming Resolution, by the NCTE working conditions study groups, and by the MLA Commission on Professional Service. The issues we face are complex and seemingly intractable. Lester Faigley, in his role as 1996 CCCC chair, wrote that "in no area has our inability to act on the concerns of our members been more painfully evident than working conditions. [. . .] We should have no illusions that these are easy battles to win, but at the same time we should not accept defeat as inevitable" (1).

Our intention in this paper is not to provide solutions to faculty overwork but rather to break the taboo that mandates silence on the issue. We are aware of many arguments against the ideas we have presented here. We are aware that the range of overwork varies considerably within departments, institutions, and fields. We are aware that, compared with many other workers in the broader culture, many of us lead relatively leisured lives. But we are also aware that tenured and tenure-line faculty members are simultaneously victims of and complicit in the overwork economy of late-twentieth-century society, and we want to start a conversation about it—one that we hope will lead to solutions.

NOTE

We would like to acknowledge the support for and the critical responses to earlier versions of this article provided by Joseph Harris, Dawn Trouard, and Mary Beth Krouse.

WORKS CITED

Abel, Emily. *Terminal Degrees*. New York: Praeger, 1986.

Aronowitz, Stanley, and William DiFazio. *The Jobless Future: Sci-Tech and the Dogma of Work*. Minneapolis: U of Minnesota P, 1994.

Barr-Ebest, Sally. "Gender Differences in Writing Program Administration." *WPA: Writing Program Administration* 18.3 (1995): 53–73.

Bellah, Robert Neelly, Richard Madsen, William M. Sullivan, and Ann Swidler. *The Good Society*. New York: Knopf, 1991.

Benjamin, Ernst. "Changing Distribution of Faculty by Tenure Status and Gender." Memo. Washington: AAUP, Committee W. 19 Jan. 1997.

Boyer, Ernest L. *Scholarship Reconsidered: Priorities of the Professoriate*. Princeton: Carnegie Foundation, 1990.

Dewey, John. *Democracy and Education*. New York: Macmillan, 1916.

Elgin, Duane. *Voluntary Simplicity: Toward a Way of Life That Is Outwardly Simple, Inwardly Rich*. New York: Morrow, 1993.

Faigley, Lester. Letter to CCCC members. Fall 1996. NCTE, Urbana.

Fassel, Diane. *Working Ourselves to Death: The High Cost of Workaholism and the Rewards of Recovery*. San Francisco: Harper, 1990.

Fellman, Gordon. "On the Fetishism of Publications and the Secrets Thereof." *Academe* Jan.-Feb. 1995: 26–35.

Fisher, Shirley. *Stress in Academic Life: The Mental Assembly Line*. Bristol: Open UP, 1994.

Formo, Dawn M. "So What Do You Do with All Your Free Time? Compositionists Respond." CCCC Convention. Phoenix. 12 Mar. 1997.

Gergen, Kenneth J. *The Saturated Self: Dilemmas of Identity in Contemporary Life*. New York: Basic, 1991.

Giddens, Anthony. *Beyond Left and Right: The Future of Radical Politics*. Stanford: Stanford UP, 1994.

Griesman, B. Eugene. *Time Tactics of Very Successful People*. New York: McGraw, 1994.

Hochschild, Arlie. *The Managed Heart: The Commercialization of Human Feeling*. Berkeley: U of California P, 1983.

Horn, Robert N., and Robert T. Jerome. "When Corporate Restructuring Meets Higher Education." *Academe* May-June 1996: 34–36.

Hunnicut, Benjamin. *Work without End: Abandoning Shorter Hours for the Right to Work*. Philadelphia: Temple UP, 1988.

Janangelo, Joseph. "Somewhere between Disparity and Despair: Writing Program Administrators, Image Problems, and the MLA *Job Information List*." *WPA: Writing Program Administration* 15.1–2 (1991): 60–66.

Lamont-Brown, Raymond. "Karoshi—A Fatal Export from Japan." *Contemporary Review* Oct. 1993: 197–99.

Leatherman, Courtney. "Heavy Reliance on Low-Paid Lecturers Said to Produce 'Faceless Departments.'" *Chronicle of Higher Education* 28 Mar. 1997: A12–13.

Mackoff, Barbara. *The Art of Self-Renewal: Balancing Pressure and Productivity on and off the Job*. Los Angeles: Lowell, 1992.

Mandel, Ernest. *Late Capitalism*. London: New Left, 1979.

Marx, Karl, and Friedrich Engels. *The Marx-Engels Reader*. 2nd ed. Ed. Robert C. Tucker. New York: Norton, 1978.

McConnel, Frances Ruhlen. "Freeway Flyers: The Migrant Workers of the Academy." *Writing Ourselves into the Story: Unheard Voices from Composition Studies*. Ed. Sheryl I. Fontaine and Susan Hunter. Carbondale: Southern Illinois UP, 1993. 40–58.

MLA Commission on Professional Service. "Making Faculty Work Visible: Reinterpreting Professional Service, Teaching, and Research in the Fields of Language and Literature." *Profession 1996*. New York: MLA, 1996. 161–216.

Nelson, Cary. "Superstars." *Academe* Jan.-Feb. 1997: 38+.

Phelan, James. *Beyond the Tenure Track: Fifteen Months in the Life of an English Professor*. Columbus: Ohio State UP, 1991.

Saltzman, Amy. *Downshifting: Reinventing Success on a Slower Track*. New York: Harper, 1991.

Schell, Eileen E. *Gypsy Academics and Motherteachers: Gender, Contingent Labor, and Writing Instruction*. Portsmouth: Boynton, 1998.

Schoening, James R. "Teletutoring Concept Ready for Demo." V-Net, the Volunteer Network. EDUTEL Hotline. 8 Sept. 1995. <http://www.jrs@aol.com>.

Schor, Juliet B. *The Overworked American: The Unexpected Decline of Leisure*. New York: Basic, 1991.

Sosnoski, James J. *Token Professionals and Master Critics: A Critique of Orthodoxy in Literary Studies*. Albany: State U of New York P, 1994.

St. James, Elaine. *Simplify Your Life*. New York: Hyperion, 1994.

Taylor, Shelley E., and Joanne Martin. "The Present-Minded Professor: Controlling One's Career." *The Compleat Academic: A Practical Guide for the Beginning Social Scientist*. Ed. Mark P. Zanna and John M. Darley. New York: Random, 1987. 23–60.

Thorpe, Anne E. "Just Teaching, Just Writing: What about a Personal Life in the Academy?" CCCC Convention. Phoenix. 12 Mar. 1997.

Uchmanowicz, Pauline. "The $5,000–$25,000 Exchange." *College English* 57 (1995): 426–47.

United States. Dept. of Educ. Natl. Center for Educ. Statistics. *The Condition of Education, 1995*. Washington: GPO, 1996.

Vanderbilt, Tom. "It's a Wonderful (Simplified) Life." *Nation* 22 Jan. 1996: 20–22.

Whitman, Walt. *The Portable Whitman*. Ed. Mark Van Doren. New York: Viking, 1945.

Recognizing Local Value:
College Service and the Problem
of Portability

MICHAEL SELMON

In *Profession 1996* the MLA Commission on Professional Service offers a lengthy critique of the traditional faculty work triad of research, teaching, and service. The product of some four years of study, "Making Faculty Work Visible" is a thoughtful and humane response to inequities in the current reward structure. Yet in important ways, ways especially visible from a small-college perspective, the proposed solution seems to perpetuate the underlying problem. In particular, the MLA report documents a systematic bias toward research, a bias that even within small colleges results in a devaluation of teaching and service work. This paper, using an analytic framework established by Bruno Latour, explores the structures that underlie our skewed valuation of faculty labor. It shows both how the MLA report retains these structures and how the small-college model provides a potential remedy for their bias. For the sake of brevity I focus on service, the least rewarded of the three areas, but the argument applies to teaching as well.

To read the articles that surround the MLA report in *Profession 1996*—indeed, to read almost any 1990s issue of *Profession*—is to be struck by a sense of crisis. Much of this impression stems from an all-too-familiar economic reality, the cuts in higher education funding during the first half of the decade. But this sense of crisis has a broader manifestation as well, a recurrent set of questions about the identity of our profession. Repeatedly

The author is Associate Professor of English at Alma College. A version of this paper was presented at the 1997 MLA convention in Toronto.

the articles of *Profession* ask, "What should be the work of the academy as we approach the year 2000? What work should be expected from faculty members, and how should it be rewarded? These questions, raised in disciplines across the academy, frame the MLA commission's effort to "redefine professional service in higher education and to formulate new guidelines for rewarding it" (161). Perhaps, as the commission notes, the "traditional triple mission of the American university—scholarship, teaching, service—has always been in tension in American education because it is an amalgam of different educational visions and intellectual traditions" (168). But recently this tension has become quite pronounced, as the "traditional triad [of] *research*, *teaching*, and *service* has increasingly become a hierarchy, ranked in order of esteem" (161).

Belonging to a smaller department does not exempt one from this hierarchy. On the contrary, studies have shown that an "emphasis on research in tenure and promotion reviews holds across all disciplines and all types of institutions, except two-year colleges" (Park 48). This emphasis has created a sense of imbalance between labor and reward. Even the traditional triad, the MLA commission notes, has been marred by "many unacknowledged or unrewarded faculty roles and activities" (162). The current research bias creates an "ethically unacceptable gap" in our profession's reward structure (187).

The commission is not alone in pointing to such a gap. Numerous studies have shown a gender bias in the preference for research, with teaching and service duties falling disproportionately to women (Park 52–54). Likewise, those who work to correct biases in the curriculum often find themselves laboring in devalued areas of the triad (56–60). Other commentators point to a different set of forces that have helped to devalue teaching and service. Lamenting the "modernist" logic of our times, Connecticut College President Claire Gaudiani argues that many campuses are "caught in an invisible web spun by the forces of modernism in conflict with the forces of tradition" (27); a prime symptom is that "teaching and advising are still often poorly assessed and lightly valued" under modernism's research bias (31). She emphasizes the cost of this impulse, noting that while "most boards and presidents have been pushing modernism into higher education to address financial pressures," they "have largely ignored the threat to relationships from lost social capital on campus" (30).

Gaudiani's comment alludes to two contexts that help explain our skewed evaluation of labor. The first is economic, for the American academy's funding and mission shifted dramatically after World War II. The cold war emphasis on technology encouraged a focus on research, both as a source for funding and as a component of faculty work. At the same time the GI Bill fueled a shift toward a middle-class clientele and an eightfold increase in enrollment between 1940 and 1980 (Pratt 38). While providing new revenues, this surge of students also changed the academy's mission.

Indeed, much of our current identity crisis is rooted in these two disparate strands of postwar growth. As the MLA report notes, "conflicts between ideas of increased student access to higher education and superior achievement in research were probably inevitable. Research places one set of demands on faculty members, academic programs, and institutional resources; accessibility creates other kinds of demands" (167). This conflict came to a head when government academic funding collapsed in the early 1990s, a time when revenues were already constrained by the baby bust and an increasingly tuition-sensitive market.[1]

Yet while research and teaching are grounded in different economic realities, Gaudiani's reference to modernism reminds us that their opposition is not absolute. Beneath the twin triggers for the academy's growth lies a common set of assumptions, assumptions that the cultural critic Bruno Latour has investigated in his recent book *We Have Never Been Modern*. Generalizing the "anthropology of science" that he undertook in studies like *Laboratory Life* and *Science in Action*, Latour argues that a wide range of contemporary disciplines and institutions are marked by a common structure. Recognizing this structure enables us to see the research, teaching, and service triad as one manifestation of a more general pattern, a pattern seemingly replicated in the MLA report.

What is modernism for Latour? To give a quick synopsis, Latour claims that "the most fundamental aspect of our culture [. . . is that] we live in communities whose social bond comes from objects fabricated in laboratories," communities where "ideas have been replaced by practices, apodeictic reasoning by controlled doxa, and universal agreement by groups of colleagues" (*We* 21). He goes on to sketch two sets of practices characteristic of the modern world.

First he notes a pervasive set of practices that create "mixtures between entirely new types of beings, hybrids of nature and culture" (10). Because these hybrids transgress established boundaries, they are difficult to describe concisely. Latour suggests that they generalize the "sociotechnological networks" discussed in recent science studies, and he labels them "quasi-objects" to reflect their equivocal location between product and producer.[2] One characteristic of the contemporary world, he argues, is that quasi-objects multiply ceaselessly. In terms of the faculty work triad, think of these hybrids as service.[3] Are committees work, or do they do work? Both and neither: they feel like work but aren't rewarded; they produce something but not academic work. The only thing that is clear about committees is that they, like Latour's hybrids, multiply ceaselessly.

In contrast to the quasi-objects, modernism creates a more ordered realm. Latour details how, through a set of practices he terms purification, moderns create "two entirely distinct ontological zones: that of human beings on the one hand; that of nonhumans on the other" (10–11). In these two purified zones we find the academic work that produces and receives economic rewards: the work of facing humans or exploring nature, of engaging in teaching or doing research. Here we see clear products: research rendered instantly measurable by an "equation that makes publication (in certain venues) synonymous with scholarship" and teaching with its "more indirect and gradual" but still assessable impact (MLA 171, 163).

The modernist impulse is to differentiate sharply between these purified zones and the hybrids. Indeed, Latour claims that the modern world is so obsessed with purification that while "everything happens in the middle [. . .] by way of mediation, translation and networks" (37), moderns "refuse to conceptualize quasi-objects as such. In their eyes, hybrids present the horror that must be avoided at all costs by a ceaseless, even maniacal purification" (112). This statement too strikingly parallels our attitude toward service, "much of which is either erased by categories that exclude it or trivialized as unworthy of close attention" (MLA 170). Thus, while a task force is our standard solution to a problem, it is almost inconceivable for us to admit that we like committees; instead, "such service is perceived as sheer labor, at worst despised as thankless scut work" (170). Even the MLA commission's praise of this hybrid labor ends up relegating it to the margins: "The explicitly or purely intellectual element of faculty work is, more than we admit, surrounded by a penumbra of professional tasks that are equally vital" (178). That which is literally central to our work cannot be acknowledged as such.

What do we learn, then, if we assume that the faculty work triad is a subset of the modernist constitution, a subset that reflects both the properties and omissions of modernism? In part, recognizing the depth of the triad's modernist roots helps clarify why an equitable valuation of faculty labor has proven so elusive. When the academy segregates and ranks the work triad even as it asserts the need for better balance (169–70), it follows the modernists' impulse to "treat the two constitutional poles as incommensurable, even while they assert that there is no task more urgent than their reconciliation" (Latour, *We* 56). Likewise the academy responds to Latour's rhetorical question, "Must there be hundreds of hybrids in order for a simply human politics and simply natural things to exist?" (30), with classic modernist affirmation. Yes, the MLA report suggests, because the service area is the sine qua non of academic life (179).

The best example of the modernist impulse in our profession, however, is probably the most familiar. The notion of portability has created a persistent problem in our valuation of service, in part because portability is highly esteemed both by professional associations and by the academy as a whole. Indeed, in the MLA report portability justifies disciplinary study. "What disciplines offer," the report claims, "is a way of understanding academic missions, and therefore a wide range of faculty work, as portable among institutions" (207). Portability likewise is seen as integral to research, an endeavor that by definition is "cosmopolitan rather than local or institution-bound" (181). Indeed, portability is so central to the MLA's identity that one commentator has described the organization as being "devoted primarily to enabling its members to add lines to their vitae" (Nelson 45).

In general Latour problematizes the notion of portability, reminding us of the innate vulnerability of our intellectual goods, of the way that "we produce only matters of fact that are created in laboratories and have only local value" (18).[4] This general reservation is intensified when we attempt to scrutinize hybrids, since honestly assessing something like college service requires that we affirm its engagement with the local at every point. Here we see part of the logic behind the "ethically unacceptable gap" in our profession's reward structure. Service, even service crucial in establishing an environment for research, implicitly threatens research, for we can't take our environments with us. Fully recognizing service work would bring us perilously close to admitting that the products of our discipline are not entirely portable and pure.

Or, at the very least, fully recognizing service work would require that we acknowledge the inequities in current notions of portability. While Latour's book largely focuses on the way modernism shapes intellectual capital, other studies remind us that research has a social function as well. In particular, Gaudiani's critique pointed to the notion of social capital developed by the sociologist James Coleman. A concept in some ways analogous to Latour's quasi-objects, social capital too is grounded "in the *relations* among persons" (S100–01).[5] Hence it is often unstable, for its "benefits [. . .] are largely experienced by persons other than the actor" (S118). The logical outcome of this disparity between individual investment and reward is "an underinvestment in social capital" (S119)—an underinvestment, that is, from the social or institutional point of view.

Here again college service provides a classic example, for when faculty members work as effective committee members to create a first-rate teaching or research environment, they rarely benefit directly. Instead it is the individual researcher and the college as an institution whose reputations are enhanced (Park 69–70). Once more, then, we glimpse the logic underlying our ambivalence toward service. Because research and reputation are not as pure or portable as we claim—because they thrive only when the laboratory runs smoothly, only when the infrastructure is in place—it is not in an institution's interest that the service providing this infrastructure be portable. The vulnerability of social capital requires that institutions protect against underinvestment.

Such utilitarian logic clarifies the achievement of the MLA commission, for "Making Faculty Work Visible" is going against the grain. The commission's effort to recognize previously unacknowledged service is a major step toward a fair evaluation of the hybrid realities of academic life. Its call for rewarding "distinguished" faculty service and its conclusion "that the quality, significance, and impact of work [. . .] are more important than its label" are equally admirable (196, 180). Indeed, the commission's assertion that "it is necessary to change both the basic organization and the underlying premises of the faculty reward system" seems absolutely correct (162).

But does the MLA report fully take on these premises? Latour's framework reminds us that the commission's proposals retain a decidedly modernist cast. The report rejects the purified modernist dichotomy that ranks research above teaching against a backdrop of unrecognized service, and it even contemplates the use of evaluations based on local criteria. Yet the commission's search for "common or universal academic values" (174) in an academy shaped by modernism inevitably leads back to a dichotomous pattern, a model positing "*intellectual work* and *academic and professional citizenship* as primary components*" (162). Likewise the commission proposes, as the remedy for the modernist refusal to recognize quasi-objects, a standard modernist solution: "the application of rigorous standards in a thoroughgoing and time-consuming process of assessment" (211). Time-consuming service on a committee to assess service—presumably this too could be assessed. But, to paraphrase Latour, must there be hundreds of such hybrids in order for ethical valuation to exist?

Our profession in fact offers an alternative model for valuing service. Within our lifetimes we have seen the study of literature shift from a focus on universals to a rich and thriving engagement with the newly visible hybrids of life. A similar strategy could help create more equitable evaluations of service. Instead of stepping back to notions of portability and other purified modernist ideals, we will obtain more ethical measures for faculty work only when we honestly recognize its local, unportable value.

Indeed, small-college departments, perhaps because they have been less pressured by the academy's postwar growth, are already well positioned for such rethinking. Latour's solution to what he sees as the failure of post-modern thought is to recognize that "we have never been modern," that we have always been centered not in purified divisions but in hybrid links. The notion should ring true to any member of a small-college department. We are generalists in our teaching, by necessity linking the experience of one field to others; our research is frequently intertwined with the classroom experience; our service work so thoroughly engages us with our colleagues that we don't need an additional committee to recognize their worth.

At small colleges, that is, research, reputation, and environment are already unmistakably intertwined. The entanglement provides an opportunity for recognizing and reinforcing areas that need support, for protecting social capital not merely through disincentives but also by establishing positive local rewards. Larger institutions could implement the strategy as well. In an age of college rankings, professional associations, and research imperatives, there will always be pressure to make portability the measure of worth. Yet we will not begin to bridge the ethical gap such valuation creates until we begin to reward what the small-college experience surrounds us with every day: the environmental links that cannot be transported, the contributions that do not result in individual gain.

NOTES

This paper is based on ideas first explored in March 1997 at Kansas State University's Sixth Annual Cultural Studies Symposium.

[1]Franklin (1–2) and Pratt (38–39) are among the many sources that provide documentation of this funding collapse.

[2]For a further discussion of these hybrids, see especially pp. 3–8 and 51–55 of *We Have Never Been Modern*. Latour notes that he borrows the term "quasi-object" from the French philosopher Michel Serres (51).

[3]The MLA report defines service by reference to its hybrid nature, noting that among the elements classified as service, "the common element, it appears to us, is the relation they forge between knowledge, learning, and practical action with real-world consequences. Professional service is distinguished from other sites of faculty work in that it is integrally active or related to practical action; if intellectual work, it has to do with ideas in action" (187).

[4]Latour argues that even such an ostensibly universal idea as a law of physics spreads only as its "network is extended and stabilized"; its "speed of propagation is exactly equivalent to the rate at which the community of experimenters and their equipment develop" (24).

[5]Coleman's full sentence helps distinguish the concept of social capital from capital's more familiar forms: "If physical capital is wholly tangible, being embodied in observable material form, and human capital is less tangible, being embodied in the skills and knowledge acquired by an individual, social capital is less tangible yet, for it exists in the *relations* among persons."

WORKS CITED

Coleman, James. "Social Capital in the Creation of Human Capital." *American Journal of Sociology* 94, suppl. (1988): S95–120.

Franklin, Phyllis. "From the Editor." *Profession 1996*. New York: MLA, 1996. 1–5.

Gaudiani, Claire. "The Soul in the Machine or the Machine in the Soul?" *Profession 1996*. New York: MLA, 1996. 26–36.

Latour, Bruno. *Science in Action: How to Follow Scientists and Engineers through Society.* Cambridge: Harvard UP, 1987.

———. *We Have Never Been Modern*. Trans. Catherine Porter. Cambridge: Harvard UP, 1995.

Latour, Bruno, and Steve Woolgar. *Laboratory Life: The Construction of Scientific Facts.* 1979. Princeton: Princeton UP, 1986.

MLA Commission on Professional Service. "Making Faculty Work Visible: Reinterpreting Professional Service, Teaching, and Research in the Fields of Language and Literature." *Profession 1996*. New York: MLA, 1996. 161–216.

Nelson, Cary. "How to Reform the MLA: An Opening Proposal." *Profession 1996*. New York: MLA, 1996. 44–49.

Park, Shelley M. "Research, Teaching, and Service: Why Shouldn't Women's Work Count?" *Journal of Higher Education* 67 (1996): 46–84.

Pratt, Linda Ray. "Negotiating Agendas? Academic Management for Quality and Control." *Profession 1996*. New York: MLA, 1996. 37–43.

Serres, Michel. *The Parasite*. Trans. Lawrence R. Schehr. Baltimore: Johns Hopkins UP, 1982.

The Construct of the Near-Native Speaker in the Foreign Language Profession: Perspectives on Ideologies about Language

GUADALUPE VALDES

The topic of this article is one about which I have worried a great deal for many years. I believe that the subject is central to what we do as a profession, to our sense of who we are and what we should be, and to the future of departments of foreign languages. Let me begin with a brief scenario.

Imagine an MLA meeting and a spacious suite at the convention hotel. Members of a department of foreign languages are interviewing junior candidates for a position in their department. Paul Fletcher, the most brilliant student of the country's leading expert in a key area of literature, enters the room. Though a bit nervous, he conducts himself well. He answers questions about his research, he tactfully avoids taking sides on a current controversy in the field, and describes and presents syllabi for a set of exciting courses. The final question is asked in the foreign language. Both the members of the department and the candidate know that this is a test. The job announcement carefully stated that native or near-native proficiency in the language is required. Paul valiantly attempts to answer the question with the same confidence that he exhibited in English. His uneasiness, however, is obvious. He has a very slight accent, and he hesitates and self-corrects a number of times. Even so, his responses are detailed and complete, although delivered in relatively simple syntactic structures.

The author is Professor in the School of Education and in the Department of Spanish and Portuguese at Stanford University. A version of this article appeared in the Spring 1998 issue of the ADFL *Bulletin.*

Paul Fletcher, like many other graduate students in the foreign languages, is an American who majored in the foreign language, studied abroad for a year, completed a graduate program, and spent time in the foreign setting. He is not, however, indistinguishable from a native speaker.

For members of the department carrying out the interview, the question is, How nativelike must a near-native be? If near-native proficiency is a job requirement, what standards should the department members apply in evaluating the language abilities of future assistant professors? Should the interviewers be guided by the evaluation of their native-speaking colleagues? Should they rely on their own sense of the candidates' ability to teach in the target language? Or should they simply ignore the matter entirely?

In Paul's case, members of the department argued for many months. Interestingly enough, faculty members who liked Paul's work (and this group included both native- and non-native-speaking members of the department) found his foreign language ability to be adequate. Faculty prescriptivists, faculty members who did not like Paul's work, and faculty members who simply opposed the appointment in the first place vigorously criticized his language ability. They argued strongly that he would be unqualified to teach even basic language courses. The latter faculty group also included both native and nonnative speakers.

As you may gather, the purpose of this article is to suggest that the notion of near-native ability as it is currently used in the foreign language profession must be examined carefully. Most job announcements state clearly that it is what members of the profession want in young colleagues. It is less clear what both native and near-native ability mean in practice.

From the point of view of the field of linguistics, the concept of the native speaker is both important and complex. Florian Coulmas, for example, points out that linguists of every conceivable theoretical orientation agree that the concept of the native speaker is fundamental. For some linguists, native speakers are the essential source of linguistic data. For others, the principal goal of the linguist is to describe a language in a way that makes explicit the innate ability (competence) of such native speakers.

In spite of the centrality of native speakers in linguistic research, however, there has been much disagreement about the use of native speakers in both fieldwork and theory building. Regardless of the position taken on the use of native speakers for linguistic research, though, the sense that native speakers are fundamentally different from nonnative speakers underlies every discussion of the concept.

In the popular mind, the concept of the native speaker is less complex than that encountered in the field of linguistics. For most people, a native speaker is one who can function in all settings in which other native speakers normally function. Moreover, to be considered fully native, a speaker must be indistinguishable from other native speakers. When interacting with the individual, other native speakers should assume that he or she acquired the language from infancy.

But the issue is not simple. As Claire Kramsch has pointed out in her recent guest column in *PMLA*, "Originally, native speakership was viewed as an uncontroversial privilege of birth. Those who were born into a language were considered its native speakers, with grammatical intuitions that nonnative speakers did not have." Kramsch argues, however, that a closer examination of the concept reveals that it has often been linked to social class and to education. She maintains that the native speaker norm that has been recognized by foreign language departments in this country is, in fact, that of "the middle-class, ethnically dominant male citizenry of nation-states" (363). By implication, the language of those who do not belong to the middle class of such nations has been considered suspect.

As I pointed out in an article published in the *ADFL Bulletin* in 1991, issues of native ability, language, ethnicity, and class are quite complex in American departments of foreign languages. Let us consider for a moment the case of departments in which the "stars" are native speakers of European origin who have come to this country as adults. Often there is a tendency for such faculty members to belittle the linguistic abilities of those Americans in the department who have elected to make the teaching and study of a foreign language their career. In those departments, so-called near-native ability in the target language is not enough. The underlying belief is that only those persons who have grown up in the original culture and who have learned the language in the course of primary socialization can truly understand both the foreign literature and its culture.

Being a native speaker does not, however, necessarily save a foreign language faculty member from being looked down on by his or her colleagues. Because the notion of which language variety is prestigious or considered correct varies considerably, being a native speaker does not automatically mean acceptance as a worthy colleague. Depending on which group is in power, the only valued members of the faculty may be those who speak, for example, Madrid Spanish or Parisian French. Speakers of other varieties of the target language (no matter how indigenous or genuine it may be in certain parts of the world) would be considered faulty models for language teaching. For instance, speakers of Caribbean Spanish or Canadian French are frequently thought of as undesirable additions to departments of Spanish or French if their speech betrays their geographical origin.

The judgment of what is bad or inferior language is, again, directly related to the views held by the group in power. Sometimes, in fact, all native speakers of the language may be found to be using the wrong type of language. The situation occurs, for example, when the majority of the members of the department are American nonnative speakers of the target language who normally teach their literature courses in English. Because they themselves do not speak the language well or keep up with the ever-changing native norms governing speech, they tend to judge native-speaker performance from an idealized, unrealistic perspective and to consider unqualified all who appear not to function according to textbook standards. In these departments, the target language seldom reflects the growth and dynamism that it displays in its natural setting. Instead, it is subjected to rigid controls based on the belief that all change is either unnecessary or simply not typical of the "best" usage. Clearly, then, members of foreign language departments who are identified as belonging to the "despised" or "excluded" minority can vary greatly. Even if one doesn't consider the variables of race and ethnic background, it is obvious that marginal status is easily achieved.

The situation becomes even more complex when one considers the place of ethnic-language speakers in departments of foreign languages. By ethnic-language speakers I mean American-born, second-, third-, or even fourth-generation members of immigrant families who have developed their original competence in the ethnic language. This group includes Spanish speakers of Mexican American and Puerto Rican backgrounds, northern New England francophones, Portuguese speakers from Massachusetts, French speakers from Louisiana, and so on. These speakers of immigrant languages are often considered undesirable in our departments. They supposedly speak the wrong kind of language, and their class backgrounds clash directly with those of faculty members who were raised in foreign countries.

Because of the complexity surrounding the question of *native* ability, then, and the politics that surround these complexities in our departments, it is not surprising that the construct of *near-native* ability is, itself, extraordinarily complex. To examine this construct fairly, let us stand back for a moment and consider why foreign language departments have an interest in the language ability of their faculty members.

What is clear is that foreign language departments carry out intellectual work in languages other than English. It is logical to expect that most, if not all, members of the faculty will be able to carry out such work in the language of the field and, additionally, that they will be able to teach *in* the target language and to serve as models of language for their students. In some departments, it is also expected that young assistant professors will be able to teach the language itself as a subject.

The question, then, becomes, How near-native must an individual be in order to carry out intellectual work in the target language, to lecture in the language, and to teach the language itself to undergraduate students?

To my knowledge, no research has been done on the question of what kinds of language proficiencies are required in order to work in the area of literary and cultural studies. A description of the demands made on language ability by the reading of texts, by research on social contexts surrounding text production, and so on does not currently exist. We have no evidence, for example, that creditable "readings" of foreign language texts demand excellent control of the structure of the spoken language. What is needed is careful research in this area, to help us understand not only what kinds of proficiencies to expect in our colleagues but also how we—as departments of foreign languages—can develop these same proficiencies in our own students.

Research on the language abilities required in order to lecture in a foreign language on a relatively narrow set of topics is also not available. A commonsense view would hold that, to lecture in a language in an academic setting to both graduate and undergraduate students, some of whom may be native speaking, instructors must be able to use the registers of the language considered appropriate for such teaching—to present information to persons who have little or no background in the subject, to explain, to simplify, to offer examples, to make links to other kinds of knowledge, and so on. Additionally, the instructors should be able to respond to questions, to read between the lines to determine the real messages being sent by students, and to manage classroom discussions. Finally, they should be able to correct both the content and the form of the written work produced by the students.

As will be noted, many of the elements I have listed above (e.g., the ability to read between the lines) go well beyond language. So too does the ability to present information to people who have little or no background in a subject. What we still cannot evaluate is the effect, on graduates and undergraduates, of a professor who is less than nativelike in the language and is an excellent teacher, in comparison with the effect of a true native who has limited abilities as a classroom instructor.

Moreover, we have little information about the impact of "deviant," or non-nativelike, language on early learners of a foreign language. Many myths abound. There is fear that students will become confused if their instructor uses an ungrammatical form. As Diane Larsen-Freeman and Michael Long point out, however, there is almost no research on the effects of experience with natives and nonnatives on second language acquisition. What we do know is that—in a natural setting—most native speakers, when addressing language learners, use "foreigner talk," a slightly modified and sometimes ungrammatical version of the language. This too is "deviant" input for the learner, as is group work with language-learning peers who themselves produce a flawed version of the target language.

The question here, then, is how good is good enough. Does the second language acquisition environment require an instructor who is largely indistinguishable from a native speaker in regard to phonology, syntax, morphology, semantics, and pragmatics, or does it demand an enthusiastic, committed individual who is likely to motivate young undergraduates to pursue further language study? In an ideal world, language teachers would be inspiring, enthusiastic, and—I might add—knowledgeable about second language acquisition. Indeed, many of us in the language-teaching field would maintain that an understanding of how language is acquired, a commitment to providing a broad set of language experiences for students, and a deep awareness of one's own language limitations might be more important than perfect or almost-perfect native speaker abilities.

A complete research agenda, focusing on the examination of the construct of near-native ability, might include the following:

- a survey of near-native-speaking foreign language professionals, asking about their experiences as nonnative speakers in the profession, their perspectives on the standard of near-native ability, and their views concerning the legitimacy or the necessity of the construct
- a retrospective study of language professionals considered to be near-native, to identify salient personal and experiential factors in the acquisition of near-native ability
- a study of the language demands made on literary scholars by the study of texts of various types
- a study of the language demands made on literary scholars who teach in the target language
- a study designed to identify the best foreign language scholars in the profession and to evaluate these scholars' actual language proficiency
- a study designed to identify the best teachers of foreign language in the profession and to evaluate these teachers' actual language proficiency
- a carefully controlled study of the impact of instructors' language proficiency on language learners
- a study designed to describe fully the grammatical and pragmatic language abilities of near-native individuals

This is clearly an ambitious agenda. There is much to be done in examining the notion of near-native ability in our profession. A more important and immediate question might be, How much does this notion affect us on an everyday level? To be truthful, I expect that the answers will vary a great deal.

I suspect that in hiring young assistant professors, most departments find themselves weighing personal characteristics, scholarship, and the like, in addition to language competence. In some cases, differences in language abilities may be used only to distinguish between two equally qualified candidates. The fact remains, however, that judgments about candidates' language abilities made by literature professors in departments of foreign languages are largely impressionistic. Each professor brings to the task of evaluating language proficiency different criteria and different expectations. Two equally competent native-speaking members of the faculty, for example, may disagree profoundly about the fluency and accuracy of a particular candidate. Not surprisingly, it is difficult for the chair of the department to reconcile vastly different conclusions based on the identical sample of language performance.

The chair, of course, could ask that the candidate be "tested," using some professionally recognized examination. Unfortunately, there are no available tests of foreign language proficiency that can establish the linguistic range of particular individuals across a broad spectrum of occupations and professions. There are certainly no instruments available that even pretend to measure a person's ability to carry out original research on foreign language texts or to lecture to both graduates and undergraduates in the target language. Although such tests could be constructed, it is unlikely, I would argue, that test scores and rankings could persuade members of foreign language departments to set aside their own judgments of their future colleagues' language abilities.

What we have in the profession, then, is a dilemma. Near-native ability is largely in the eyes of the beholder. As a construct, it is both difficult to define and difficult to defend. It may well be, however, that in our hiring practices we have learned how to negotiate around this issue and have come to recognize when objections to a particular candidate are a question of language competence as opposed to a question of politics. The issue is not quite so simple for the PhD students we are preparing to compete in a highly constricted job market. PhD-granting foreign language departments have many obligations to the Paul Fletchers of the world. If our PhD students are to be judged on their language proficiency, we cannot pretend that we have no responsibility in helping them to develop the language skills they will need in order to carry out their obligations as members of language- and literature-teaching departments.

There is much, however, that we do not know about how near-native ability is produced. The second language acquisition literature is limited in what it can offer us, because it has not approached the problem from precisely this perspective. We do know that in order for students even to get past an interview, they must sound confident and fluent. They must defend an opinion, seem appropriately deferential in the terms of the target culture, and present themselves authentically in the target language. This is a tall order indeed.

The question we must ask ourselves is whether the PhD curriculum enables students to develop such proficiencies. The challenges are many. In most departments, courses designed to develop language skills are limited to the first two or three years. Attention is seldom given to evaluating the language strengths and weaknesses of future PhD students. For the most part, they are expected to take care of their continued language learning on their own. Although we often suggest to weak students that they spend a year or more in a country where the language is spoken, we seldom make clear to them the kinds of language experiences they should seek out during their stay abroad to help them develop needed skills.

In some graduate departments, the problem is completely avoided. Only those students considered to be already near-native are admitted for graduate study. All too often, however, the policy of giving preference to highly proficient graduate students results in large numbers of students who are foreign nationals and who have been educated in their own countries in the target language. As is evident, the implications for American departments of foreign languages of such enrollment and admissions policies are many. I am not the first to suggest that these policies and their consequences need to be examined closely and evaluated carefully over time.

The notion of near-native ability is deeply embedded in the culture of foreign language departments. Most of us view it from a commonsense perspective. Indeed, I would wager that many of my readers are wondering why I think it is an issue worth their attention at all. Of course the faculty members of a language department must be able to function in the target language!

As I pointed out, I have no quarrel with this perspective. My concern is with the unquestioned acceptance of a language policy and its implementation in the absence of research evidence that such *near-native* ability, as variously defined, is (1) commonly acquired, (2) essential to the carrying out of professional duties in teaching and research, and (3) designed to bring about the creation of the strongest and best foreign language departments.

In suggesting that the entire concept needs to be examined, I am influenced by researchers who, working in the context of critical language study (e.g., Fairclough, *Awareness and Power*; Tollefson), have demonstrated that language is never simply neutral. Indeed, they have strongly argued that language conventions and language practices are invested with power relations and ideological processes of which people are often unaware. What is evident from the work of these scholars is that language—in spite of our best intentions—contributes to the domination of some people by others. Ideologies about language—that is, commonsense notions about what is correct, appropriate, and necessary—directly depend on structures of power.

The notion of near-native ability and the language policy operating in most departments of foreign languages today are, in fact, the institutionalization of language for the purpose of making distinctions among different groups of individuals on the basis of accidental characteristics. As James Tollefson points out, such policy is one mechanism for locating language within social structure in such a way that it determines who has access to political power and economic resources.

As a profession, we may decide that distinctions between the "right" and "wrong" kinds of speakers are indeed vital to what we do. However, we should reach such a conclusion only after we carefully examine the notion of near-native ability as an indicator of professional competence.

The truth of the matter is that learning a foreign language is the project of a lifetime. As one scholar put it:

> In the beginning it has to be like a love affair. It comes at the time in life, adolescence or early youth, when the individual is seeking an ideal fulfillment which will complete the ego's secret view of itself. . . . No sane explanation can account for this possession, this demonic urge, that impels the student, not only to seek an unpopular undergraduate major (that would be just a passing aberration, later corrected in graduate school or professional life), but to choose to pursue an ill-defined goal, to persist through years of graduate study, to haunt the doubtful corridors of the job market, and finally to embrace a life in the classroom where, once arrived, the individual can enjoy an alienation from native culture and a second-class citizenship in an adopted one. (Dudley 57–58)

More important, perhaps, Edward Dudley reminds us that becoming a member of our profession is not without extraordinary costs. As if anticipating our examination of the concept of near-native fluency, Dudley adds:

> It should be recognized that the pursuit of native fluency imposes a condition of perpetual slavery to a goal that can never be possessed. Nor can it be pretended to without constant dedication to the maintenance of skills, equal in difficulty to the daily drudgery of a concert pianist, a prima ballerina or an operatic athlete. (58)

I know that there are many equivalents of concert pianists and prima ballerinas among my readers, many individuals who have dedicated their lives to the continued study of the language they teach. There is much that we can learn from each other. I would ask you to initiate conversations with your colleagues about their own near-native abilities. Ask them to share with you how they became near-native. Find out how they have managed to maintain language abilities over time and how practices of what I call linguistic one-upmanship in their departments have affected them in their professional lives.

The construct of near-native ability is fundamental to our future as a profession. I hope that you will join me in examining it and in exploring its many implications in your own departments.

WORKS CITED

Coulmas, Florian. *A Festschrift for Native Speaker*. The Hague: Mouton, 1981.

Dudley, Edward. "Profess and Confess: Reflections on a Cultural Displacement." *American Attitudes toward Foreign Languages and Foreign Cultures*. Ed. Dudley and P. Heller. Bonn: Grundmann, 1983. 57–67.

Fairclough, Norman. *Critical Language Awareness*. London: Longman, 1992.

———. *Language and Power*. London: Longman, 1989.

Kramsch, Claire. "The Privilege of the Nonnative Speaker." *PMLA* 112 (1997): 359–69.

Larsen-Freeman, Diane, and Michael H. Long. *An Introduction to Second Language Acquisition Research*. London: Longman, 1991.

Tollefson, James W. *Planning Language, Planning Inequality: Language Policy in the Community*. London: Longman, 1991.

Valdés, Guadalupe. "Minority and Majority Members in Foreign Language Departments: Toward the Examination of Established Attitudes and Values." *ADFL Bulletin* 22.2 (1991): 10–14.

Night Thoughts on Retiring Early; or, Reflections on How the Tail Wags the Dog

BARTON R. FRIEDMAN

One day, now two years past, I found myself on the elevator to my department's eighteenth-floor offices, inveighing to a friend about what I no longer remember—maybe students who took my demand they demonstrate ability to reason as outrageously unreasonable; or maybe colleagues who, like electricity, chose the path of least resistance by passing such students on to become someone else's problem or who, following the equally sound principle of nothing ventured, nothing lost, were disinclined to protest cuts in the library's already meager book-buying budget or to challenge our dean's easy assumption that we should sacrifice literature offerings to increase sections of service courses, mainly freshman English, or to oppose administrative priorities that had shrunk our department to the point where such invidious choices became necessary.

Exiting the elevator, we encountered one of my by now several successors as departmental chair. "At it again, Bart," he smiled in passing.

"To most people around here," I remarked to my friend, "I've become a curmudgeon."

She laughed, meaning to be sympathetic. "But you're *our* curmudgeon." At that moment, I glimpsed retirement beckoning.

When I told a former student I'd retired, she responded that, unlike me, she still loved her job. I loved the work, but I'd grown increasingly disaffected from the job. This essay is my effort to discover, like Bishop

The author is Professor Emeritus of English at Cleveland State University.

Berkeley reflecting on his motive for publishing, whether I have colleagues out there who think as I do.

The best advice I ever got about teaching came from the worst teacher I ever had. "In the classroom," he said, "always be yourself."

An authority on Irish literature, he was the quintessence of bad. The stereotype of the soporific professor relentlessly droning scholarly minutiae might have been invented to describe him. He sat before us—all two who stayed the course—reading from aged notecards that yielded, even on Yeats and Joyce, only slogging columns of facts: background; parentage; birth and death dates; major works, when and where published; literary allies, literary adversaries; political allegiances; religious convictions, or lack thereof; on and on. Never did he venture into what we intellectual children of the New Criticism supposed was the business of English professors: explication of texts. He seemed an academic Rip Van Winkle, who, having slept twenty years, had now (in 1956) resumed his duties, oblivious to the revolution fomented by Brooks, Warren, and their fellow mental travelers.

Yet he was an encyclopedia of biographical and bibliographical data that, I later realized, provided useful, sometimes crucial, support for the kind of interpretive work on which I set out to build a career. He could, I imagine, have made his courses stitcheries of New Critical readings (he wrote delicate lyrics in the manner of early Yeats), and he would have enjoyed less embarrassing enrollments as his reward. But he would have thought such a concession equivalent to the bargain a previous scholar made with that exemplary provost Mephistopheles. He knew explication as the spell by which his colleagues enthralled students, and he decided that from him we should get something else that, by his lights, we needed more. I don't say he was right, though I've come to believe he wasn't wholly wrong. Despite the pain he must have felt at the sentence students regularly passed on him with their feet, he remained resolutely himself.

Strangely, he recalls one of the best teachers I've ever known, William M. Sale, who taught modern fiction at Cornell. His classes consisted of elegantly crafted essaylike lectures, packed with what back then we labeled insights. There was one catch: he mumbled. Not, it transpired, because of weak vocal cords. One spring day in 1957, as his son Kirk conducted an overture to the Berkeley Free Speech Movement, noisy enough to have elicited the *New York Daily News* headline "COEDS RIOT FOR SEX," outside his window, he showed he could raise his voice at need. He mumbled as a pedagogical stratagem. He wanted only those students willing to stretch for every word. Either you arrived early to claim a seat in one of the front rows or you strained to keep his voice from settling into a monotonous hum. Students who couldn't or wouldn't tolerate his needling style usually drifted off as the semester wore on.

When I later enrolled in his Faulkner seminar, I anticipated learning from him in a setting where the sheer effort to stay with his words would drain less energy. But he simply changed tactics. Instead of mumbling, he meditated. He seemed to wonder out loud. It appeared he might traverse the whole semester without uttering a declarative sentence. Maddening! He provoked us—that is, he taught us—to read Faulkner as a novelist of subtlety and power demands to be read. We came out of his seminar stronger readers than we were when we walked in.

Today neither of these teachers would be tolerated, not alone by students but by typical university administrators, perhaps even by colleagues. They would all be wrong. The classes each taught drew no throngs of satisfied customers—the happy state that presidents aspire to report to the accountant-heads controlling most boards of trustees. But each launched apprentice scholars who learned to read perceptively, write cogently, and meet exacting standards of accuracy and thoroughness in their research.

I don't mean we should devote ourselves, as scholar-teachers, solely to reproducing ourselves, though we must reproduce ourselves if universities are to have scholar-teachers for the twenty-first century. I mean we must graduate people who can think clearly and independently if our technocracy and, more to the point, our democracy are to survive in the twenty-first century. After Congress reneged on its original commitment to fund the building of the supercollider, the director of the project is said, in his postmortem to the press, to have attributed its death to the revenge of C students. As a society, we must decide whether we want—whether we can afford—public policy made by C students.

Having read that, many of you, I suspect, will stamp me elitist and have done. And I might reply, "If this be elitism, let's make the most of it." For elitism is as un-American as Thomas Jefferson, though he called it "aristocracy of talent." Jefferson saw that among the first requisites of a democratic (he would have said republican) society is a citizenry capable of informed, intelligent choices—which is why he became a founder not only of the United States but also of the University of Virginia.

Our current version of the public, and especially open admissions, university institutionalizes elitism in reverse. Instead of privileging good students, we in effect penalize them. For they are too few, their presence overwhelmed by the mediocre that many administrations recruit, and pressure faculties to retain, as an economic strategy for survival. Precious resources are expended to "retain undecided students," most of whom have as much business being students as I, in my advanced middle age, would have becoming an astronaut. Meanwhile, talented students—those we should be recruiting into the Jeffersonian aristocracy—are left to find their own way, or lose it, among the crowd. My university, now in its thirty-third year, has no honors program. Yet it boasts a dean for retention, with a million dollars or so a year to spend, while its roster of classroom instructors dwindles and genuine instruments of remediation, like the English department's writing center, are fed on leavings. Few tails could wag their dogs better than that.

I'm not simply playing that popular faculty parlor game Pin the Tail on the Administration, though senior administrators—removed as they often are from the true "mission" of every university, teaching and research—have much greater influence than professors over how our constantly diminished budget pie gets sliced. The professoriat is, I suppose, the last consulted on how well or ill universities spend their money—or, more important, on how they might spend it better—largely because most Americans who think about universities think them businesses, in which administrators are management and faculty labor. Some faculties, my own included, have encouraged this misperception by unionizing. I have colleagues who view themselves less as members of a faculty than as members of a bargaining unit.

The damage done by this thinking, by the whole analogy between universities and business, is manifest in the contradictory roles it assigns students. They're customers, who have a right to expect their money's worth from the product their tuition buys; and they're the product, rolling off assembly lines, packed with information and know-how, to be bought by corporations requiring their services. Either way, studentship reduces to passive reception—like watching television. As customers, students assemble to receive the course content from the professor; as products, they sit still for the period allotted the professor to enter the content into their synapses.

Under neither model must they take responsibility for learning. If they fail to learn, it's because they were badly taught. We've graduated from the draconian academy of the past, which tolerated martinets like William Sale, to a user-friendly institution. Students need feel no guilt over deficient performance. Even for the misguided remnant, who may yet suspect they've had a hand in determining their Ds and Fs as well as their As and Bs, we've devised an instrument to restore their self-esteem: student evaluation. Student evaluation enables the aggrieved to strike back, officially, at faculty members who haven't recognized their talent, to rate instructors on a reassuringly precise numerical scale as unprepared, unclear, unfair, unsympathetic, or all of the above.

No faculty members I know—good and popular teachers though most believe themselves to be—would stake next year's raise, much less tenure, on the reliability of any evaluation their students might make. At one of my last department meetings, when the chair informed us that our newly anointed union had agreed to student evaluation in every course as a provision of its first contract, a colleague, himself a union activist, asked, "Surely the dean won't rely on student evaluations as the only measure of our teaching . . . will she?" But the misgivings this colleague expressed behind closed doors almost no one is willing to assert in the open and out loud. Since the sixties, to suggest that students are in most areas unqualified to vet faculty members has been bad form.

Those worst served by this turn are the students themselves. Many readers of *Profession* will recognize the student who's missed half the class meetings (he or she has to work, of course) but expects a satisfactory grade or the student who can't write a coherent paragraph and regularly confuses homonyms like *there* and *their*, *affect* and *effect*—even *to*, *too*, and *two*—but waxes indignant at the suggestion that such lapses, say in a letter of application, might provoke questions about the applicant's literacy. And some readers, at least, will recall students who've acted on their indignation, assuming the stance of angrily dissatisfied customers to complain to the department chair (the boss, as they doubtless thought) that the failure was not theirs but the instructor's: they deserved more for their money.

But I don't blame such students for their unpreparedness or their attitudes. We're the Frankensteins who've created this monster. We've repeatedly declined to defend the integrity of our disciplines against the pressure of our administrators, the politicians, the public, not to mention the students themselves, consenting instead to clerk in what the pseudonymous author of *Generation X Goes to College* calls A-Marts (Sacks). Small wonder eighteen-year-olds treat their writing instructors to pronouncements like these:

Genuine education is an idea whose time has come and gone.

or

If the bridge I design collapses, no one, NO ONE, will ask me if I had learned Spinosa's [sic] geometry.

These students have grasped the lesson taught by, among others, a recent governor of my state, whose nostrum for sustaining a malnourished system of public education was, "We must learn to do more with less."

There remain, I trust, some politicians intelligently concerned about public education; dedicated students still turn up in our classes; and I'm as interested as anyone else in crossing bridges that won't collapse. But my instances of hostility to "genuine education," harbored by the very people we're supposed to be educating, seem surprising (if they do) only in their openness about expressing attitudes that weigh on us like the Dark Lord's Ring. For people to whom these attitudes seem so normal, so inoffensive, that they feel no reticence at sharing them, even with their instructors, learning as we understand it is meaningless. The university is a licensing bureau: you pay your tuition, you serve your time, and you emerge with a ticket to economic opportunity.

A common complaint. It's usually met with regretful admonishments that students must be practical. To some, it's no complaint at all. In a 1979 essay confronting the plight of the liberal arts, Mark C. Ebersole quoted a "successful management consultant" as warning:

> A lot of these people [liberal arts graduates] are wasting their futures and educational careers by choosing the wrong fields. What society is saying today is that most jobs are of a technical, marketing, or financial variety. Some of the faculty that have been teaching things for which society seemingly has little need are going to find themselves without students.

At Cleveland State, hardly a citadel of humanistic studies, something funny has happened along the way to fulfilling this prediction. We haven't lost students. We've lost instructors for teaching them. When I arrived to chair the English department in 1978, we had 120 majors. That number has increased by two-thirds. Our faculty has decreased by one-third.

CSU practices the gospel of Ebersole's management consultant: that since jobs for college graduates are in technology, marketing, and finance, colleges should train students—not educate them—in technology, marketing, and finance. I'll resist comment on the long-term prospects for students seeking such jobs, given the infatuation with downsizing in corporate America, which has indeed learned how to do (or make?) more with less. But I believe it important to comment—loudly—on policies that, in downsizing universities to high-class trade schools, institutionalize ignorance of, or indifference to, the history of science and technology itself.

For our capacity to do—and make—more with less has emerged from the work of a few great scientists, situated mainly in universities, where they were free to pursue their curiosity into arcane corners of nature. Who in 1905, or 1935, dreamed that those ghostly traces eventually rendered visible in cloud chambers would one day dance to our will on computer screens? What management consultant, if management consultants existed back then, would have advised a student, "Go into physics; society needs you there whether it says so or not"?

The same cost-benefit mentality that, by constricting higher education, is choking the humanities is also, if more slowly, choking science. Where nowadays but on a campus can an environment friendly to *basic* research survive? The import of this question is underscored by no less a scientist than James D. Watson, whose memoir of how he and Francis Crick discovered the structure of DNA includes a paean to Cambridge as itself a collaborator in one of the major scientific achievements of our time:

> The following morning [after their breakthrough] I felt marvelously alive when I awoke. On my way to the Whim [where Watson breakfasted] I slowly walked toward the Clare Bridge, staring at the gothic pinnacles of the King's College Chapel that stood out sharply against the spring sky. I briefly stopped and looked at the perfect Georgian features of the recently cleaned Gibbs Building, thinking that much of our success was due to the long uneventful periods when we walked among the colleges or unobtrusively read the new books that came into Heffer's Bookstore. (116–17)

Lest anyone dismiss as mere nostalgia this hymn in praise of the leisure to think, here's Crick on the same event:

> People often ask how long Jim and I worked on DNA. This rather depends on what one means by work. Over a period of almost two years we often discussed the problem, either in the laboratory or in our daily lunchtime walks around the Backs [. . .] or at home, since Jim occasionally dropped in near dinnertime, with a hungry look in his eye. Sometimes, when the summer weather was particularly tempting, we would take the afternoon off and punt up the river toward Grantchester. (68)

Crick's "deconstruction" of "work" brings to mind a summer afternoon I spent by Lake Mendota on the University of Wisconsin, Madison, campus, at a time when legislators were pushing one of their recurrent campaigns to make those professors at the other end of State Street "accountable." A mathematician friend and I were standing on the beach while our children splashed in the water. "I can be working," he said, "while I watch my kids swim."

Wisconsin is hardly unique in electing legislators who suspect the faculties in their state's universities of malingering. And the conviction that *tenure* is synonymous with *sinecure* is hardly confined to elected officials, as books like *Profscam* make clear. I want to meet the grant reviewer who'd seriously entertain a proposal that had built into it time for creative walks by the water or conversation over drinks and dinner.

Yet to shrug such diversions off as amusements that professors should leave for weekends, "like the rest of us who punch time clocks," is to miss the obsessive power of the work. David L. Hull remarks that to scientists research "is not just an occupation; it is a compulsion" (245). It's no less a compulsion to humanists. When scholars walk away from desk or lab bench to escape problems that have proved, for the moment, intractable, what they'll usually end up discussing with colleagues they may meet over coffee or under a tree are the problems they've tried to escape.

That an essential function of campuses is to supply opportunity for such moments of productive idling squares, I'd wager, with the experience of most readers of *Profession*. Here, for example, is testimony by two scholars, whose courses in literature and in philosophy I recall with gratitude and respect. The first is M. H. Abrams in his preface to *Natural Supernaturalism*:

> Suppose one were [. . .] to imagine an ideal place for writing a work on Romantic literature. He might envision a study in a commodious old university building surrounded by the studies of scholars, generous of their learning, whose provinces include both ancient and modern literatures and philosophy; a minute's stroll distant there would be a major research library with a notable collection in the age of Wordsworth, reached by a path commanding a Wordsworthian prospect of hill, wood, lake, and sky. This was in fact my situation in 171 Goldwin Smith Hall, where this book was planned, worked out in lectures and discussions, and largely written. (15–16)

The second is Max Black, reflecting at his life's end on a distinguished academic career:

> When I became a professor of philosophy, after a decade of teaching mathematics to children and their prospective teachers, I needed to learn as much as I could about a wide variety of disciplines, ranging from linguistics and literary criticism to psychology, sociology, and, in recent years, economics. ONLY AT Cornell University could I have found so many conversable colleagues, willing to relieve my ignorance and to engage in extended cooperative investigation. (2)

I quote Abrams and Black not only because both are great scholars, from whose teaching I benefited greatly, but also because both attest to a truth about universities, and about themselves as university professors, that critics of universities want badly to disbelieve: contrary to what passes for popular wisdom, no necessary conflict exists between teaching and research. They should—often do—reinforce each other. Abrams alludes to how he developed the argument of *Natural Supernaturalism* in his classes (including, as I know from experience, undergraduate classes).

I also encountered Black in an undergraduate course. What draws me to his preface, though, is less my recollection of being a student in his classroom than my realization that he always thought of himself as a student among students. I've occasionally (half) jested that professors become professors because they remain arrested in postadolescence: they want never to stop being students. Cornell seemed idyllic to Abrams and Black as an ongoing seminar that gave them freedom to follow wherever their interests led.

Most of us, that is, find ourselves teaching, I think, not primarily because, like elementary or high school teachers, we want to teach but because we want to learn. "Aha," readers of *Profscam* will chorus, "I always suspected some such hypocrisy." At the risk of inflating their moral indignation, I might add: in universities, there's little wrong and a lot right about privileging learning over teaching. It makes better teachers—teachers who believe their disciplines important enough to warrant the dedication of maximum energy to teaching and who require that students dedicate comparable energy to studying.

I'm not describing a customer-friendly institution here. I'm describing an intellectually challenging one. I'm probably also describing an ideal that in practice exists nowhere. Harold Bloom dissects the academy with ruthless candor:

> We are destroying all intellectual and aesthetic standards in the humanities and social sciences in the name of social justice. Our institutions show bad faith in this: no quotas are imposed upon brain surgeons or mathematicians. What has been devalued is learning as such, as though erudition were irrelevant in the realm of judgment and misjudgment.
>
> (35)

Bloom is, I surmise, looking mainly at Yale. What would he say were he situated in the typical public university, with its politics-ridden board of trustees, its enrollment-driven budget, and its narrowly defined "mission" of preparing students for Workworld?

Lewis Thomas, in the essay "How to Fix the Premedical Curriculum," attacks the curriculum's single-minded focus on biomedical science, proposing instead that "classical Greek [wow!] be restored as the centerpiece of undergraduate education." He deplores the "depressing [. . .] drift toward special courses for prelaw [. . .] and even prebusiness students," arguing that "English, history, the literature of at least two foreign languages, and philosophy should come near the top of the list, just below Classics, as basic requirements [. . .]." Homer would replace the MCATs "as a shrewd test for the qualities of mind and character needed in a physician" (200, 201).

The trouble with Thomas's program lies in its assumption that we humanists will do our part; that we'll insist on rigorous standards of performance in our classes, though, since the end of the sixties, we've been drifting the other way. In what I can only ascribe to a failure of nerve, we've recurrently allowed ideological bias to overwhelm intellectual judgment and encouraged students to believe that anything they truly feel should be treated as critically respectable, lest their egos be bruised.

That such stratagems will shield us from enrollment entropy—a more than incidental motive for adopting them—seems to me no less Pollyannaish than James Clerk Maxwell's fable of a demon with the hand-eye coordination to sort fast molecules from slow, thus arresting entropy in nature. If we don't respect the integrity of our disciplines, why should anyone else? Bloom would have us simply thumb our noses at the head counters, to which most deans and provosts have been reduced: "We need to teach more selectively, searching for the few who have the capacity to become highly individual readers. The others, who are amenable to a politicized curriculum, can be abandoned to it" (17).

That sort of elitism we should resist. We need instead to adopt some reasonable version of Thomas's program, not just for premeds or Bloom's highly individual readers but for all students. By restoring traditional standards to curriculum planning and to our expectations for our classes, we may regain good students we've lost.

Regaining those students is the last thing anyone with a management consultant's mentality wants to accomplish, not because he or she fears for their economic futures but because people with ears for language and a capacity for critical thought aren't easily manipulable. And manipulation is a management consultant's business: "Marketing is a technique—millions of dollars are expended to induce us to consume certain products. Surveillance is a technique—ingenious instruments can monitor every detail of our public and private acts. Political campaigning is a technique—candidates are conditioned in authentic Skinnerian fashion [. . .]" (Ebersole).

Not all totalitarianisms rise to power out of the barrel of a gun. I taught in a city whose mayor has given millions in tax abatements to corporations but purports to think that it's the adults teaching in the system's underequipped and undermaintained schools who "have failed our children" (McQueen). I have also taught in a university that boasts a big-name basketball coach, hired at a modest $100,000 (Maxse) plus an unspecified amount for recruiting, but that seems unable to find dollars for building its library collection. By letting permissiveness creep into our classes, we've contributed to producing citizens who detect no incongruity in conduct Pope would have savored as grist for *The Dunciad*. We've cooperated in easing the way for a form of totalitarianism particularly insidious because it masquerades as democratic choice.

To paraphrase a famous conclusion of Norman Mailer's, then, we are killing us. If much of my argument sounds like leftover Matthew Arnold, rewarmed and served up anew, we could do worse that to read *Culture and Anarchy*. For between culture (in Arnold's sense) and, if not anarchy, a progressive decline of democracy our choice may well lie.

WORKS CITED

Abrams, M. H. *Natural Supernaturalism: Tradition and Revolution in Romantic Literature*. New York: Norton, 1971.

Black, Max. *Perplexities: Rational Choice, the Prisoner's Dilemma, Metaphor, Poetic Ambiguity, and Other Puzzles*. Ithaca: Cornell UP, 1990.

Bloom, Harold. *The Western Canon: The Books and School of the Ages*. New York: Harcourt, 1994.

Crick, Francis. *What Mad Pursuit: A Personal View of a Scientific Discovery*. N.p.: Basic, 1988.

Ebersole, Mark C. "Why the Liberal Arts Will Survive." *Chronicle of Higher Education* 21 May 1979: 48.

Hull, David L. *The Metaphysics of Evolution*. Albany: State U of New York P, 1989.

Maxse, Joe. "Cleveland State Picks an Experienced Hand." *Cleveland Plain Dealer* 1 May 1996: D1.

McQueen, Anjetta. "Social Services in Schools." *Cleveland Plain Dealer* 19 Apr. 1996: B2.

Sacks, Peter. *Generation X Goes to College*. Chicago: Open Court, 1996.

Thomas, Lewis. "How to Fix the Premedical Curriculum." *A Long Line of Cells: Collected Essays*. New York: Book-of-the-Month, 1990. 199–202.

Watson, James D. *The Double Helix: A Personal Account of the Discovery of the Structure of DNA*. Ed. Gunther S. Stent. Norton Critical Edition. New York: Norton, 1980.

This Is Not a Hypertext: Scholarly Annotation and the Electronic Medium

BRUCE E. GRAVER

It is the purpose of this paper to raise questions about the hypertext model (or, more accurately, the hypertext synecdoche) for electronic scholarly editions. These questions arise from my experience as an editor for the Cornell Wordsworth, a project that, according to Jerome McGann, "has put a period to codex-based scholarly editions" ("Rationale"), and my experience as the coeditor of *Lyrical Ballads* for Cambridge University Press, which will be among the first of the new generations of electronic editions. I focus on the issue of annotation, partly because my Cornell Wordsworth volume is, for the series at least, heavily annotated and because the annotations in my *Lyrical Ballads* edition will seem, for an electronic edition, unusually spare. The reasons for this difference emerge in the course of my discussion, but here, at the outset, I would like to suggest that the everexpanding, "radiant" model of the hypertext archive, eloquently envisioned by McGann and others (McGann, "Radiant Textuality"), is, in my view, something of a mistake.

But before I get too far ahead of myself, let me step back and talk about the problem of annotation in my Cornell volume, Wordsworth's *Translations of Chaucer and Virgil*. The Cornell Wordsworth has usually avoided annotation of the historical or interpretive kind. Because of their extraordinary effort to present the full textual record of Wordsworth's poems, from the earliest drafts down to the last lifetime (or first posthumous) publica-

The author is Professor of English at Providence College.

tion, its editors have maintained that annotations not concerned with textual matters add an undesirable layer of clutter to volumes that are already very large and very full. But for my translations volume, a significant exception was made. Why? Because, in the words of an anonymous NEH reviewer, "this promises to be one of the least interesting volumes in the series." Wordsworth's translations are virtually unknown even to Romanticists, they do not have the cultural significance of the translations of Dryden or Pope, the bulk of them were left unpublished, and many are unfinished. So there is little apparent reason to devote editorial energy to them, except to complete and remain consistent with an ambitious editorial enterprise.

My challenge, then, was to find reasons why these poems are interesting and to make those reasons apparent. My means for doing so was annotation. A typical page of my edition of Wordsworth's *Aeneid* has four bands of text: one containing the reading text of the translation and three in smaller type underneath. The top band in smaller type gives Coleridge's unpublished notes to the translation, a wonderful find that, to my knowledge, only Robert Woof and Stephen Parrish had examined before I did. The middle band provides the critical apparatus of verbal variants, such as one would find in any variorum edition, and the bottom band contains extensive annotations about Wordsworth's methods of translation—comparisons between the translation and the Latin, suggestions about ways in which his translation may have been influenced by prose paraphrases and scholarly commentaries, passages in his original poems that allude to the *Aeneid*, and, of course, obligatory attempts to explain Coleridge's comments. In addition, after the reading text, a lengthy set of editorial notes records Wordsworth's borrowings from four earlier translations of the *Aeneid*: the translations of John Ogilby (the 1650 edition that Wordsworth owned, which is now in the Wordsworth Library, Grasmere), John Dryden, Joseph Trapp, and Christopher Pitt. Now all of this means that in addition to tracing the full textual history of Wordsworth's poems, I have attempted to illustrate Wordsworth's methods when translating and assess (or present the evidence for assessing) his place in the history of English translation. As my reviewer for the Center for Scholarly Editions realized, the volume thus incorporates a monograph on Wordsworth as a translator, and in this respect it is unique in the Cornell Wordsworth series.

The volume also has the most complicated page layout of the entire Cornell Wordsworth series, a fact that caused me and the editorial board more than a few moments of anxiety. But I ultimately came to regard the complexity of the pages as a kind of rhetorical statement about the value and interest of my little-regarded texts. Moreover, the page layout, with its various layers of annotation, enforces a special discipline on those who at-tempt to read the volume: readers are constantly led away from the text and back to it again; they are forced to keep track of different kinds of an-notation, sometimes in different parts of the volume. In short, they cannot lightly skim. Annotation, in this respect, is a rhetorical means of impress-ing readers with the significance of the poetry, and it is also a means of re-habilitating the poetry, by forcing readers to scrutinize Wordsworth's efforts as a translator in unprecedented ways. If one chooses to read the edition at all, one must read slowly, painstakingly, and in that way impart value to the poetry that it has not previously been accorded.

Late in the preparation of this volume, I received a mandate from Cor-nell University Press, requiring me to deliver my work in camera-ready copy, typeset in PageMaker according to series specifications. When I had more or less gotten over the shock, I counted my pennies, called Aldus, Adobe, and Gateway 2000, and entered the computer world in a very big way very suddenly. Sometime in the fall of 1994, after the volume was type-set and I was checking cross-references, I noticed that there were seven windows open at once on my computer terminal, all of which showed pages that refer to the same passage of text but that appear at different places in the volume, some of them several hundred pages apart. I could switch from one window to another quite easily, put them side by side for close comparison, change the size of a window to focus my view: all this the computer environment allowed me to do. But to do the same thing in the printed book, I realized, would be difficult at best, if not impossible. Now the fall of 1994 was also about the time that Netscape released the first version of its World Wide Web browser, instantly making a word like *hypertext* part of the everyday vocabulary of educated people. I acquired a copy, started surfing, and was fascinated. Here, I thought, was a medium that would make the kind of edition I was preparing much easier to use. I jumped in feet first and in just a few weeks found a collaborator, Ronald Tetreault of Dalhousie University (we met by e-mail); in just a few months we were contacted by Kevin Taylor of Cambridge University Press about preparing an edition of *Lyrical Ballads*. It was breathtakingly fast.

Initially, our plan was to develop a McGann-inspired hypertext archive. In the project description submitted to Cambridge University Press, we proclaimed that our edition

> will include all the print versions of the [*Lyrical Ballads*]—1798 (both the "Lewti" and "Nightingale" printings), 1800, 1802, and 1805—and, for the poems by Wordsworth, all of the versions of *Lyrical Ballads* works that the poet reprinted in the various collective editions of his poetry. We will

also include the printer's manuscripts of *Lyrical Ballads*, both in digital reproduction and transcription, and any other manuscript notebooks and letters that contain drafts and corrections of *Lyrical Ballads* material.

We would also bring together source material, authorial comments, unauthorized publications (including the American *Lyrical Ballads* and the chapbooks of individual poems), and even reviews of the collection: everything that had anything to do with *Lyrical Ballads* and the individual poems published in it. Virtual space, we thought, was virtually unlimited, and we could prepare an edition of *Lyrical Ballads* that combined traditional variorum, facsimile, bibliography, and illustrative commentary in ways unthinkable to those whose sense of editing was defined by the limits of the printed book. We set to work collecting this material, giddy with enthusiasm.

The enthusiasm has not subsided—much—but the giddiness has, as we have confronted the practical realities of delivering an actual product. The limitations of software, the awkwardness of SGML markup (not to mention learning how to do it), the difficulties and costs of digital reproductions of manuscripts, and the simple fact that *Lyrical Ballads* is a very well edited text forced us over and over again to rethink our project and change its scope. One of our biggest challenges was to differentiate ourselves from the Cornell edition of *Lyrical Ballads*, edited by James Butler and Karen Green and published in 1992. We saw pretty clearly that pursuing our original plan would mean merely repeating much of their work, and that was not acceptable. Anyone who has examined the draft manuscripts of Wordsworth's "Michael," for instance, and has looked at Karen Green's painstaking transcriptions of them in the Cornell volume knows that this is work that need not be done again. Anyone who has checked James Butler's collations of the collective life editions of Wordsworth's contributions to *Lyrical Ballads* (as I have done) will not see much use in yet another variorum collation. Coincidentally, the Butler-Green edition provided the solution to our dilemma. There, in describing their reading text of *Lyrical Ballads* (1800), the most bibliographically complex of all Wordsworth's publications, they write:

> A reading text based on [the 1800 printer's manuscripts] emphasizes what Wordsworth actually wrote [. . .]; a text based on the printed volume, despite its flaws, highlights *Lyrical Ballads* as an influential historical artifact. Both goals, contradictory as they are, are valid: our aim, though, is to stress Wordsworth as author more than *Lyrical Ballads* as book.   (127)

That is, Butler and Green were in pursuit of that elusive idea, authorial intent. In so doing, they neglect (and in one case were even forbidden to report)[1] the characteristics of the printed books that people actually read. Those interested in the material form of *Lyrical Ballads* may find, buried in footnotes, manuscript descriptions, and appendixes, some of the information that they need. But reconstructing what the printed volumes consisted of in 1802 or 1805 or even in 1800 is very difficult, and in an age when bibliography and scholarly editing are no longer a standard part of graduate education, it is nearly impossible for many active scholars to do.

So we decided to present in our edition the history of the various artifacts, published in Wordsworth's and Coleridge's lifetimes, that called themselves *Lyrical Ballads*.[2] We have keyed our texts to specific copies of the collection; we will present digital images of the various states of the published pages, including the canceled "Christabel" leaf from the 1800 "Preface" and the "Michael" cancels and the "Michael" paste-in from *Lyrical Ballads* (1800); and we will present full texts of each of the five "Lewti" copies of *Lyrical Ballads* (1798), bearing the Bristol imprint, each of which survives in a bibliographically different state. Manuscript material will be largely avoided, except when revisions have been entered in printed copies by the authors or their amanuenses or when the material is clearly part of the printer's manuscripts of *Lyrical Ballads*. Our edition will also include unauthorized printings of the collection, if they called themselves *Lyrical Ballads*, and our chief witness of this kind will be the Wordsworth Library copy of the extremely rare 1802 Philadelphia printing, a copy presented by Professor Henry Reed of the University of Pennsylvania to Wordsworth himself in the late 1830s. There is no library that has all these books, and no traveling exhibition, even in the bicentenary year of 1998, will ever bring them together in one place. This is the kind of thing that the electronic environment can do, and do very well.

This edition will of course have many hypertextual features: the ability to move directly from the text to an image of the printed page or from the text to a critical apparatus, the ability to set different versions of poems side by side for purposes of comparison, and even (we are told) simultaneous scrolling of open text windows. But it would be a mistake, I believe, to regard it simply as a "hypertext," at least in the sense in which promoters and theorists of hypertext have intended the term. We are not interested in "nonlinear" modes of thought; rather, we are intent on providing scholars with evidence that will allow them to draw very "linear" conclusions about this collection of poems. We are not interested in creating a vast, complex web of documents, at the center of which is a *Lyrical Ballads* poem, but which is so rich in annotation that the poem is buried beneath the weight of its associated texts. Rather, we are interested in providing a limited set of documents, annotated only with bibliographical descriptions, that will allow for careful, focused study of the history of the printed artifact, *Lyrical Ballads*, one of the most important collections of poetry ever published in our language.

But, even more, we realize the necessity of convincing skeptical, technophobic colleagues of the usefulness of the electronic medium. These are people, on the whole, for whom "nonlinear" modes of thought have little appeal; they sneer at all the hype about hypertext and return to their studies or their library carrels to hold in their hands the objects they revere. Such scholars are not simply going to retire or disappear, and we need them, if a market for electronic editions is to develop. They can, with only slight difficulty, navigate a complex scholarly book like my Cornell volume, because they understand the organizational principles of such objects, principles that have gradually developed over a half millennium of print-based scholarly editing. But turn them loose in an electronic environment, and they tend to get lost: the conventions of organizing electronic books have yet to be established; there are few of the organizational signposts, such as page numbers or clearly marked cross-references, that they are familiar with; and the text they are investigating often seems buried in a wealth of commentary, associated texts, parallel versions of texts, images, and even film clips. Frustration sets in, they turn off the computer, they don't go back, and as a result publishers may become increasingly reluctant to invest money in experimental electronic projects. In short, it is incumbent on those of us making electronic editions to make them as easy to use as possible for the inexperienced user, and the nonlinear, hypertext model, at least as it has been described and projected, won't do.

My main point, then, is simple: extensive annotation can work in print, primarily because the organizational principles of the medium are firmly established and implicitly understood by most readers. Extensive annotation in the electronic medium, however, is more problematic. On the one hand, it is extremely tempting to create superannotated editions, bringing a given text together with all its sources, all its commentary, all its reviews, all its illustrations, even all its parodies and film adaptations. But until the conventions of the electronic edition are securely established, too many potential users will find these editions too difficult to navigate. In the early days of the computer era, we do not need to dazzle people with our scholarly editions; we need to give them things they can use today and find editions in some ways better or more useful than what they have in print format. To do so, we need to keep things simple and obvious. And we also need to have finished projects, not just cyberdreams of promises we are not likely to be able to keep. With a body of such editions, we can begin to learn just what the electronic edition can do, from the perspective of some-one other than a member of an inner circle of enthusiasts. We can discover and establish the most sensible means of organizing electronic editions; we can establish conventions of organization that will gradually allow us to organize them more complexly. And then we can begin to see the ways in which this new medium can radically change what we, as scholars, actually do.

NOTES

[1]No account of the publisher's advertisements published in *Lyrical Ballads* (1798) can be found in the Butler-Green edition.

[2]A fuller account of this project can be found in Graver and Tetreault.

WORKS CITED

Graver, Bruce, and Ronald Tetreault. "Editing *Lyrical Ballads* for the Electronic Envi-ronment." *Romanticism on the Net* 9 (1998). 15 Mar. 1998 <http://users.ox.ac.uk/~scat0385/electronicLB.html>.

McGann, Jerome. "Radiant Textuality." 15 Mar. 1998 <http://jefferson.village.virginia.edu/public/jjm2/radiant.html>.

———. "The Rationale of Hypertext." 15 Mar. 1998 <http://jefferson.village.virginia.edu/public/jjm2/rationale.html>.

Wordsworth, William. *Lyrical Ballads and Other Poems, 1797–1800*. Ed. James Butler and Karen Green. Ithaca: Cornell UP, 1992.

———. *Translations of Chaucer and Virgil*. Ed. Bruce E. Graver. Ithaca: Cornell UP, 1998.

Faith and the Profession

PATRICIA HOWELL MICHAELSON

Let me admit this right away: I am very ambivalent about our profession. I love literature unreservedly—like most of us, I read avidly, incessantly, addictively—and there should be nothing better than getting paid to read and talk about books. But though I would like to participate wholeheartedly in the profession and though I envy people who do, I cannot. I love reading, I love teaching, and writing is—well—okay, but something has always held me back.

A couple of years ago, I had one of those "click" experiences feminists used to talk about, when I finally got it. At a major conference, I attended a lecture by a senior scholar whose "dammits" were at least as frequent as a rapper's "f---s." I became more and more distracted by this, and I cannot now remember anything else about his talk. As I listened, I wondered: Is he just unaware that his language offends? Is he deliberately cultivating a naughty boy persona? But what took my fancy in the end was imagining the reaction from the audience had I responded, as I was tempted to, "Friend, is thee aware how often thee takes the Lord's name in vain?" Had I been less shy (or already tenured) I might have made the gesture, which surely would have evoked a stunned silence—or laughter, perhaps. Mention of religion (our own, I mean, not our authors') is strictly taboo, except in the negative. Click. I cannot fully participate because I cannot at the same time be a scholar and a Quaker.

The author is Assistant Professor of Literary Studies at the University of Texas, Dallas.

But why not? It is not at all obvious that religion and literary criticism are incompatible, especially given the robust pluralism that now characterizes our profession. Having toppled the positivist claim to disinterested research, postmodernism seems to have made room for scholars who make no bones about their interestedness. Religion should be able to claim the status of any other "theory": not a means of automatically reaching prejudiced or predictable conclusions, thus easily discounted, but a set of basic assumptions from which argument can begin. Religion makes powerful claims on its adherents, but so do other theories on those who are fully committed to them. Yet religion still seems, to this believer, to have a curious status by which in my faith community it is the *only* subject and in my profession it is unmentionable. This creates a sometimes paralyzing ambivalence. I cannot make invisible what is dearest to me, nor should I have to. Our profession must be open to people of faith.

That said (and few people, I believe, would reject that claim out of hand), the question becomes, What inhibits people of faith from full participation in the profession? And here, the qualifications and caveats must come first. Like our profession, American religion is remarkably pluralistic; almost any generalization about people of faith will be wrongheaded. Our vibrant faith communities include people of vastly different political perspectives, cultural traditions, and epistemologies. I would not dream of speaking for all of them. I can only explain what inhibits me from full participation in the profession, knowing that I am probably unrepresentative. My own sect is so tiny that there may be only a handful of MLA members who share my beliefs. And since Quakerism may be congruent with, say, feminism in some ways and with conservative Christianity in others, few will find all of my positions comfortable. Still, since I can only speak from my own experience, I will have to trust my readers to translate my examples into those appropriate to their own faith traditions.

In recent years, two questions about the very complex relations between faith and intellectual endeavor have been addressed, if not resolved. One is the changing institutional status of religion, as universities that were originally denominational increasingly segregated religion into an academic department. In *The Making of the Modern University*, Julie A. Reuben demonstrates that by the late nineteenth century, liberal critics believed that the "scientific" study of religion would keep religion relevant to the modern world; their goal was not to destroy religion but to reconstruct it by utilizing a progressivist model of free inquiry leading to new, more certain truths. But, she says, this endeavor was seen to have failed by early in this century, when the truth of religion (faith) was felt to be different in kind from the truth of science (knowledge). George S. Marsden tells a similar story, but with added advocacy: in tracing the path "from protestant establishment to established nonbelief," he laments "the near exclusion of religious perspectives from dominant academic life" (6) and argues that while some religious perspectives may indeed preempt intellectual inquiry, "there seems no intellectually valid reason to exclude religiously based perspectives that have strong academic credentials on all other grounds" (431). The issues remain murkiest for religion as an academic discipline, which at one and the same time explores the power of faith and seems to demand a "proper" distance from it. Recognizing the growing interest in this problem, *Academe* in 1996 devoted a special issue to the ways in which religion might be taught in a secularized setting without being false to its very nature (*Freedom*). Our field should have rather less difficulty with this problem: literary studies does not make the same truth claims that religion does, and secular kinds of criticism are not self-contradictory.

A second important problem is that of advocacy in the classroom: how might one express one's religious views while teaching, without inappropriately imposing those views on students? M. D. Walhout argues that religion can be returned to the classroom if it is framed as part of a debate, in the same way that political advocacy can be included if we follow Gerald Graff's program of "teaching the conflicts." This problem, while important, is not the source of my own unease about the profession: my religious beliefs are simply not what I teach. This is not to say that I avoid teaching religious works of literature. In one core course (Western Literary Tradition: Homer to *Frankenstein*!), I teach both Dante's *Inferno* and *Paradise Lost*. I find that students at my Bible Belt university are eager to share their knowledge of religion: the Catholic students explain the papacy to fundamentalists who are not even sure whether Catholics are Christians; the fundamentalists astonish us with their ability to catch every biblical allusion. Having students of different faiths does invite discussion of reader response: why does *Paradise Lost* resonate more for some students than for others? But when we discuss theology, it's Milton's that matters, and while I feel that it's important for them to understand Milton's theology, I never ask them to either agree or disagree with it.

The risks of direct advocacy are, I hope, minimized in my classroom. In a more general way, though, my faith leads me to choose certain kinds of pedagogies. We Quakers emphasize a continuing revelation rather than solely the historical revelation of Scripture. We believe that we cannot predict where Truth may arise and trust that we will be led to it by God; to help discern whether the leadings we feel are truly divine, we test them against the wisdom of our gathered community. Our epistemology is thus nonhierarchical and communitarian. It is consistent with a mode of teaching as shared learning, with a participatory, nonhierarchical style, like that described by Mary Rose O'Reilley in *The Peaceable Classroom*.

And here, at last, is the rub. The culture of the classroom is each teacher's to create. It may be agonistic or consensual, characterized by lecturing or by mutual discovery. In the classroom, while the content of my teaching is not obviously derived from my faith, my epistemology is. My faith community has its own answer to the question, How is Truth discovered?, one that I believe meets George Marsden's criterion of not preempting intellectual life. But the profession as a whole insists on a hermeneutics of doubt—secular, adversarial, individualistic—that keeps me from joining wholeheartedly.

This attitude strikes me most powerfully at conferences, where junior members are socialized into our community and where our rituals are played out. Though I can't deny the inspiration gained from hearing new ideas, I feel alienated—never a member of the community. I especially dread the question-and-answer periods, which seem dominated by agonistic models of truth seeking. The "proper" attitude is contestatory, what Nancy K. Miller calls "this Critical Warriors business" (61). In a reflection on her own career, Miller acknowledges the oedipal battles she fought with senior scholars but says she now admonishes her students not to assume that they must be "Critical Terminators" (62–63). Whatever the causes of the change, the sense that the profession is growing meaner is shared by many.

More is at stake here than civility: the meanness has epistemological roots. The imagery of violence pervades the metaphors we use for success in the profession (Don't deans want us to be on the cutting edge, for example? in the avant-garde of the battle against ignorance?) because we envision the discovery of truth as adversarial and aggression as necessary to the fight. As Janice Moulton puts it, this tendency is simply a cultural assumption: "Aggression may have no causal bearing on competence, superiority, power, etc., but if many people believe aggressive behavior is a sign of these properties, then one may have to learn to behave aggressively in order to appear competent, to seem superior, and to gain or maintain power." This "conflation of aggression and competence" is typified by what she calls the "Adversary Method" in philosophy, in which work is evaluated by trying to prove it wrong (149, 151, 154).

The habit of debunking is well ingrained in our professional culture. But what if our faith leads us to seek truth in other, less adversarial ways? Feminist scholars have made excellent cases for nonadversarial modes—modes that may make women feel more comfortable and thus more inclined to participate. Yet there is a fundamental difference between a commitment to consensus seeking based on inclusiveness and one based on faith: we Quakers believe not simply that consensus leads to the best decision but also that it is the best we can do to discern God's will for us— which we call Truth.

Am I claiming that there is divine Truth in literary criticism? Not exactly. Traditionally, Quakers who chose academic careers went into science, in which it is easier to feel that one is exploring God's creation. In fact, until recently Quakers frowned on imaginative literature altogether, for all the standard Puritan reasons: it is frivolous, a waste of time, and not truthful. Thankfully, Quakers now allow more wiggle room in their concept of Truth, and though I am hesitant to believe in a God who urges a particular interpretation of *Pride and Prejudice*, I can easily justify reading literature as a way of following the Quaker commandment to seek "that of God" in every one. Literature is the best way I know of seeking to understand people of the past, by imaginatively experiencing their hopes and fears. Reading is an especially attentive form of listening to an other, in which (if we so choose) understanding can replace—or at least precede—judging. For example, a work that glorifies war (like the *Iliad*) is not easy for a Quaker to appreciate. Being fully committed to pacifism, I do not feel threatened or put much energy into being a resisting reader. But if I truly listen, I may develop more sympathy for the author's values. My reading may help me to understand why the author values war or to appreciate the virtues war calls forth. At the very least, I can learn to respect the energy and thoughtful hard work (craft) of someone I disagree with. And in this direction, I believe, lies God's Truth.

When I write for a professional audience, I am generally willing to translate my understanding into words that can pass for secular. Some accommodation to linguistic context is always necessary. But while I may be willing to speak in a mode that is different from the language of my faith, I cannot speak in one that contradicts it. Thus, a subset of my ambivalence about our professional ways of testing knowledge is a concern about our professional use of language. Among its many functions, language use serves to establish solidarity with other members of a speech community. We are all accustomed to tailoring our habits of language to the local culture of the classroom, the soccer field, the dinner party, or the office, each of which has norms prescribing the appropriate vocabulary, level of formality, turn-taking etiquette, and so on. Our professional culture obviously privileges certain kinds of discourse over others, though this is a matter of some contestation. The use of specialized vocabulary is felt by some to be not only unavoidable but also the most economical way to allude to a web of ideas; for others, jargon serves only to draw a ring around an "in" group and exclude all others. Both these points of view have value: any speech community, in order to include, must also exclude. We must only be careful that we are not excluding people willfully or for bad reasons.

In a diverse community, it is easy to misunderstand the behaviors and language of others. In recent years, our professional culture has become more open to different assumptions about the world, human nature, and what matters in literature. Because religion is not visible, though, members of our profession tend to assume that we are secular, assume that we are playing the game of "critical warriors" whether we are or not. For example, one custom that sets us Quakers apart is our nonadversarial use of silence. In our highly verbal professional culture, silence is often read as lack of engagement; it is a bad sign if your paper is the one no one asks about. But for Quakers, silence means allowing time to absorb and opening a temporal space in which the Divine may lead us to speak. Rushing to speak cuts off this space and may prevent Truth from arising from an unexpected source. If my colleagues "read" my silence as lack of engagement, they are misunderstanding me.

If the profession is to become more open to people of faith, it must recognize that other ways of speaking, acting, and seeking truth are valuable and heartfelt. I often feel "closeted" in professional situations, pretending to be something I am not. Our institutions are powerful and tend to reinforce secular and adversarial modes, but surely they are staffed by people of good will who would willingly change their assumptions if the flaws in those assumptions were exposed. There is no necessary connection between adversarial modes of interaction and the quality of literary insights. The styles of interaction and linguistic habits of our colleagues may or may not conform to secular and adversarial norms. Conversely, if people of faith made themselves more visible, the profession would surely accommodate them; if we used a language of faith more often, ears would adjust. In the end, perhaps it is my responsibility to insist that the profession make room for me. I should have reminded that speaker that his language excluded a segment of his audience. I should just go ahead and use Quaker language (names instead of titles, the occasional *thee* to mark affiliation, simplicity above all); how can I expect my audience to understand that I follow a hermeneutics of faith if I speak the language of skepticism? I should, I should, I will. Let me end with a traditional Quaker query: How does Truth prosper among you?

WORKS CITED

Freedom of *Religion or Freedom* from *Religion?* Spec. issue of *Academe* 82.6 (1996): 14–42.

Marsden, George S. *The Soul of the American University: From Protestant Establishment to Established Nonbelief.* New York: Oxford UP, 1994.

Miller, Nancy K. "Time Pieces." *Narrative* 5 (1997): 60–66.

Moulton, Janice. "A Paradigm of Philosophy: The Adversary Method." *Discovering Reality: Feminist Perspectives on Epistemology, Metaphysics, Methodology, and Philosophy of Science.* Ed. Sandra Harding and Merrill B. Hintikka. Dordrecht: Riedel, 1983. 149–64.

O'Reilley, Mary Rose. *The Peaceable Classroom.* Portsmouth: Boynton, 1993.

Reuben, Julie A. *The Making of the Modern University: Intellectual Transformation and the Marginalization of Morality.* Chicago: U of Chicago P, 1996.

Walhout, M. D. "Beyond the Wars of Religion: How Teaching the Conflicts Can Desecularize American Education." *Profession 1996.* New York: MLA, 1996. 138–45.

REGINA M. SCHWARTZ

There are days when teaching the Bible feels like being a prophet: you are slow of speech like Moses, want to escape to the ends of the earth rather than convey certain messages like Jonah, you feel alone like Amos (who was not in one of the professional bands of prophets) as you forge ahead, interpreting the Bible without the authorization of a church community, and you feel persecuted by everyone—by those who think you ought to be teaching the canon of Western literature and by those who wonder why you are not doing something hip and noncanonical rather than the Bible, so in general you often wish you had never been born, like Jeremiah. But there are also days when you do feel inspired like the prophets, not because the word of God has been conveyed to you, but because you have to rise to the challenge of making the most familiar myths of Western culture, stories like the Creation, the Fall, and the Flood, unfamiliar to students, and because you must face the challenge of making unfamiliar stories, like the rape of the concubine in Judges 19, alien purity laws in Leviticus, and horrific curses in Deuteronomy, sound less strange. There are freedoms gained by teaching narratives that enjoy such cultural currency. First, the chances are good that nothing your students say hasn't been said before. When a timid student ventures, "I know this is going to sound stupid, but what if," and what follows is a wacky interpretation of Mark 14, you can respond to that student by saying, "No, that does not sound stupid; as a mat-

The author is Professor of English and Religious Studies at Northwestern University.

ter of fact, that is precisely what Zwingli, one of the leaders of the Reformation who changed history, said about the passage." Your student is empowered, and the whole class loosens up. There are other benefits of that cultural currency. In our efforts to make the literature we are teaching pertinent to the present, we often come up with embarrassing analogies: *The Faerie Queene* to *Star Wars*, et al. But because the Bible is so alive in our culture, we can cull examples of its uses and misuses directly from the presidential addresses of Lincoln or Clinton, the paintings of Giotto or Rembrandt, Christmas carols or operas, political rhetoric from South Africa or Israel, and films like *Salome* or *The Last Temptation of Christ*, to say nothing of the literary legacy in Milton, Blake, Melville, Faulkner, Zora Neale Hurston, or just about anything else students read in their Western culture classes.

The other challenge arises because this text is held to be sacred, and not just literature, by the living, breathing faith communities of Christianity and Judaism. What impact does that have on the classroom? I raise that very question, early in the course, and the Babylonian creation story affords a good opportunity for my students to consider it. The *Enuma Elish* (literally, "when on high," the opening words of the narrative, just as Genesis opens with "in the beginning") was once held to be sacred by those who believed that Marduk was their god, that he created the heavens and the earth (in the same order that Genesis 1 describes it), and who turned to the creation story for explanations of how the cosmos was constituted and governed. In ancient Babylonia, where it was held to be sacred truth, there was an organized religion, a priesthood, and rituals, and this narrative of the defeat of chaos and the creation of the cosmos, of Marduk assuming lordship, was at their center, authorizing all that activity and belief, just as it was authorized by the priesthood. But now, the Babylonians have disappeared, and what they have left of their culture is no longer believed by a faithful community. Those with faith commitments to Judaism or Christianity would say that this is because the Babylonian story was partial and imperfect and was supplanted by a greater truth, the truth of how the real God—Yahweh, not Marduk—really created the world: not by dividing the body of the Goddess of the waters of the Deep, Tiamat, but by dividing the waters of the Deep, Tehom. For secular students, the Babylonian creation narrative teaches a different lesson: not that an inferior religion has been displaced by a superior one but that what is deemed sacred is contingent upon a living community with the authority to make the claim that it is sacred stick. According to this logic, if Babylonians were still around and had managed to keep their hegemony, Marduk would still be worshiped, and the Babylonian creation story would still be deemed sacred—not relegated to the status of an ancient epic that is often compared to Genesis in the spirit of comparative literature.

This same logic could be deployed to resituate works of literature. If *Paradise Lost* had a cult and a priesthood (say, the members and officers of the Milton Society of America), and if it had a liturgy (say, the weekly recitation of the poem), and if it claimed that it was a divine revelation made to Milton (who regarded himself as a prophet of God), and if a community believed that *Paradise Lost* describes God as he really is and events as they really occurred, and that all of human history derives its meaning from the sacred history of redemption contained therein, and if the text were ceaselessly interpreted so that a revered tradition of interpretations could be consulted, then it too would qualify as a sacred text. But of course, as students hasten to point out, Milton *did* claim to be a prophet and the text *is* recited weekly in the context of an institution that *does* authorize it and ceaselessly interpret it. And this is not only true of *Paradise Lost*: there is a reason the *Norton Anthology of English Literature* and the Bible are both called canons. Perhaps the *Norton Anthology* is held to be sacred too, by some, and its editors regarded as the scribal priests who mean to pass that sacred tradition on to future generations of believers. Perhaps, too, the virulence of the attack on this sacred literary canon is evidence of its religiocultural authority, one that many want to call into question. But isn't this analogy becoming exaggerated, for isn't one text, the Bible, *really* the word of God and the other, the *Norton Anthology of English Literature*, *really* the word of men and (in more recent editions) women? Aye, there's the rub. Who is to say? Some say men and women wrote the Bible too. Whom do we believe?

At this point, I would intervene in this imaginary dialogue to point out that whatever communities may believe about them, sacred texts are, like any works of literature, *representations*, caught in the fallen realm of language. Why is the story of Joshua's conquest of Jericho held to be sacred while the story of Aeneas's siege of Troy is not? Even if the answer lies outside the text, in the beliefs of communities with authority, nonetheless the two stories themselves share the same power and the same limitation: language. And whether your theory of signs is informed by Augustine, Derrida, or whomever, these texts are *representations*, and as such, only approximations, not unmediated truth. How speak of God when language cannot adequately signify him? Augustine, following Paul, explained that ever since the Fall we are condemned to a realm of interpretation, one in which our interpretations are decidedly limited. For if we inhabit a realm of signs that must be interpreted, behind them await truths that are independent of these signs (for believers, that is). By the Reformation, a theory of accommodation had become current, wherein God had tailored signs, accommodating them to fallen, human understanding.

> Immediate are the Acts of God, more swift
> Than time or motion, but to human ears
> Cannot without process of speech be told
> So told as human notion can receive.
>
> (*Paradise Lost* 7.176–79)

My students who have deep faith commitments are already equipped with this intuition long before they come to college (even if they could not articulate it), and so the versions of God they encounter in biblical narratives rarely lead to a crisis of faith. One might expect that prolonged looks at portrayals of God as threatening his people with all manner of abuses if they don't obey him—portrayals of the deity as exclusive, possessive, tyrannical, and violent—could challenge their convictions. One might even expect that classes on the Bible as literature could easily turn into virtual dens of heresy. It does not happen. My students' intuitive Augustinianism kicks in, and these depictions of God immediately strike them as inadequate representations, portrayals that are drawn more in the image of *man* than in the image of God. They'll grant that God is often depicted as a punitive parent in Deuteronomy, a glory-seeking tyrant in Exodus, a vindictively jealous husband in Hosea, a bloodthirsty conqueror in Joshua, but these depictions—I call them the dark side of monotheism—are in the all-too-human image of man, reflecting his preoccupations with possessing women, possessing land, and possessing power, preoccupations that are projected onto the deity, who in turn is supposed to authorize these all-too-human ideologies of possession and domination. On the day that the veil lifts and students have read enough portrayals of monotheism to assume that humans have not adequately portrayed their God, they also understand that the Bible is not only a sacred text but also a work of literature, deeply embedded in our immanent culture—and not, in any simple sense, a transparent window onto transcendence. They stop asking questions like, Why did God accept only one sacrifice when both Cain and Abel offered sacrifices? and instead they ask, Why does the narrative *describe* God as accepting only one sacrifice? Why does the narrative *depict* God as demanding allegiance to himself alone—"You will have no other gods before me [. . .] for I, the Lord your God am a jealous God" (Exod. 20.3–4)—and why does it *depict* him as conferring favor on one alone—"God looked with favor upon the sacrifice of Abel but not on the sacrifice of Cain" (Gen. 4.4–5). And then they are ready to explore the vast political and cultural legacy of such a narrative: the real-world violence that is perpetrated by the elect under the banner of divine wrath against the infidel—the slaughters by Crusaders, the exiles by Inquisitors, the conquest of the New World, the hate crimes of the Christian Identity movement, and the ongoing legacy in the secularized versions of racial and ethnic supremacy—genocide throughout Europe, in Bosnia, and in Rwanda. Are we the heirs of Cain because we murder our brothers? Students discover, as they read biblical narratives, that the violent rivalry that breaks out between the first brothers is repeated, ad nauseam, among the sons of Noah, the sons of Abraham, the sons of Isaac, the sons of Jacob, and even the sons of David, where murder erupts again. But the longer they look, the more they note the variations on that theme. Sometimes the rivalry issues in murder, sometimes not. Sometimes the parents, human or divine, seem at fault, sometimes not. Sometimes the motif of sibling rivalry raises its ugly head only to be resolved. Joseph painfully and painstakingly teaches his brothers that they must be responsible for one another instead of being murderous rivals. Before the sons of Israel are qualified to be forged as a nation, they must learn the lesson so dramatically denied by Cain: that they are their brothers' keepers. Even my most cynical students cannot get away with claiming that the dark side of monotheism is the only side.[1]

Amid all the variety of representations of God, two poles of monotheism can be discerned. One depicts God as infinitely charitable, infinitely giving, with blessings for all. In the other, divine favor and blessings are scarce, inspiring deadly rivalries, like Cain and Abel's, in which some are blessed and some are cursed. As a drunken Cassio puts it in *Othello*, "God's above all, and there be souls that must be saved and there be souls must not be saved" (2.3.99–101). And as an anguished Abraham Lincoln put it in his "Second Inaugural Address," "Both [sides] read the same Bible and pray to the same God; and each invokes His aid against the other" (333). Why does monotheism so often suggest that one people can only prosper at the expense of the Other? Remarkably, Esau is given that very question.

> After Isaac finished blessing him and Jacob had scarcely left his father's presence, his brother Esau came in from hunting. He too prepared some tasty food and brought it to his father [. . .]. His father Isaac asked him, "Who are you?" "I am your son," he answered, "your firstborn, Esau." Isaac trembled violently and said, "Who was it, then, that hunted game and brought it to me? I ate it just before you came and I blessed him— and indeed he will be blessed!" When Esau heard his father's words, he burst out with a loud and bitter cry and said to his father, "Bless me—me too, my father!" But he said, "Your brother came deceitfully and took your blessing." "[. . .] Haven't you reserved any blessing for me?" Isaac answered Esau, "I have made him lord over you and have made all his

relatives his servants, and I have sustained him with grain and new wine. So what can I possibly do for you, my son?"

And then Esau asks that profound question, "Do you have only one blessing, my father? Bless me too, my father!" "Then Esau wept aloud" (Gen. 27.30–38). There will be no blessed future for the sons of Esau, for the Edomites, a people who will be portrayed as the enemies of Israel. What if the narrative had depicted the Edomites and Israelites enjoying equally blessed futures? or the Moabites and the Israelites? Would the cultural legacy of the Bible have been a less violent one? Would it have been more difficult to use the Bible as a weapon to degrade those who have strayed from the one jealous God, peoples who have been classified as infidels, pagans, and idolaters? Surely, we would still have had the Crusades, the Inquisition, the Christian Identity movement, but would the perpetrators have had to look elsewhere in their cultural legacy, other than to representations of the will of God as recorded in his authorized text, to authorize their hate crimes?

In the book of Exodus, before a whole host of laws are enumerated to curb the aggression induced by a world of scarcity, a moving version of paradisal plenitude is offered. It is, to be sure, a fallen paradise. This is the wilderness and not the garden, and the children of Israel are not as innocent as the children of Eden, having just escaped the bonds of slavery in Egypt. But here, God is depicted not as withholding but as providing. When he offers bread from the heavens he asks the receivers to count on his sustenance, to live with the assumption—despite all the evidence of their experience to the contrary—that there is enough to go around, that each person's basic needs will be met. And it is this glimmer of ideal plenitude, and not the prevailing real-world scarcity, that is intended to school the ancient Israelites in ethics.

> "That," said Moses to them, "is the bread Yahweh gives you to eat. This is Yahweh's command. Everyone must gather enough of it for his needs." When they measured in an omer of what they had gathered, the man who had gathered more had not too much, the man who had gathered less had not too little. Each found he had gathered what he needed.
>
> (Exod. 16.15–18)

Any who fail to accept this divine distribution of wealth succumb to greed. And when they hoard their food, it rots and rots them.

> Moses said to them, "No one must keep any of it for tomorrow." But some would not listen and kept part of it for the following day, and it

> bred maggots and smelt foul; and Moses was very angry with them.
>
> (Exod. 16.19–20)

Reading selectively, the way biblical interpretation has always proceeded, can produce a Bible that fits a particular ideological or theological agenda. The manna story can offer up a vision of a generous egalitarian God, and it can suggest a divine dispensation of charity. To bolster that case, we can add deutero-Isaiah and many other passages: "The poor and the needy ask for water, and there is none, their tongue is parched with thirst. I Yahweh will answer them, I the God of Israel will not abandon them [. . .]. In the wilderness I will put cedar trees, acacias, myrtles, olives. In the desert I will plant juniper, plane tree, and cypress side by side" (II Isa. 41.19). The miracle of the loaves and fishes revisits this motif of a miraculous generosity, a transcendent generosity, one elaborated recently in philosophy by Jean-Luc Marion and in theology by Hans Urs von Balthassar. But—and as teachers of literature who highlight the mechanisms of interpretation, it is important to point this out—even these passages can be interpreted to endorse not an ethic of charity but its complete opposite, greed. An op-ed written by a spokesperson for the Italian right shows how easily the Bible can be used in culture for any purpose, turning the sentiment of charity around 180 degrees, all the while invoking biblical authority: "We can offer them a plate of pasta but not open the cafeterias. Even Jesus who multiplied bread and fishes did not open trattorias. He transformed water into wine, but, it seems to me, only once, and even then, for a wedding. Albania, like Bosnia, is not our problem, but the problem of Europe." It is the cultural appropriations, the acts of interpretation, like this, and not necessarily the narratives themselves, that turn the Bible into a weapon.

On the question of the Other, the foreigner, the narratives are decidedly inconsistent. If the book of Ezra recommends separation from the Other, advising the Israelites to put away their foreign wives acquired during their exile, in contrast, the book of Ruth embraces a foreign wife—Ruth the Moabite—and gives her the honorific role of progenitor in King David's lineage. If the book of Exodus depicts wrath against the Other, plagues against the firstborn Egyptians, drowning of Pharoah's army and all the while a hardening of his heart, the book of Jonah depicts such forgiveness of the Other, such compassion for the people of Nineveh—Israel's historical enemy—that the prophet is furious with God for being so merciful. And if the God who curses with dearth and with death is depicted in Amos and Deuteronomy, in Genesis we are offered a God who blesses the creation with fecundity, enjoining all created things to be fruitful and multiply and fill all the earth. Even the God of Cain and Abel, who accepts one sacrifice but rejects another, and the God of Jacob and Esau, who has only one blessing, is also challenged by the God of Exodus, who rains manna from heaven, enough for everyone. For the closer we look at these narratives, the more difficult it becomes to name the Other and so to hurt the Other. Who is an insider and who is an outsider is perpetually negotiated, and these are not the only options: there are also "outsiders within" or outcasts who are not altogether cast out. Divine fidelity and sexual fidelity are homologous throughout the biblical narratives. (According to the prophet, because David has committed adultery with Bathsheba, the kingdom of ancient Israel unravels when it is at its height.) Students typically ask, isn't God overreacting? but then we point out that the king has violated all the commandments and that the promise of the kingdom depends on obeying them. These preoccupations with fidelity are preoccupations of a narrative that tends to construct identity as someone or some people set apart, with boundaries that could be mapped, ownership that could be titled: "You are my people, my very own." But the parameters of "the people" are always shifting and blurred: a people who are bound by a law they refuse to obey, a people defined by their nomadism but who are promised a land, a people who remember (or adopt) a shared history only to constantly forget it.

How do students, with their youthful craving for certainty, react to all this uncertainty? How do they negotiate blatantly conflicting interpretations? No sooner do they open the Bible than they are confronted with two different stories of the Creation, one that begins with God creating "the heavens and the earth," the second reversing that word order to the "earth and the heavens"; one in which a universe of waters must be divided to create the dry land, the other in which sweet waters flow in rivers through the land to irrigate it; one that articulates an entire cosmos, with the sun, moon, and stars, before man is created last of all, another in which man is created first, and the garden is articulated around him and for him. And what about David, the heroic vanquisher of Goliath, the godly fugitive from the disfavored and tormented Saul, who becomes in other narratives an abuser of power who lolls about at home at the season when kings are to lead their troops to war, ravishing his loyal servant's wife and then murdering him to try to cover his crime. The Bible harbors both a narrative in which a powerful woman uses her sexuality as a deadly weapon to defeat ancient Israel's enemy—Judith seducing Holofernes so effectively that he literally loses his head—and a narrative in which an unnamed, hapless woman becomes a sexual victim who is gang-raped, left for dead, and then hacked into pieces. And it harbors a God whose prophet announces that he will punish Israel mercilessly—"For the three crimes, the four, of Judah I have made my decree and will not relent [. . .]" (Amos 2.4)—and a God whose prophet is angry that justice is not satisfied by divine universal mercy, so angry that he tries to escape his prophetic commission to warn Nineveh to repent, only to wind up belched ashore from the belly of a whale commissioned to deliver his message.

If for some students—believers—these conflicting versions confirm the sense that God cannot be adequately represented, for others—who are secular—truth does not lurk beneath or behind signs, separable from them. For those students, it is signs all the way down. Conflicting interpretations do not signal that a single inviolate truth has been poorly conveyed; rather, these conflicts confirm their sense that the notion of "one truth" is a fiction, carrying the potential tyranny of certainty—"my truth must be your truth or you are an infidel"—and to their surprise, they come to appreciate the Bible, relieved that it is not just full of pious Sunday-school injunctions they rejected in their childhood but full of narratives recounting the grittiness of peoples struggling to find their identity in a world of violent competition for scarce resources. They note how the experiments with social order keep being provisional: that a tribal confederacy gives way to judgeship, that when that fails, the experiment of kingship follows, that the monarchy is critiqued by the prophets, that the prophets are reinterpreted in the New Testament in a new light as fulfilled, and that after all the experimentation to achieve a social order, from the military leadership to kings and priests and prophets, in the end justice doesn't reign in this world at all—but reigns in a new heaven and a new earth where the rivers that once watered an earthly paradise now become the rivers of eternal life in a heavenly paradise—and that vision is not about our political order at all, for it is utopian. They do not experience this multiplicity and provisionality as a satanic plot against the One Truth; the conflict of interpretations does not lead them into spiritual angst, moral turpitude, and emotional despair. If God is depicted as excluding and unforgiving in some narratives and including and forgiving in others, the students find that discrepancy allows them to make value judgments, and they discover that they respond to biblical narratives, like other literature, with values that are already in place, with the human sympathy and compassion they have derived from other cultural sources, a sympathy that makes them worry about the Egyptians and the Canaanites. For these students the sacred peeps out of the nooks and crannies of narratives chiefly preoccupied with power and greed and lust and violence in small acts of kindness, forgiveness, sympathy, or charity, in sporadic efforts to rise above humanity's worst instincts with compassion and thanksgiving. Not only the social dimension but also the philosophical dimension offers such glimpses, for the Bible poses profound questions about divine justice. For such students, if the Bible is a sacred text, calling evil into question rather than assuming its unavoidability, so too is *Paradise Lost*, so too is the *Divine Comedy*, and so too is *Star Wars*—not because they are authorized by a community of believers but because they take up a sacred question: how to live justly in a world of injustice. For such students, the question we face is less how to teach sacred texts as literature than how to teach literature as sacred texts.

Of course, students do not always divide neatly into these two broad categories, "religious" and "secular." Actively engaged in the process of self-discovery, most are in the midst of defining their religious commitments. They know what their families have asked them to believe, to do, and even to think, but in college they are constantly either altering, confirming, or rejecting those childhood injunctions. Nonetheless, teaching the Bible in literature courses with these heuristic poles in mind helps to move students from both fundamentalist extremes toward a less certain middle, one in which, on the one hand, signs are not always readily transparent to divinity but, on the other, they do not refer, in an archly secular way, only to their own referentiality. The philosopher Jean-Luc Marion offers a key to this middle realm with his helpful distinction between the idol and the icon. The idol—and this can include any object of knowledge, a concept, a word—stops the gaze for it satisfies its aim; there is no reason to go beyond. If we see the divine in the idol (meaning *as* the sign) it is according to the measure of our own gaze. The icon, in contrast, points beyond itself, to the invisible, the unthinkable, the unutterable. As a sign, the icon neither refers naively to its signified, nor does it arrest the gaze. Rather, it points beyond itself to an immeasurable source: "The icon recognizes no other measure than its own and infinite excessiveness [*démesure*]; whereas the idol measures the divine to the scope of the gaze of he who then sculpts it, the icon accords in the visible only a face whose invisibility is given all the more to be envisaged that its revelation offers an abyss that the eyes of men never finish probing" (Marion, *God* 21).[2] In this middle realm, one in which signs do not just coldly denote or fail to denote but mysteriously reverberate, echoing mysteries, we interpret the immanent and its vexed relation to transcendence, albeit variously understood and represented, but we do not just use one to decode the other. Am I suggesting that one's theory of signs is an index to their theology? Absolutely, and any theologian worth their theology would agree. Either the bread is God, stands for God, or is bread. But not necessarily *mere* bread—rather, it is a "saturated phenomenon," as Marion would say, or even a resonant cultural inheritance, as in "bread and circuses" or "bread and chocolate" or "loaves and fishes." Students gradually learn that the very activity they are engaged in—interpretation—can be a sacred one, for it has been not only the privileged job of English professors,

Bible scholars, lawyers, and leaders in all religious traditions but also one shared by all human beings in the world.

And so, while students may find themselves abandoning the hankering for the depiction of one truth, one version, one ideology, one theology, one access to the sacred, their sense that the Bible is a sacred text is rarely sacrificed in the process of discovering these conflicts. To the contrary. I sense from their papers that their understanding of the sacred becomes more capacious, and less fragile, as the term proceeds. For some, the sacred emerges in the biblical ideals of social justice, despite all the evidence to the contrary of real injustice. By the end of the term, they are pointing to the way Amos insists that greed is appalling, citing the injunctions against Israel in Amos for "selling the righteous for silver and the needy for a pair of shoes" (2.6), the generosity of Boaz to Ruth and Naomi, Jeremiah's impatience with social injustice and ritual hypocrisy in his warnings to corrupt worshipers on the steps of the Temple. For this sense of the sacred, they could also turn to Erasmus, who, in his humanist version of a critique of identity politics, was impatient that monks worried too much about the color of their habits and not enough about feeding the poor, or to Matthew Arnold, who defined religion as heightened ethical sensibility. The sacred also emerges from the aesthetic, from the spare haunting verses of the sacrifice of Isaac that Erich Auerbach so brilliantly contrasts with Homeric verse in *Mimesis*; for this, they could also turn to George Herbert or Mark Strand. Or the sacred emerges from the repetition of a metaphor like the parting of the waters, as it accrues its penumbra of referentiality, from the parting of waters at Creation to the parting of the Red Sea to the parting of the Jordan to baptismal waters; for this, they could also turn to Mozart's *Magic Flute* or Lincoln's address at Gettysburg. For others, the sacred emerges from the sheer effort humans make with language to represent what is beyond language—transcendence. Somehow, the ancient peoples who wrote these texts managed to convey a sense of wonder, a sense that something transcends themselves and their immanent concerns even if it defines them and circumscribes them, and this is reflected in portrayals of a deity who creates humankind, yes, but also a whole cosmos; for this, we could also turn to Blake's *Book of Urizen* or *2001*. When we return to the creation story after the book of Revelation on the last day of my Bible class (like Milton's Angel sent to teach Adam, I want to leave students not with the conclusion that this world is to be destroyed but with the reminder that it is newly created), students are frankly amazed—and moved—that the Bible includes narratives of creation at all. Since the Hebrew Bible tells the story of a people's struggle, why not begin with the father of those people, the call to Abraham in Genesis 12? Since the New Testament is devoted to the redemption from sin made possible by the incarnation and sacrifice, why not begin with man's first sin? The creation story is incredibly evocative of humankind's wonder before the cosmos and of our sense of the sacred, with its blessings of proliferation—to be fruitful and multiply—even if they do quickly degenerate into the first brothers committing the first fratricide. But the blessing to all creation stands alongside the curse of Cain; a transcendent generosity flows in the face of human violence.

Vested, as we inevitably are, with the responsibility to ask students to forge their ethics, often in the face of the monolithic institutions that are only too happy to hand them one of self-aggrandizement, I have come to believe that teachers of literature, whether or not that literature is *officially* deemed sacred, are purveyors of the sacred. "Woe is me, for I am ruined!" said Isaiah,

> "Because I am a man of unclean lips,
> And I live among a people of unclean lips
> For my eyes have seen the king, the Lord of hosts."
>
> Then one of the seraphim flew to me, with a burning coal in his hand which he had taken from the altar with tongs. And he touched my mouth with it and said,
>
> "Behold, this has touched your lips;
> and your iniquity is taken away, and your sin is forgiven."
>
> (Isa. 6.5–7)

While some days teaching the Bible feels as if you are walking on hot coals, on others, it feels as if a hot coal is pressed against your lips.

NOTES

[1] The political afterlife of biblical narratives and the ensuing discussion of "the dark side" of monotheism are elaborated more fully in Schwartz. The brighter side of monotheism—its emphasis on charity—is the focus of my current work.

[2] As a phenomenologist in the wake of poststructuralism, Marion recently made important distinctions about signification and the impossible in a debate with Jacques Derrida (Caputo and Scanlon; see also Blond).

WORKS CITED

Auerbach, Erich. *Mimesis: The Representation of Reality in Western Literature.* Princeton: Princeton UP, 1953.

Blond, Phillip, ed. *Post-secular Philosophy: Between Philosophy and Theology.* London: Routledge, 1998.

Caputo, John D., and Michael J. Scanlon. *Religion and Postmodernism.* [Tentative title].
    Bloomington: Indiana UP, forthcoming.
Lincoln, Abraham. "Second Inaugural Address." 4 March 1865. *The Collected Works of
    Abraham Lincoln.* Ed. Roy P. Basler. New Brunswick: Rutgers UP, 1953. 332–35.
Marion, Jean-Luc. *God without Being.* Trans. Thomas Carlson. Chicago: U of Chicago
    P, 1991. Trans. of *Dieu sans l'être: Hors-texte.* Paris: Fayard, 1982.
———. "Le phénomène saturé." *Phénoménologie et théologie.* By Jean-Louis Chrétien,
    Michel Henry, Jean-Luc Marion, and Paul Ricoeur. Paris: Criterion, 1992. 79–128.
Milton, John. *John Milton: Complete Poems and Major Prose.* Ed. Merritt Y. Hughes. New
    York: Odyssey, 1957.
Schwartz, Regina. *The Curse of Cain: The Violent Legacy of Monotheism.* Chicago: U of
    Chicago P, 1997.
Shakespeare, William. *Othello.* Ed. Alvin Kernan. New York: Penguin, 1963.

Narratives, Tricksterism, Hyperbole, Self-Image(s), and Schizophrenia: The Joys of Chairing an English Department

ZACK BOWEN

As I cast my thoughts back to the after-dinner scene that was the occasion for this talk, I distinctly recall looking out from the podium and detecting behind the many encouraging smiles a certain habitual submission, the product of countless interminable guest speakers and poetry readings, of suffering intellectual fools gladly during office hours, anti-intellectual administrative bureaucrats during university meetings, and self-serving politicians at legislative hearings (at tax-supported institutions), or corporate idiot-trustees (at private schools). To paraphrase Gilbert and Sullivan, "A chairperson's lot is not a happy one." Still, it teaches us to assume a semblance of forbearance, humility, and tolerance and, like Prufrock, to prepare "a face to meet the faces that you meet." Well, my aim here is to resurrect Prufrock's specter, to spit out the butt ends of my days and ways.

My argument wends its way through tedium and switches from conditional to past tense to answer Prufrock's and now my overwhelming question, Was it "worth it, after all?" Being more of an optimist than that fastidious, whining, coffee-slurping little prig, I think it was. Indeed my whole life as a chair was the inevitable outcome of my early training at the Wharton School and my later practical experience as a used-car salesman and eventually manager (of the one other salesman) at the automotive establishment C. Jamstremski, Polish Purveyor of Fine Used Cars. While

The author is Professor of English at the University of Miami. A version of this article appeared in the Winter 1997 issue of the ADE Bulletin.

this was not exactly a *Fortune* 500 firm, its lessons for academic life were priceless. Cutting a semblance of tread into bald tires became an indispensable lesson in revitalizing the teaching of older, jaded faculty members; financing the unfinanceable buyer, a recipe for preparing the department travel budget; haggling over the price of an untrustworthy machine, a textbook case for obtaining funding for a new program; mollifying an irate buyer with a rod through the engine block, a strategy for appeasing apoplectic faculty members after they receive their annual raise notices; offering meaningless fifty-fifty guarantees on parts and labor, a pattern for calming the anxieties of publicationless faculty members approaching tenure decisions—the list goes on and on.

I was prepared for life as a corporal in the administrative army by a mother who was both an opera singer and an A. F. of L. organizer in the Ladies Garment Workers Union and by a father who was manager of an automobile agency. Two more disparate characters one is not likely to find: she a vociferous leftist and he a resolute conservative; their common tie, indulging me (their only child) in showing off. I am at it again here. My parents' after-dinner side-porch battles were epic, their voices, particularly my mother's—trained as it was and cultivated on the picket line at the Gotham Hosiery Company—rising in incantation to gender, social, and political diversity. I grew up precocious and fat, each condition militating against the other in terms of social acceptance. To counterbalance my inflated, egomaniacal inner self, I had my overinflated, socially denigrated corporeal exterior. Used to satiating every legally obtainable desire, I tried to make the best of two noxious traits by counterbalancing them into a virtue, hardly an Apollonian ideal but nevertheless one I am here to share with you in all its permutations in my life as a chair.

My paper is about making the most of our imaginaries to construct helpful dialogical self-narratives—or simply split personalities that work to advantage in solving administrative problems. The process is not much different from becoming an antihero with a thousand faces. Constructing a rationale for one's place in the universe comes easily to people who make a living pontificating on the meaning, or, more recently, the meaninglessness, of literary metaphors and mirror-image reflections. Like many of you, I began at an early age to identify with characters in the literature I read, lavishing my self-identification with comic hyperbole. "Why comic hyperbole?" you may well ask (but probably wouldn't).

I think I did so because I already had a sense of inherited schizophrenia, coupled with diametrically opposed ego problems. A coping maneuver was to develop a mindset that stressed comic exaggeration as an art form and to cling to the disparate hope that a round peg might after all fit into the square hole of life. Exaggeration of spirit seemed to go hand in hand with the fleshy exaggeration of my body. Thinking big has its drawbacks, however; it inspired dark suspicions, as I am sure some readers are even now beginning to harbor, of sincerity, commitment, veracity—that sort of thing. But I was always viscerally opposed to righteousness as an announced agenda and to people firmly even if quietly rooted in the absolute strength of unalterable conviction.

Of course, certainty need not always be harmful. I remember one day back in Binghamton when I was on the university tenure appeals board. The academic year had officially ended, and members of the panel were desperate to finish our last meeting and get away for the summer. The case involved a neighbor of mine in the philosophy department. He insisted, in the twilight hour of our last afternoon of the spring semester, on beginning his case with an hour-and-a-half-long definition of education. Six o'clock came and went, and his tedious recitation showed no signs of abatement. As the committee members grew increasingly restive, the chair finally forced closure to the philosophic peroration and began to call witnesses. Nearly all the department faculty members enlisted to testify, but only three survived the definitional preamble. Despite the late hour, all three, including the chair, testified that my neighbor's teaching was superb, his publication record strong, his university services unimpeachable. So what was the problem? On philosophical grounds (opposition to any system of hierarchical values or concept of permanence), the plaintiff was unalterably opposed to the university's decision to grant him promotion and tenure, and the appeals committee had to decide whether he could be forced to accept the new rank and status. He threatened to quit rather than suffer the indignity of cooperating in any such anathematized scheme, but he was, despite his abberant behavior, as valuable and accomplished a faculty member as his colleagues claimed. The argument for finding for (that is, against) him was that if he were allowed to reject the new appointment, somehow the whole tenure and promotion review process would be jeopardized. Near comic convulsions, I tried to listen with a reflective seriousness, knitting my eyebrows thoughtfully, biting the corner of my lower lip, and gripping the chair arm so hard that my knuckles turned white. After we finally put the entire tenure process at risk by granting the plaintiff his wishes, it occurred to me that no narrative I had ever invented was as apt a metaphor for academic life. But the incident had confirmed my worst tendency to regard academe as something to be savored, like *Alice in Wonderland* or some Nabokovian comic permutation. So I chose the trickster road as one that, if less traveled by, was the more interesting and a lot more fun.

I have survived for more than a quarter of a century as a minor university administrator by applying the same schizoid narrativizing strategy to the art of running, and being run by, an academic department. When hyperbole infuses narrative formations, particularly dialogical ones, they become caricatures, easier to understand, harder to dismiss simply because of their ludicrousness. Take my introductory paragraphs, involving Prufrock and the used-car salesman as a demonstration of competing paradigms of an old department chair—a fat man in the delicate position of dealing with intelligent people ever ready to devise their own defensive narratives of themselves in interaction with him. The point is to have them come away feeling amused and slightly superior but sensing the entire action was not a total waste of time and maybe even a little fun.

Should you choose to embark on the devious course of trying to have fun being a chair or a director of graduate studies, choose your paradigms from literature. I read both parts of *Henry IV* early on and immediately identified with Falstaff, whose clever comic self-exaggerations mitigate the damages of his grubby, hedonistic antiheroism. I adopted him as my coordinating trickster figure. It was the Falstaffian persona that marshaled my other fictive personalities. I looked a lot like Falstaff, so it didn't take a lot to convince people of the similarity. Then I recognized myself in both Quixote and Sancho Panza, the absurd bookish idealist and the grubby, fawning servant who is his comic alter ego. Like Quixote, I was taken with the notion that I could actually help my colleagues and the department, that I might bring about some sort of Camelot where we would all sit at a round table with no head or foot to plan the ideal curriculum and establish a disciplinary utopia together. Like Quixote, I needed the scheming Sancho in me to scrounge budgets, TA and faculty lines, and a share of the merit raise treasure from the worldly provost. When Sancho got to be governor of his island, he wasn't so bad.

In the absence of any Aristotelian poetics of comedy, I had no theoretical basis for my applied schizophrenia. Then from deep in the wastes of Kazakhstan came Bakhtin's revelations on the carnivalesque and on the low comic side of life, which I had always instinctively embraced. Now with the scriptures at hand, I was able to throw off the shackles of self-pity for systematic, productive comic delusion. Like many other chairs, I had spent years convinced that my idealistic, tender concern for others resulted in my being a self-condemned tragic hero or scapegoat enslaved by circumstance and fate, surrounded by the embittered and the power-hungry.

After Bakhtin, I began to think in terms of carnivalesque spectacle and conceived the idea of constructing an enormous wooden cross and bearing it to the department meetings to inform the faculty of my martyrdom on their unpitying, uncooperative behalf. I could hardly lift the wood, and, unwilling to risk a herniated martyrdom, I finally settled for a blood pressure machine. During uncivil exchanges, I wrapped the strap around my arm and began vigorously pumping the ball, wheezing slightly all the while. Department members invariably quieted down as they silently watched the column rise.

This attempt to instill pity was only one aspect of my Sancho persona as a bumbling, humble, defeated idiot, a persona especially useful for covering mistakes. Incidentally, all errors should be accompanied by a major grovel (groveling being a necessary part of every chair's repertoire), especially when the errors are trivial boo-boos. Such appeasing insincerity silences the offended faculty member, and at the same time conveys the uneasy impression that the display of humility is so disproportionate to the insignificance of the offense that, despite all protestations, the chair is not half so addlepated or abject as he or she claims to be. I often apologized profusely for things I was sure I hadn't done, since an apology takes the onus off the real malefactor while underscoring the malefaction's insignificance and inspires guilt without triggering a righteous faculty defense mechanism.

Dealing with the upper levels of administration evokes another set of alter egos, most of them habitually antagonistic. In these roles at least I was my mother's shop steward. Anyone who wants the job of chair badly enough to participate in what is not in the department's or its members' best interests should not be a chair. Anyone who sees the role of chair as a stepping stone to exalted administrative office should join a corporate enterprise, like the ones many administrators try so hard to emulate. For chairs, satisfaction must ultimately lie in small victories like the granting of a deserved but disputed promotion, the funding of a new line or program, the long-awaited publication of a good book after years of encouragement and support, or praise in a peer review for a remarkably well taught hour— in short, in the achievements of the people chairs represent.

But even in good times, chairs should never let the administration know they like the job. I used to keep a stack of purple dittoed resignation letters on my desk. I dated and signed one to put on the dean's desk whenever I entered his office simply to assure him that I regarded the matter to be discussed as serious. I don't know that this stance is for everyone's stomach, but I always regarded my interaction with the administration essentially as labor negotiations, and I learned never to admit any departmental weaknesses I thought the dean or provost didn't already know about.

I always tried to add a layer of hyperbolic humor to mitigate the insults I regularly heaped on the higher-ups. It didn't always work. Once in a spirited and public debate with our president over his exercise of university charter prerogatives during a dean's search, he drew himself up and announced that he had chosen the deans for twelve of the university's thirteen schools. I suggested that perhaps any dozen random derelicts off the commuter-rail platform would have had a better statistical chance of success than the crowd he had hired. This remark was not entirely true and even a bit out of line, but I thought its hyperbole was funny. I guessed from his apoplexy that the president didn't appreciate all the comic subtlety of the comparison.

I ultimately discovered how convenient it is to pick out an administrative scapegoat, some doddering, fawning, or vindictive associate vice president or sub-subprovost who can't really retaliate against the department for whatever slander is heaped on him. There are a lot of nincompoops in business suits wandering around every administrative building, people who richly deserve whatever vilification they get. Choose a scapegoat (preferably male, for political purposes) and publicly and loudly blame everything that happens on him—you can't find your glasses because he or his minions have stolen them, or your parking space was taken by one of his operatives, or it began to rain as you were walking to class—nothing is beneath him. Then when you screw up something meaningful—you can't find somebody's sabbatical leave form or a travel reimbursement check—you can blame the scapegoat and comically undercut your need for perpetual penance.

Now that I have left the faculty-administrative wars, I can admit that many of the administrators I dealt with over the years were decent, warm people and that I count several among my best friends. But that is all personal, not business. If professionally I responded to administrators antagonistically, it was because I always felt it my primary, if admittedly patriarchal, obligation to protect and enhance the careers and programs of those who elected me by challenging the false sense of infallibility and privilege power conveys. I was lucky over the years that most of the administrators with whom I crossed verbal swords were good, tolerant people, and when I wrote them to that effect after I left the position of chair, several seemed surprised, and I'm not sure they believed me. I was sincere. I am sorry about that, but as Don Corleone tells Sollozzo, "Business is business."

All Sancho's grubby, low-life tricks finally give way to a few Quixotic admonitions. I have already pontificated that sort of advice in the yellowing *ADE Bulletin*s of yesteryear. But in one last strain on your patience and credulity, I offer a final Polonius-like ("politic, deferential, glad to be of use") admonition or two. I am sure this is to most of you the oldest, most self-evident nonnews anyone could impart, but like the national anthem before a prize fight, it has a traditional purpose.

For new chairs and for chairs of long experience, established written departmental procedures are indispensable. People should know exactly what is expected of them for tenure and promotions and raises, in terms as explicit and realistic as the department can devise. Any and all department policy should be approved by the collective group. Your first allegiance is to the people who depend on you to represent them, and in the rare instances when you feel you have to oppose a departmental decision, give everyone all the reasons you can without embarrassing the affected party. You must be able honestly to doubt the wisdom of the decisions you make regarding meaningful aspects of faculty members' lives: salaries, jobs, the quality of teaching and scholarship, service to the department and the university. Whenever possible, you should solicit collective decisions; I have honestly found such decisions to be generally better than my own. Pedants and kooks abound in departments, but when trusted with shared responsibility, department members more often than not collectively become thoughtful, sensible people.

The illusion of power is a dangerous delusion to harbor consciously or unconsciously in either its comic or heroic form. The experience of being a chair points toward just the opposite. Our worst enemy is the frustration of any long-term goals we have for our departments—the department's or the college's failure to cooperate, an administrator's refusal to fund a project, the unavailability of outside funding, and a whole litany of other problems.

With teaching, where interaction is instantly gratifying, parameters are set, success is measurable, and feedback is honest if baffling, but chairing is a whole other ball game. Programmatic changes seem glacially slow, and when they do come, they are always the product of an entire faculty or at least of a major segment of it.

Even keeping a detailed year-by-year departmental statistical record of changes (an absolute necessity for use in budgetary battles) does not necessarily afford any measure of one's individual worth as a chair. The growth of enrollments may result from changes in general education or major requirements or from increasing demands that law school applicants be literate—in short, from things for which individual chairs cannot take credit. It is self-delusion to identify oneself completely with the department, to see the department's progress or regression as one's own. Yet the responsibility of the everyday nuts and bolts, of keeping the ship afloat, is to a large extent the chair's. It is a task made problematic by increasing paperwork and even more dramatic by the evolution of our discipline as a whole.

I want to close with what I think are the two most difficult issues academics, particularly English department chairs, face. Though these issues are seemingly separable, they are intrinsically related. The first is the state of the academic economy. This June the news commentators trumpeted the robust job market for college graduates, average starting corporate salary offers in the mid-thirties, and a new high in the Dow Jones index. But as Archangel Greenspan, guardian of the gates of prosperity, let us know, the whole house of cards depends on fear. People insecure in their jobs don't ask for more money, better working conditions, or anything remotely resembling tenure. The lesson for many academic administrators, in what used to be the last bastion of some semblance of freedom of speech and thought, is to reduce whatever interferes with corporate efficiency, including the impediments of outspoken professors, the sticky business of full-time personnel with fringe benefits and ever-increasing salaries in a world where everyone except CEOs must expect to hold down inflation by working more for less.

How can we think that academe can escape this all-pervasive tendency? Our job market in English is apparently eroding at the same time that more and more kids and adults are going to college. I think the need for English teachers has never dropped; rather, increases in course loads, class size, and, most important, the use of part-time labor have turned us into a McDonald's with billions of fast-fried, semiliterate students made on the cheap by part-timers and a faculty grateful on good days to have any work at all. At the University of Miami, our newly created postdoctoral teaching fellowships, whose recipients must teach six courses a year, pay one half the announced rate for a BA or BS job. The salary was decided by a vote of the graduate students themselves, whose collective fear made them choose more fellowships at lower salaries. The point is that, as chairs, the lowest, most functionary level of university administration, we have been and are in some measure to blame for letting our institutions get away with it. If we submit to corporate fear or to some aspiration to join exalted ranks by willing submission, we have let our faculties and our profession down. To whatever extent we are able to resist unwarranted incursions into the rights of our faculty members, their economic well-being, or the health of our programs, I think we are obligated to do so. Many chairs may be surprised at how much weight their simple refusal to go along will carry. If chairs don't give the power structure maximum grief over some arbitrary or inhuman scheme, nobody else will.

If all faculty positions were filled with full-time PhDs, there would be no glut of English teachers, and perhaps undergraduates would be able to read with understanding and write with alacrity by the time they pick up their diplomas and start drawing $35,000 salaries—even the business majors.

The second issue is of course related to the economics of our profession but is more overtly political than even corporate capitalism in academe. Inspired by the evolving gender composition of our faculties and the political effect of official pronouncement during the Vietnam War, the intellectual and academic community has increasingly questioned our culture's stability, its resistance to change, its power structure, its verbalizations, and even the validity of its existence. Whatever these insights may be, the evolution or revolution of disciplinary thought ushered in a new era of thinking as profoundly important as it is radical, even as it settles and devolves into the continuum of intellectual history. Our job is first to try to understand what it is all about, then to recognize its existing importance in our discipline and to make the most of it. The ideas expressed in our departments, what we teach, and our ways of teaching it are neither moral nor philosophical issues so much as observable phenomena, part of continuing cultural and intellectual evolution. We as department chairs should do our best to accommodate intellectual diversity. When we have found demons, they are us. Our enterprise is about intellectual curiosity, about constructing and reconstructing our personal narratives as well as the narratives germane to the world around us, and at least to me the whole business is interesting. The heat of the evangelicals on either side involves overtones of both morality and religion, and it is our job to try to replace righteousness with understanding, polarity with intellectual curiosity, censoriousness with whatever comic sensibility or grotesque masks we can raise and to ensure that we and our colleagues get on with the stern task of surviving by enjoying the whole enterprise as much as we can.

Career Possibilities in Administration; or, How That Job Helped Me Get This One

LINDA K. KARELL

In the Fall 1995 *ADE Bulletin*, Erik D. Curren succinctly represents the graduate student point of view:

> Approaching the PhD, we have found that [. . .] the tenure-track jobs for which we had been training do not exist or that the competition is so intense that our chances of getting a satisfying English teaching position compare unfavorably with the proverbial lightning strike.   (45)

For job seekers, this grim outlook can be despairing and demeaning, and recently, well-deserved attention has been given to making the job search more humane for candidates. For universities, too, however, the outlook is depressing: while a buyer's market when hiring *is* possible, too often lines go unfilled, sometimes to disappear altogether. In many English departments, adjunct hiring is replacing tenure-track positions, class size and committee responsibilities are increasing, and overall morale is declining. It is no longer any surprise that the academic job market, which has been extremely bad for years now, may never rebound to a state of health. Furthermore, even if the job market does improve, it may take years, and in the meantime new technologies such as distance learning and other forms of computer technology, as well as reconsiderations of time-honored academic cornerstones such as tenure, may alter the face and function of English departments as we currently know them.

The author is Assistant Professor of English at Montana State University.

It is important, then, to address job-seeking and career-building strategies with these realities in mind. In this paper, I discuss ways in which administration—whether as a temporary career strategy or as a long-term commitment—can provide job seekers with additional (and satisfying) career options. Let me begin with some personal contextualization: I received my PhD from the University of Rochester in 1994. A year earlier, I had been on the market and even had a few—very few—interviews at the MLA convention, but nothing came of them. Wary of the depressed job market for English PhDs and increasingly aware of my student loan repayment schedule, I took an administrative position at a private university in New York State, where I was responsible for developing and directing a campus-wide retention program for underperforming students. This program was new on campus, and I was its first official director. It was a moderate-level administrative position, but it catapulted me from a graduate student training to enter the faculty ranks to the director of a major campus program with a staff, an annual budget in excess of $300,000, and considerably different responsibilities and expectations regarding my performance. My two-year stint in administration ended when, after lengthy searching, I accepted a position as an assistant professor at Montana State University at Bozeman, the same university where I had received my BA some eight years earlier. This series of moves and removes, along with my return to my home, remains poignant and startling to me; the support of several colleagues was crucial, and I also freely acknowledge that some element of profound good fortune was present. But specific experiences in administrative work during graduate school helped me land the retention program position, and in turn experience gained while I was an administrator helped me move laterally into this faculty position.

University administration has always been a career option for faculty members. It is also a career option for graduate students who, for reasons of choice or inevitability, find themselves struggling in the tenure-track race but enjoy the challenges, atmosphere, and benefits of higher education and want to remain there. While there are a range of opportunities outside the university, jobs that often pay exceedingly well, I believe some people like myself are happiest and most productive in a university setting. Despite downsizing, administration still offers those with advanced degrees a variety of career opportunities within the university environment. My own experience suggests that an administrative career, if not a candidate's first choice, can create a remarkably satisfying second choice.

An administrative career has much going for it, and it offers excellent tangible as well as intangible benefits. Administrative positions are frequently more lucrative, both in salary and in fringe benefits, than faculty positions. Particularly in this era of temporary and adjunct positions, the salary and security of an administrative position can be almost plush. Even ABD, my starting salary as the director of this retention program was several thousand more than my beginning salary as an assistant professor. A career in administration may also offer a wider variety of advancement opportunities and greater mobility than a faculty position, which can be especially helpful for partnered candidates or those for whom a particular geographical location is paramount. An administrative career can put excellent teachers on the front lines of student advocacy, and like good teachers, committed administrators can profoundly and positively affect students' lives. Many universities and colleges also offer administrators opportunities to teach from time to time, without the obligation to produce research in their teaching area. A dual appointment arrangement between administration and faculty can also sometimes be negotiated at the point of hire. The PhD, now required for college-level teaching at all but the community college level, is equally attractive in administration and frequently commands more prestige. In most faculty departments, everyone has a PhD. This is not true in administration, where the PhD can supply leverage in salary and benefits negotiation. Finally—and admittedly among the reasons I chose it—an administrative career can be broadly useful. First, it can be a sincere career path within higher education. Second, it can buy a job seeker time while it builds skills, creates contacts, and provides invaluable experience. It may even become a back door into the faculty ranks that today so often appear closed to young PhDs. Third, important educational changes often originate at the administrative level—changes that are much harder, or even impossible, to effect from the professoriat.

The variety of administrative positions graduate students may consider is enormous, although the particulars of any job depend on the educational structure in which it exists. Some general options include student support, minority recruitment and development (at both the student and the faculty levels), retention programs, residence life administration, grant writing, program evaluation, recruitment, financial aid, career services, honors programs, learning centers, and international student services. The broadness of this range can be intimidating, but it can be sorted out on the basis of the highest degree held: a bachelor's degree is sufficient for most entry-level support positions, while a master's degree is generally required for positions with some independent supervisory responsibility. Comparable experience, usually at the hiring university, will sometimes substitute for the master's degree. A PhD is now required for most directly supervisory leadership positions. A PhD will overqualify job seekers for most entry-level administrative positions, particularly in student services, while directorships such as the one I held, assistant dean–level positions, or assistant or associate director positions for prominent campus programs such as financial aid, advising, or recruitment generally require demonstrated experience in addition to an advanced degree.

It is essential, then, to get this experience while in graduate school. Graduate programs must accept more responsibility for the current plight of job seekers and begin heeding the elephant in the faculty lounge: many, perhaps even most, graduate students will not find a reasonable approximation of their dream jobs, and some will not find tenure-track jobs at all, becoming the adjuncts whose exploitation we are now only beginning to acknowledge or leaving higher education in pursuit of a financially and emotionally feasible lifestyle. Guiding graduate students toward traditional research jobs that most of them are unlikely ever to hold is irresponsible, immoral, and economically untenable. Rather than provide a narrow focus on the faculty track, graduate departments must additionally encourage their students to prepare for jobs that require supervisory experience and leadership skills. Nostalgia aside, colleges and universities are businesses, and they seek the same things we tell our undergraduates to demonstrate: leadership, responsibility, creativity, and experience that can translate to a variety of job situations. The graduate student with a nonteaching fellowship will be a less attractive administrative candidate than the student who has taught, worked part time, and amassed evidence of leadership responsibilities. Graduate departments, pressed by the current job situation, are revising their programs and decreasing the numbers of students they accept. In addition to these appropriate changes, I want to encourage them to support graduate students' forays into alternative careers by providing guidance, mentoring, recommendations, and other pertinent resources.

As much as graduate schools can rise to the challenge presented by the job crisis, the responsibility is not theirs alone. Graduate students must also share the responsibility for becoming employable. When possible, they should try to choose part-time and summer work that carries with it supervisory or decision-making responsibilities. That part-time work is most beneficial when it is situated within the university, because a lingering distrust between corporate business and the university can hamper candidates seeking an administrative career without specific experience in the university. Graduate students can seek part-time positions that allow student advocacy, that enable students to get to know various program directors and show initiative, perhaps by suggesting program development or coordinating teaching efforts. The population of any university is surprisingly mobile; in the years it takes to graduate, a former administrative colleague may have advanced to a high-level job and will be in a position to write or call on the candidate's behalf. And just as academic search committees look primarily at their scholarly colleagues' assessment of a candidate's qualifications, administrative search committees want to hear one's praises sung by other administrators. Graduate students need to expand the networking they have been forced by a grim job market to learn to do so well. But now they need to make contacts not only with authors, theorists, and professors but also with administrators whose careers stand out.

Candidates considering a particular administrative job at a particular university should do their homework. Reading the ads in the *Chronicle of Higher Education* and seeing what kind of experience is required or preferred for particular positions and what the salary levels are nationally are a solid beginning for accumulating the information needed to decide well and negotiate successfully. Another way to aid decision making is to examine the pattern of promotions in general at the university being applied to: What job historically leads to what next job? Who has been in a position "forever," and is that an indication of job security or of a paucity of advancement opportunities? At what level do women seem to disappear from visible positions of authority? Are minority administrators chiefly in charge of minority programs, promoted to assistant and associate but never dean? Whom does the position report to, and what is his or her record of supporting the career advancement of the people he or she supervises? These questions can help distinguish a position that is a stepping-stone from one that is a millstone. Those making the transition to administration should aim as high as possible and try to start in a leadership position, preferably as the director, assistant director, or coordinator of a program, and avoid primarily service positions, such as career counselor or academic adviser. These positions, however valuable they may have been in providing experience for a graduate student, tend to be career dead ends: repetitive duties at low pay and minimal intellectual or creative opportunities. Successful job candidates should also volunteer for a major college committee or two as quickly as possible—this is the place where change happens and reputations are built. It is also where to meet, greet, and interact with the university big guns.

As a stepping-stone, an administrative career can have a high payback in the faculty job market within two or three years. I continued a confidential job search for a faculty position throughout my time in administration, and all the interviewers I met with at the MLA convention pointedly told me that my administrative experience was what made me stand out amid dense competition. Whether they planned to use my administrative background directly in the position they were interviewing for was not the issue—some did, most did not. The point seemed to be that beleaguered academic search committees, seeking one person to complement a possibly ravaged faculty, sought as many skills in one package as possible.

If moving from an administrative to a faculty position is the goal, candidates should be aware that there are drawbacks to this strategy. Those choosing the backdoor approach should realize that, for the months or years in administration, they will be working double duty. Their administrative position, which may include research and professional development requirements, is likely to be demanding of their time and energy. They must also stay current in their literary research area, revise the dissertation or write articles for publication, attend professional conferences, and, of course, survive the exhausting annual job search. This double life is a drain, certainly, and it takes a cumulative toll on candidates and their families and friends. In a world of imperfect options, however, I found it no harder than graduate school or the frustration of cobbling together adjunct positions, and it paid significantly better. Finally, this strategy is not endlessly usable. Spend too much time in administration and the move to faculty becomes more, not less, difficult, as job seekers come to be seen as a "them" to the faculty's "us." Having an administrative position that requires some student advocacy can help deflect this attitude, because faculty members tend to identify themselves as student advocates and can identify with the rebel administrator.

I also want to mention the inevitable, but often repressed, area of political maneuvering. I am certainly advocating a version of political maneuvering when I speak of career strategies more than I do of career missions, callings, or the love and dedication we bring to our work. This is not because I don't value the moral or ethical imperative behind teaching and research. I do. But the competition for jobs is too keen for candidates to rely on others to recognize the inherent value of their work or their worth as persons. Job seekers have to be demonstrably effective, efficient, productive, and politically savvy individuals. They must astutely prepare themselves by acquiring experience and seeking out otherwise hidden opportunities. Administration is not unilaterally the savage and inhumane place it is often described as being. Some very fine people work there and are committed to its possibilities. Along with all the advantages an administrative career offers, it can be a place of enormous educational importance by offering energetic individuals an opportunity to revise some of the very structures that disempower students at all levels. Individuals prepared in the humanities can have a positive effect on higher education through administration, although a humanities background is no defense against the inevitable priority shifts administration requires.

For ill or well, a position either in administration or on the faculty will speedily divest a new hire of any dependency on the infantilizing structure of graduate school. Although awkward and sometimes painful, this period of growth can be useful. Less acknowledged is the toll that the arena of politicking can take, particularly on new hires. The distrust—so rampant as to be self-evident—between administration and faculty looks different from each side of the fence, whether perceived as justified or ridiculous. Yet when moving from one arena to the other, I capitalized on exactly this insider-outsider vision. When seeking my administrative job, I drew on my experience as a student and stressed my ability to work with faculty members. By the same token, candidates applying for faculty positions that require the development of some arm of the department (a women's studies program, for instance, or an advanced degree program) can emphasize their ability to work with administrators. Graduate students and junior faculty members are often encouraged to lie low, remain politically naive, and wait first for the PhD and then for tenure, while the same philosophy of passivity in administration frequently works against acquiring a favorable reputation across campus, particularly for female and minority administrators. In either arena, gendered expectations, racial prejudices, pay inequities, and historical animosities are present and can make productive work difficult to achieve and evaluate. These political realities shouldn't dictate one's state of mind to the point of paranoia, but neither should they be ignored.

In closing, let me mention a few pointers to aid the transition from graduate student to professional. First, whether they are entering administration or the faculty, it is especially important for new hires to get a mentor. Mentoring is crucial, but because the mentoring relationship is at heart characterized by generosity, risk, and trust from both sides, assigned or prescribed mentorships are often only remotely useful. Choose your own mentors, preferably two or three people whose achievements, political outlooks, or job duties you respect. Make sure they are not all in the same department or unit and be direct: ask for their support and mentoring. Chances are they will be flattered and you will have to spend less time later, apologizing for intruding when asking them for their perspective or suggestions. I could not have survived my administrative job without the reliable and generous support of several female colleagues, and I have already relied on the support and generous spirit of mentors in my current faculty position. Second, quickly acquire a range of perspectives on your new department or position. Perceived histories are always present and affect every department. It may not be either necessary or advisable to measure the bones of the skeletons in the closet, but it helps to know they are there. Third, have a clear and consistent set of standards. Knowing what your own standards are and being able to apply and to meet them are crucial in maintaining your own sense of integrity, not to mention sanity. Fourth and finally, create a support system composed of people not involved in the university. Self-care and clearheadedness are essential and are often most consistently and delightfully provided by people who care more about you than they do about your job. Good luck.

WORK CITED

Curren, Erik D. "Response to John T. Day." *ADE Bulletin* 111 (1995): 45–46.

Jouissance *and the Job Market*

GEOFFREY T. WILSON

Like other commentaries on the employment crisis in higher education, the *Final Report* of the MLA Committee on Professional Employment paints a stark picture. The oversupply of PhDs and the downsizing of higher education have led to a multitiered job market in which academics at the bottom end, if employed at all, move from school to school, working harder and harder for less money and no job security. A host of paradoxes and ironies amplify the cruelty of this market. For instance, diminishing resources for hiring full-time teachers have led to increased dependence on graduate teaching assistants for staffing courses, so that we create more and more job candidates precisely because there are fewer and fewer faculty positions (Gilbert et al. 7). Another irony: we grieve that the corporate economy of layoffs and "flexibility" has fully penetrated higher education, when in fact the employment outlook has been much more favorable in the corporate sector than in academia over the past few years. These are distressing conditions, yet many job seekers return to the MLA convention year after year in the hope of getting that elusive tenure-track position.

As terrible as all this is, we can nevertheless draw some profit from the job crisis, as it can usefully illuminate some points from Lacanian psychoanalytic theory. In particular, the dialectic of desire between job candidate and the profession demonstrates the Lacanian logic of alienation—that process in which the neurotic subject sacrifices a piece of being or *jouissance* and in doing so provides for the Other's enjoyment. In the academic job

The author works in the computer industry. A version of this paper was presented at the 1997 MLA convention in Toronto.

market the job seeker forgoes pleasure, satisfaction, and comfort, and this renunciation appears to increase enjoyment somewhere else. I propose that the transfer of *jouissance* from subject to Other accounts for the reluctance of many perennial job seekers to leave academia. We are reluctant to leave behind a piece of ourselves that is now possessed or enjoyed by what I call the profession as Other.

For Lacan *the Other* is a broad term for, among other things, the "place" of symbolic-social authority to which a subject relates. The Other can be an individual person—a parent, a judge, a boss, a psychoanalyst—or an abstraction such as academia or society. According to Bruce Fink, the function of the symbolic Other is "generalizable"; it is originally embodied by our parents but is extended to "the academic Other, the law, religion, God, tradition, and so on." Our sense of duty or ethical obligation is produced in relation to this Other. The symbolic Other—whether it be a parent or academia—designates or is imagined to demand certain objects and goals we feel we ought to pursue: "grades, diplomas, success, marriage, children—all the things usually associated with anxiety in neurosis" (*Lacanian Subject* 87). In other words, most of our "socially valorized" pursuits can be thought of as objects "prized by the Other, associated with the Other's approval or disapproval" (189n).

In academic life many of our goals and objectives can be understood as just such objects. The desire for publications and good teaching evaluations or even the more basic desire to lead an academic life can be construed as emanating from the Other's demand. At bottom many people become academics to gain recognition by some Other, whether a parent, an admired teacher, or society. Having an academic parent, for instance, might cause one to feel that being an academic is an appropriate, socially valued career goal, simply by virtue of the esteem in which the parent is held, irrespective of whether the parents actually urge that choice on their child. For the subject, such social valorization is equivalent to a demand or expectation.

The problem with such demands addressed by the Other to the subject is that they are ambiguous, open to interpretation. The parent says, "You can be anything you like" or "Do what most makes *you* happy," but we continue to wonder, "What do they *really* want" (Fink, *Clinical Introduction* 54). In fact, this uncertainty constitutes the basic question asked by the subject in the dialectic of desire: "What does the Other want from me?" The subject tries to "interpret" or "read" the Other's desire, to figure out what the Other wants and thus transform vague desirousness into the specific, manageable demand for something (61). However, the most plainly stated demand—or even the lack of a demand—can conceal ulterior desire. Despite their protestations, our parents may in fact unconsciously want us to reproduce their lives or pursue something they wish they had pursued. Children perceive and respond to such unstated desires but also act on what they presume to be the Other's (concealed) desire, which may bear no relation to its real hopes for us.

What does the profession as Other desire for us? In the job search this desire is unknowable. Many job seekers are familiar with the experience of applying for positions that apparently suit their preparation and credentials exactly—never to receive any response beyond the EOE form. Conversely, after applying for positions they do not quite fit, many applicants have been surprised to receive those cherished calls. The arbitrary and unpredictable response of the Other to our applications suggests that we don't really know and can't anticipate what the Other wants. It is not uncommon for an advertisement to specify a candidate who is, say, both a Shakespeare and Milton specialist with secondary qualifications in linguistics, anthropology, and women's studies. Since we know there is no such person and assume that the advertisers know there is no such person, we ask, "What does this committee really want? Which of these things is most important?" Clearly the department is trying to solve all its needs in a single hire, and the candidate is left to puzzle over an impossible set of demands. "Should I apply, even though I can't possibly satisfy these demands?" Interpreting the committee's ulterior desire is made still more difficult by the "fake" job search, conducted to accommodate institutional hiring guidelines although an inside candidate has already been identified. The job listing might conceal a contradictory real desire—"We've already got this person and are therefore not really seeking the candidate described at all." This effort to read the Other's desire, of course, occurs at the interview stage as well: we prepare for interviews by looking at catalogs and Web sites, trying to glean the school's needs; we look for clues in the questions, facial expressions, and parting comments during interviews themselves.

Generally speaking, job candidates are persons who have always enjoyed success as students—we've always attained the academic Other's recognition and approval in the form of scholarships, outstanding grades and evaluations, and the acceptance of papers and manuscripts. These rewards show that we have been successful at interpreting and satisfying the Other's demands. The institutions and organizations, our mentors and colleagues, all tell us that we're doing it right—that is, until we try to find a tenure-track job. The academic employment crisis means we've suddenly reached a point at which the Other no longer exhibits signs of approval. The only such tokens that matter at this level—jobs—are not forthcoming. Our advisers offer consolation: "It's not you; it's the job market." But it is hard not to read the failure to get interviews, campus visits, or job offers as a judgment of one's worth. In the absence of these rewards, academia actually appears to disapprove of the job candidate.

That we seek the Other's approval rather than actual jobs is easily demonstrable. Consider the importance of interview calls in the weeks before the MLA convention. They become a kind of currency for measuring academic success, and we quietly compare the number of interviews we get with those of our friends and colleagues, offering tepid congratulations to peers who enjoy more success. We value interviews even with schools we have no real desire to teach at (those that require 4/4 loads, that are thousands of miles from spouse or partner, and so forth). In this respect, they are undifferentiated; we simply count them. What's at stake, therefore, is not the job per se but its status as a token of approval or recognition. Unlike objects of the Other's demand (what's expected of us), these are signs of the Other's love (signs that we've satisfied its demands).

We can of course recognize these tokens as Lacanian *objets a*. When we insist that the Other show us love and approval, the specific object by which it responds is unimportant. As Joan Copjec puts it, "Whether one gives a child whose cry expresses a demand for love a blanket, or food, or even a scolding, matters little. The particularity of the object is here annulled; almost any will satisfy—as long as it comes from the one to whom the demand is addressed" (148). The objects are now something more than themselves; they contain a surplus insofar as they bear the Other's love. Moreover, we most seek from the Other precisely what it cannot give, what it does not even have—for the object *a* is precisely the lacking object. "Love's deception," Copjec continues, is that "the object *a* can be given" (148). In the academic job search we are insisting that the Other show its love by giving us objects made that much more meaningful because they don't exist. The failure to receive these signs of love causes us to feel inadequate but also implies that the Other is withholding the object *a*, keeping the imagined surplus for itself.

We receive form rejection letters in March telling us that we did not satisfy this or that particular instance of the academic Other. Of course, the reason good people don't get jobs lies in the economic conditions of higher education. But we tend to psychologize those conditions; we imagine that arbitrary economic effects express specific purpose or desire, and we consequently feel inadequate to that desire. "I could have done more." "I should have said [x] in the interview." Often, however, there is nothing we could have done to elicit the sign of approval (the callback or job offer). We've dutifully done everything that the academic Other seems to demand—we publish, read conference papers, develop smart classes—but it remains voracious and unappeasable, demanding ever more work. We've given it the satisfaction of acceding to its demands, but this is never enough.

The unappeasable, incomprehensible Other is clearly reminiscent of Freud's abusive "primal father" of *Totem and Taboo*—the "violent and jealous father" who "keeps all the females for himself," leaving no satisfaction for his sons (175). Like the mythic father of the primitive horde, the profession seems to have accrued to itself all the pleasure and satisfaction available in the system, leaving the company of brothers (the job seekers) out in the cold. This analogy is not as farfetched as it seems. It is a profession, Cary Nelson tells us, "that eats its young" (167). Consider the various "abuses" of hiring departments: committees' requirements, for instance, that applicants send expensive dossiers and transcripts up front or that candidates pay their own expenses for campus interviews (Gilbert et al. 36; Nelson 161). The discourse about these practices implies not only that the hiring departments are indifferent and arrogant but also that they obtain a certain perverse pleasure and should be restrained by rules and hiring guidelines. Consider, as well, the common impression among graduate students that our competitors for the limited number of jobs are people who already have jobs—even our own dissertation directors may be applying for the good positions in our fields. When someone leaves a tenure-track or tenured position to take another, the post vacated will most likely be eliminated or converted to a temporary line. Those who are already inside the profession seem to absorb all the jobs for themselves, consuming them.

Slavoj Žižek reminds us that "there are always two fathers" (149). In the neurotic landscape the primal father is complemented or superseded by what Copjec calls the "*unvermögender* Other." The term comes from Freud's *Fragment of an Analysis of a Case of Hysteria*, better known as the "Dora" case. Dora describes her father as "ein vermögender Mann," a man of means, but Freud argues that the phrase conceals by negation the opposite: Dora actually considers her father to be an impotent "man without means" (Copjec 150, 255n). Copjec correlates this impotent Other (the hysteric's master) with the "ideal father" installed by the clan of brothers after they have killed the primal father. Compared with the ferocious primal father, the ideal father is a relatively weak figure who articulates rules and prohibitions, dispassionately enforcing the taboos of the clan that are intended to prevent the return of an obscene father of *jouissance*. In the discourse of the job crisis, is not the MLA as professional organization—with its various resolutions, good-practice guidelines, and so forth—often cast in this second role? We find numerous appeals to the MLA to do something about the abusive Other qua profession, and we hear an equal number of denunciations of the MLA's failures and impotence in this regard.

Cary Nelson argues, for instance, that the MLA's "response to the anguish of hundreds of young scholars has been wholly inadequate" (165).

Our impression of an unappeasable, primal Other is sustained by the logic of alienation, a term that provides another way to express Lacan's most basic revision of the Freudian topography of the psyche. Instead of the dynamics of the ego-id-superego, Lacan gives us the subject divided in language, the split or barred subject. Because of our assumption in language, we lose access to a part of our very being—we are alienated from some *jouissance* that becomes inaccessible or barred. The *jouissance* we have renounced doesn't just disappear; it is enjoyed elsewhere. Marx's conception of alienated labor helps to explain this logic: "If the product of labour does not belong to the worker, if it confronts him as an alien power, this can only be because it belongs to some *other man than the worker*. If the worker's activity is a torment to him, to another it must be *delight* and his life's joy" (78). In other words, the factory owner takes pleasure in the very sacrifices and torments experienced by the worker.

Psychoanalysis describes a similar economy. Freud and Lacan identify the parental model for social-symbolic authority with the father, traditionally the bearer of a symbolic intervention prohibiting enjoyment of the mother. It is the father, they tell us, who insists that the child sleep in her or his own room and so forth—that the child give up some pleasure or *jouissance*. The father keeps this pleasure for himself even as the child is excluded from it: he takes over the child's position in the mother's love (or in the mother's bed). Indeed, in addition to its primary valence as pleasure and sexual satisfaction, *jouissance* specifically implies the enjoyment or possession of some thing (such as real estate). It is, in other words, a satisfaction in reference to which one can have rights of possession or use; like the ownership of real estate, it can be transferred. According to Lacan, we relinquish certain rights of enjoyment with the entry into language. We give up access to some *jouissance* because language as such is an interdiction against it. The symbolic order, the *nom-du-père*, is literally the same thing as prohibition, the *non-du-père*. Enjoyment sacrificed here surfaces somewhere else in the system.

Can academia be said to cause alienation from *jouissance* in the same way as the mythical moment of accession into language does? We might think in terms of sacrifice. As graduate students, we give up many years to the profession. The countless hours spent writing seminar papers, preparing for qualifying exams, completing the dissertation, conducting the job search—these are all in their way sacrifices of pleasure performed at the Other's behest. We give up "jouissance in the hope of gaining esteem, recognition, and approval—a symbolic equivalent" (Fink, *Clinical Introduction* 172). The academic Other makes demands of us; it has explicit and implicit requirements we are expected to satisfy. The cost of complying with those demands is that we give up some pleasure, but we also give the Other the satisfaction of our complying with its demands. The Other derives satisfaction (or is imagined to do so) from our very actions of dutiful renunciation. A loss of *jouissance* on our side simultaneously yields a gain in *jouissance* on the side of the Other.

This transfer of *jouissance* helps explain our reluctance to leave academia and seek the rewarding, better-paying careers that really do exist elsewhere: because the Other to whom we sacrificed now possesses the very pleasure we renounced—it gained pleasure in our renunciation. We want to keep our proximity to this enjoyment and not to let it out of our sight. We are stuck, fixated on the lost *jouissance*, and therefore we agree to low-paying, temporary jobs at the fringes of the profession in order to stay somewhat near it. This situation is surely a final cruelty of the academic job market—with its unappeasable master who cannot show satisfaction and its dutiful servants who cannot break off.

WORKS CITED

Copjec, Joan. *Read My Desire: Lacan against the Historicists*. Cambridge: MIT P, 1994.

Fink, Bruce. *A Clinical Introduction to Lacanian Psychoanalysis*. Cambridge: Harvard UP, 1997.

———. *The Lacanian Subject*. Princeton: Princeton UP, 1995.

Freud, Sigmund. *Totem and Taboo*. Ed. and trans. James Strachey. New York: Norton, 1989.

Gilbert, Sandra M., et al. *Final Report, MLA Committee on Professional Employment*. New York: MLA, 1997.

Marx, Karl. "Economic and Philosophic Manuscripts of 1844." *The Marx-Engels Reader*. 2nd ed. Ed. Robert C. Tucker. New York: Norton, 1978.

Nelson, Cary. *Manifesto of a Tenured Radical*. New York: New York UP, 1997.

Žižek, Slavoj. *Enjoy Your Symptom!* New York: Routledge, 1992.

*How We Got Contracts
for Lecturers at the
University of Vermont:
A Tale of (Qualified) Success*

ROBYN R. WARHOL

I am here to tell the story of the three-year process of getting renewable
four-year contracts and other benefits (including sabbatical eligibility) for
non-tenure-track and part-time lecturers at the University of Vermont
(which—for obscure reasons having to do with the Latin name of the university and two hundred years of custom—we call "UVM"). As a semi-
private, semipublic research institution, UVM has no faculty union. Until
fall 1996, lecturers had no job security: they were asked to sign nine-month
or four-month contracts and often did not know whether they would teach
in a given September until July or August. Getting longer-term contracts
meant a significant shift in the structure of the base budget for the university, which had paid lecturers using "one-time funds" every year for
decades. Our experience might therefore be instructive for faculties in
many kinds of institutions.

I contend that we were able to accomplish as much as we did because
we recognized that most non-tenure-track and part-time faculty members
(whom we call lecturers at UVM) are women and that their bad situation—low pay, no job security, no faculty-development support, limited
benefits—can be framed as a feminist issue. I acknowledge the serious
problems associated with universities' heavy dependence on lecturers to
teach undergraduates: I know that administrators view the use of lecturers

*The author is Professor of English and Director of Women's Studies at the University of Ver-
mont. A version of this article appeared in the Fall 1997 issue of the* ADFL Bulletin.

as a cost-cutting device and that the dollars paid to lecturers might otherwise go to support graduate students or to create (or unfreeze) tenure-line faculty positions; I know that this allocation means an erosion of the tenured faculty whose responsibilities include active research programs; I know that the lecturers have no obligation to contribute service or research to the university beyond what is required for their teaching and that service and research might decrease if a university includes lecturers among the permanent faculty.

When I joined the UVM faculty as a recently divorced, tenure-track assistant professor in 1983, I thought I also knew that the lecturers were in their positions by choice: I assumed those lecturers who held MAs could have gone on for their PhDs and that those who held PhDs (whose spouses—husbands, mainly—were all full-time employees at UVM or neighboring institutions) had simply decided that family life was more important than the pursuit of an independent career. I knew, of course, that the job market for PhDs was as tight then as it is today (judging by the helpful and painful statistics the MLA publishes each year), and I was dimly aware of the arbitrariness of the crapshoot (excuse me: I mean "search process") through which I parlayed my Stanford PhD into a tenure-track job, one that had attracted over seven hundred qualified applicants. I knew, for instance, that my having been invited to Brown for a campus visit (which did not, by the way, yield an offer, nor did the seventy-eight other applications I filed that year) played a part in my invitation to UVM, as did the UVM dean's insistence that the English department invite a female candidate. I was, in effect—and believe me, I am eternally grateful for the way that effect has benefited me in the long run—an affirmative action candidate. Even so, I believed—with all the arrogance, privilege, and wisdom of a twenty-seven-year-old—that the best PhDs would get tenure-track jobs and would, of course, be the best teachers. Thirteen years of faculty experience and a feminist perspective have changed my mind.

What a feminist perspective made me see is that the "choice" to be a lecturer is overdetermined because of the feminization of the position. At UVM, lecturers make up approximately 19% of the teaching faculty; 34% of the faculty (including all the lecturers) are women, but 66% of the lecturers are women. Any academic who takes an honest look at his or her acquaintances will have to admit that heterosexual professional couples who follow the geographic imperatives of the wife's career are rare indeed. And every academic knows the geographic strictures of academic jobs: while spousal hiring policies may be making a small dent in the problem at some institutions, the phenomenon of two wedded faculty members with tenure in the same town is rare too. I would argue that the gay man or lesbian who follows a partner's tenure-track job to become a lecturer, as well as that unusual heterosexual husband who does the same for his wife, is in a feminized position carrying all the disadvantages of a job that has long been institutionally derogated as women's work. This is what a feminist perspective has made me see. What thirteen years of faculty experience has made me see is that the lecturers who do that work at UVM are doing a splendid job. They teach as only those who love to teach can, and many are active in research, advising, and committee work as well, although they are hardly paid to be. That twenty-six of the twenty-eight tenure-line faculty members in my department signed a petition supporting the concept of contracts for lecturers suggests I am not alone in admiring the work that lecturers are doing for the department.

I will not say more here about the merits of lecturers or about whether universities should perpetuate their existence: I concede the broader view of the situation to the American Association of University Professors. Instead I turn to the logistics of getting contracts for lecturers, given that lecturers do exist and that their conditions of employment have been unbearable. I begin with a summary of the rationale we used in organizing support for the movement among the faculty, and I end with a list of the players who made this effort possible.

We presented the following reasoning to the faculty and the administration: If lecturers could hold five-year, renewable contracts and received the same support (such as travel funds, sabbatical eligibility, and faculty-development grants) as tenure-track faculty members, then

1. Departments that regularly needed lecturers could plan their curricula in five-year, rather than one-year, segments, thus improving academic programming, and they could depend on greater continuity in the teaching staff from year to year.

2. Lecturers could benefit from regular evaluation and faculty development, which would ensure the quality of teaching.

3. Lecturers who had long-term commitments to the university (some had been teaching at UVM as long as twenty-six years) would not have been marked as "temporary," while those who preferred to maintain flexibility could choose to teach without contracts.

4. Tenure-track faculty members would be free to teach more courses in their areas of specialization. To support the faculty members working toward tenure, the institution must give them adequate opportunity to focus on their research while continuing to teach. Probationary faculty members need the opportunity to teach courses (at the advanced as well as the introductory levels) in their fields. Teaching these courses enables them to

produce work commensurate with the research expectations at UVM, where the annual teaching load may be three and three or three and two, depending on the department, and where tenure-track faculty members are expected to build national reputations in their fields. Employing lecturers to help cover sections of introductory undergraduate courses makes this possible.

5. UVM could continue to attract strong tenure-track faculty members. To recruit top candidates for tenure-track jobs and to retain tenured faculty members, the university must offer an appealing teaching load in spite of the requirement that faculty members teach five or six courses a year. If all the current lecturer positions were converted to tenure-track positions, the jobs UVM offers would become less competitive because junior faculty members would be asked to carry the bulk of the introductory teaching. Employing lecturers enhances faculty recruitment.

Note the strategic emphasis here on the advantages to the tenure-line faculty members of having lecturers as colleagues. While some traditionalists at UVM maintained that they would prefer carrying heavier teaching loads and teaching more introductory courses if it meant having more PhD-holding, tenure-track colleagues, they were a tiny minority. The appeal to the self-interest of the tenured and tenure-track faculty was instrumental in organizing support for lecturers' contracts.

I organize my narrative of the campaign as a list of the players who were involved in the process. On a campus like ours, it would be necessary to mobilize the following groups or the equivalent to support the lecturers' cause:

The Faculty Women's Caucus. The effort began with the Faculty Women's Caucus, an unofficial and unsanctioned body, open to all women who teach at UVM, including lecturers as well as tenure-track faculty members. The Steering Committee of the caucus includes a dozen or so senior faculty women from across the university and meets mainly so that its members may exchange what might be called gossip about administrative decisions that affect faculty women. The Steering Committee meets once or twice a month, and when anything is happening that requires grassroots action, it calls a general meeting for all women faculty members on campus. The general meetings are also brainstorming sessions on issues the caucus needs to address: the question of contracts for lecturers came up in more than one of these meetings. We put the names of the women who come to the general meetings on a mailing list, which we use to generate support for feminist candidates for university-wide committees or the Faculty Senate. To date we have had amazing results: we nominate candidates for every major position that opens up, and in the five years of the caucus's existence every candidate we have endorsed has won. The first step in the lecturers' movement was for the Faculty Women's Caucus to get a tenured woman professor elected vice chair of the Faculty Senate. Organizing the women's vote made this possible, even though the candidate had not been actively involved in the senate and indeed had almost never attended a Faculty Senate meeting before the election.

The Faculty Senate. At UVM the lecturers are full voting members of the Faculty Senate, the body that includes all sixteen hundred or so faculty members of the university. As members of the senate, lecturers are eligible to serve on senate committees and to vote at general senate meetings. Of course, the vast majority of UVM's 184 lecturers do not attend senate meetings; neither do most tenure-line faculty members, for that matter. The largest senate meeting in recent memory (in the spring of 1996, when the Faculty Women's Caucus called for a censure of the president and provost for their failure to address racism on campus) involved only about three hundred voting members, and fewer than two hundred stuck around long enough to vote, even on a matter as controversial as that; the number in attendance is usually closer to fifty. Therefore, even a portion of the lecturers can significantly affect a senate vote. The vice chair, whom the Faculty Women's Caucus had nominated and helped elect, formed an ad hoc senate committee to address the question of terms of employment for lecturers.

An ad hoc committee of the Faculty Senate. Chaired by the vice chair of the Faculty Senate, a tenured professor, the committee consisted of five part-time, non-tenure-track lecturers; the ombudsperson; and one assistant professor who had moved into her position after ten years as a lecturer. The group gathered data from the Office of Institutional Studies about the number, gender, and longevity of lecturers at UVM and researched the situation of lecturers at institutions that had reputations for handling the employment of lecturers progressively. The committee produced a document containing a rationale and proposal for granting five-year contracts to lecturers after a probationary period of two years. The committee asked for responses to the document from faculty members serving in the president's and provost's offices and from chairs of the departments involved, particularly those chairs known to disapprove of lecturers; their comments were then incorporated into the document's argument. The document was circulated through the various committees of the senate and ultimately came up for debate on the senate floor. The lecturers' community had received plenty of advance notice of the meeting and turned out in force. The vice chair of the senate led the discussion and arranged for the chairs of departments that are heavily dependent on lecturers (e.g., foreign languages, math, English, music, art) to speak in favor of the proposal.

Department chairs. Each chair who endorsed the proposal at the senate meeting brought a petition in support of lecturers' contracts, signed by the vast majority of tenure-track faculty members in his or her department. (The present chair of one department preferred a strategy of converting lecturer funds to tenure-track lines and did not support the referendum. We asked a former chair of that department to speak in that chair's place.) The spectacle of five chairs giving impassioned testimony on the necessity for longer-term commitments of funds for lecturers was impressive. (Was it a coincidence that each of those chairs but one happened also to be married to a lecturer? Or that the one who was not married to a lecturer had been herself a "faculty wife" and lecturer at UVM for many years? Again, I say these matters are overdetermined.) No one spoke against the proposal. It passed the senate with a strong majority of those present (many lecturers were there) and subsequently went through the process of revision into language that could be adopted into the *Faculty Handbook*, the code that governs contracts at UVM. Through that process the proposal changed to allow for the possibility—not the certainty—of a lecturer's being offered a contract for up to four years, not five. A carefully reworded version of the ad hoc committee's original proposal—revised by the chair of the English department in consultation with the chairs of various senate committees and with representatives from the offices of the provost and the president—was adopted by the senate as a set of formal guidelines to be followed by the provost in future dealings with lecturers. These guidelines are not yet policy, though some lecturers have received contracts, depending on the fiscal optimism and general good faith of their deans and department chairs.

The President's Commission on the Status of Women. After the senate passed the motion to revise the *Faculty Handbook* to allow for lecturers' contracts, the President's Commission on the Status of Women, a group of students, staff, and faculty members, which advises the upper administration on campus women's issues, maintained pressure on the president and provost. Regular meetings between the commission and the upper-level administrators made it difficult for the issue to go away once the Faculty Senate had approved it.

We sought five-year contracts for lecturers after a probationary period of two years; we ended up with the possibility of a four-year contract for lecturers who have passed a second-year and a fourth-year review. While the provision is less than we were hoping for, it's much more than the non-tenure-track and part-time faculty had before: hence I call it a qualified success. I believe the key element in that success was the existence of the President's Commission on the Status of Women and the Faculty Women's Caucus. While it is relatively difficult to introduce a group like the former into an institution, a group like the latter is easy to establish. All you need to get the process started are a small group of senior faculty members committed to activism on behalf of faculty women (to form a steering committee) and one tenured faculty woman willing to take a position of leadership in your campus's equivalent of our Faculty Senate. That person must do a considerable amount of work, but the work is feminist activism, which that person is likely to be doing as part of her university service anyway. Feminist academics who share some vestiges of "male privilege"—academic women who for whatever reason have achieved the potential for influence that comes with tenure (such as women like me, who have greater access to tenure than others do because of our whiteness, middle-class status, heterosexuality, and nationality)—have had to reassess their relations with "other women" (women of color, working-class women, lesbians, immigrant women) inside and outside the academy. It is time for us to recognize the mark of otherness that has been placed on non-tenure-track and part-time faculty members and to do some "women's work" on their behalf.

The first draft of my paper ends here. I asked my former officemate, my friend and colleague Brian Kent, to read the draft, and his response forced me to acknowledge a note of smugness in what I had written, a tenure-track centrism that permeates my sincere attempt to see things from a part-timer's point of view. His points brought into focus an anxiety I had felt all along in preparing this paper to read at the MLA, a feeling that it was perhaps inappropriate for me to speak for part-timers on one of the few MLA panels devoted to their concerns. And while one member of the audience at the session characterized my qualms as an expression of "liberal guilt," I want to reproduce here the rhetorical gesture I made at the end of that presentation, which was—after all—part of a panel consisting entirely of tenured faculty members discussing the situation of part-timers. Because Kent speaks directly to the exclusion of part-timers from the process of improving their working conditions in his response, I give him the last word.

RESPONSE TO ROBYN R. WARHOL

In responding to Robyn's description of how lecturers at UVM got contracts, I should note that I have benefited directly from the effort. After twelve years of being hired to teach introductory English courses on a semester-to-semester basis, in 1996 I received a contract to teach three courses a semester for the next four years. I must confess this change improved my sense of my relation to the department in a number of ways. And on a more general level I recognize that the shift of continuing one-time funds to the English department base budget is a significant achievement for lecturers.

Nonetheless, when I look back on the process that brought about the changes, I'm left placing much more emphasis on the "Qualified" than on the "Success." Despite my own experience, the effect of the changes Robyn describes is largely theoretical and likely to remain so, given the language adopted in the *Faculty Handbook*. More important, the fundamental relation of lecturers to the university has not changed at all—lecturers remain a group with no voice and dependent on the good graces of others who are not lecturers. In the end, as ungrateful of me as it may seem, the process primarily underscored that status.

Like Robyn, I feel the need to acknowledge that this whole discussion dances around the issue of whether lecturers should exist on college and university campuses. My remarks are premised on the simple fact that they do. I believe that a separate teaching line for lecturers benefits all faculty members, students, and, yes, administrators concerned about the bottom line, but if tenure-line faculty members and administrators decided there should be only one kind of instructional employee, I would consider their position honorable (many lecturers would disagree with me, I'm sure). I would certainly lose out in such a system because I don't wish to become a tenure-line faculty member as that position is now defined. But I still have to grant an integrity to the ideal of a fully tenured teaching staff, assuming, of course, that racial and gender imbalances had been rectified.

What seems dishonorable to me is that this ideal gets lip service while year in and year out lecturers serve as a kind of invisible faculty. Either they should have a place in the structure of higher education, or they shouldn't. Right now they are there because they are needed and because most of them are fine instructors, yet they are not recognized as full participants in the university community, because administrators and some tenure-line faculty members do not want to grant them any kind of formal status. Robyn sees this condition as a feminist issue, and given the percentages it's hard to argue with her reasoning. I can't claim that sense of injustice based on gender, but I do recognize the way my job has been feminized.

I agree with Robyn that my job carries all the disadvantages of historically derogated "women's work." That's what makes the issue of status so important. The contracts address the issue by offering some measure of institutionally recognized continuity of service. In a strict, limited sense, four-year contracts do erase the stamp of temporariness from a lecturer's forehead. But in a larger sense the stigma of temporariness remains because of lecturers' status in relation to tenure-line faculty members and because of the relative status of teaching and research. As long as teaching is seen as the stepchild of research and as long as lecturers are primarily teachers, lecturers will be viewed as lesser beings.

I was pleasantly surprised by the level of support in the English department for our petition to improve working conditions and I have come to believe tenure-line faculty members genuinely admire the work lecturers do, but I'm still convinced that most of those who signed think we do less important work than they do largely because we are in some way incapable of going the route that would lead to tenure-track positions. I can't even begrudge them that attitude since they *did* labor through what I consider an odious process to get where they are.

I don't mean to suggest that this attitude is expressed meanly or maliciously, although I wouldn't be surprised if it is in other departments and at other schools. I feel fortunate to be in a department where I'm treated with kindness and respect. Still, given the professional priorities and ambitions of tenure-line faculty members, it is not surprising that when they consider lecturers' role and lack of formal status, they wonder why anyone puts up with the situation. This thought occurs to me most when I listen to tenure-line faculty members discuss the importance of upholding academic standards. Even among those who are sympathetic to lecturers' less-than-ideal circumstances and who see lecturers as necessary to the functioning of higher education, one can detect the assumption that relying on lecturers automatically compromises those standards.

So the mark of otherness Robyn mentions will remain, whatever the changes in working conditions. That structural and hierarchical component of the lecturer's position may or may not go beyond the feminist considerations Robyn has outlined. Personally, I no longer care about being perceived as a lesser being for doing what I do as opposed to what tenure-line faculty members do (however, I won't claim it was easy to arrive at that state of mind). Ultimately, though, this all raises a more important issue about power and having a voice in the decisions that affect one's job and one's life.

Robyn and I have discussed before the issue of appealing to the self-interest of tenured and tenure-track faculty members in organizing support for lecturers. This approach seems politically and procedurally expedient. But consider its implications for lecturers. The process Robyn has described left me with, above all, a sense of the utter powerlessness of lecturers as a group. When all the bureaucratic procedures necessary to creating change at the institution had finally been navigated, the president simply said no; so to salvage something from the two-year process, the committee accepted a change in the language of the proposal that created the *possibility*, rather than the certainty, of a contract once a lecturer qualified. More specifically, the wording went from "shall" to "may." This is a huge change. And it reveals two important aspects of how lecturers are perceived.

First, let us examine the practical effect of the language, of the *possibility* of a contract. A lecturer colleague of mine referred to this provision as the "whatever clause." Because when it comes right down to it, what the new guideline says is that department chairs and, more important, the administration are free to give or refuse to give contracts for any reason. Nothing in the language ensures lecturers a chance at a contract even after long years of effective service, and the language certainly offers them no recourse when they feel they have been treated unfairly.

What the language boils down to is that if a lecturer is fortunate enough to have a chair who will fight the administration on his or her behalf, then maybe the lecturer can obtain a contract. We lecturers in the English department at UVM have had such a chair, but still only slightly more than half of us have received contracts. And since the department chair serves a three-year term, every time a given lecturer's contract comes up for renewal there will be a new chair who may or may not see the value of setting aside base-budget funds for lecturers.

That's the practical failure of the language. The more damaging aspect of it is the casual request that lecturers rely on the good graces of others to secure just recompense for their services. That position is professionally humiliating. And as for the guideline's chances of improving conditions, all one has to do is look at the situation lecturers are in right now to see where such paternalistic dependence has got them. This is not to knock tenure-line faculty members. They have their own battles to fight. Why should we lecturers expect them to fight ours?

Which leads me to the second way the change in language reveals perceptions about lecturers. Robyn describes how faculty members and department chairs marshaled support and made passionate pleas on lecturers' behalf at the Faculty Senate meetings. I will admit I was happily taken aback by the statements of support offered for the work lecturers do. But another thing struck me as well—that lecturers (myself included) did not offer their own defense of their role at UVM. In part, their silence has to do with the hierarchy of the institution. I understand that. But it is a big obstacle to lecturers' making real gains. Within the larger culture of the university it is somehow unseemly for lecturers to argue their importance. If they protest their value too vehemently, they risk alienating even those tenure-line faculty members who generally support the move for improved working conditions. And without that support, there will be no improvement. Lecturers' place in the hierarchy is very clear.

The status of lecturers was quite apparent in the way the administration dealt with the proposal for lecturer contracts. As Robyn indicates, the key factors in the process were the President's Commission on the Status of Women and the Faculty Women's Caucus. Both are admirable in their pursuits, and I appreciate that they worked on my behalf, but they also represent a top-down approach that allows lecturers to remain invisible. Even the caucus, which is open to all women, relies on the Steering Committee of senior women faculty members to set the caucus's agenda for women's needs. As for the commission, Robyn makes clear its meetings with upper-level administrators ensured that the issue could not go away. But shouldn't lecturers have that responsibility themselves? That they don't reflects many aspects of their working conditions, including the influence of status on how they perceive themselves as well as on how they perceive their relation to the university and their tenured colleagues.

From the start, the proposal for contracts was aimed at tenure-line faculty members. They have power to make change at institutions. Lecturers do not. And that's the situation that institutions must address if lecturers are to improve their lot.

The effort to pass the final proposal and have it accepted in its revised form by the administration took two academic years. I am sure administrators followed the events carefully. I am also sure that if administrators had had their way, the issue would have simply disappeared. As Robyn suggests, the reason it didn't go away was that committed people, working within bureaucratic structures put in place to effect change at the university, wouldn't let it. But as administrators responded at each stage, they responded because of the authority and respect accorded tenure-line faculty members, not because they felt the need to recognize the work of lecturers. Only at the end, when it appeared that lecturers would get language in the handbook that required contracts once certain conditions were met, did administrators put aside the influence of tenure-line faculty members and deal with lecturers directly. And then they simply said no. Because, ultimately, what could lecturers do about it?

In a familiar administrative ploy, the final vote on the proposal was delayed, as most votes on potentially messy issues are, until the last senate meeting of the academic year. Thus if tenure-line faculty members were to continue this battle on lecturers' behalf it would mean beginning the process again next fall.

I don't believe administrators will ever take lecturers seriously until lecturers begin to demand change for themselves, by themselves, using tenured and senior faculty members as much as they can in support but not having faculty members run all the interference. The university hierarchy makes that difficult, if not impossible, which is why it has to be done out-side that structure. This means organizing separately from the tenure-line faculty. If lecturers must align with other groups, it makes more sense to organize with graduate students and staff, whose working conditions re-semble lecturers' more than tenure-line faculty members' do.

Will this happen? Probably not. It's hard to imagine a group of employ-ees more vulnerable to the risks of union activity than lecturers. But lectur-ers will never know their own strength until they begin speaking with their own voice, rather than through the voices of others. Otherwise, administra-tors will continue to simply say no, because, as they see it, they are ad-dressing only shadows.

Brian Kent
University of Vermont

Bob's Jobs: Campus Crises and "Adjunct" Education

SANDRA M. GILBERT

Adjunct—n. 1. Something joined or added to another thing, but not essentially a part of it.

—Webster's New Collegiate Dictionary

I offer these words in tribute to the memory of Robert J. Griffin, a dear friend, former colleague, and fellow member of the MLA's ad hoc Committee on Professional Employment, who died in early November 1997 after a grievous struggle with cancer. For the past five years Bob had eked out a precarious living as a part-time composition teacher at a community college in the San Francisco Bay area, where he had lived on and off (but mostly on) for almost forty years. Like many other academic workers in his position, he had no benefits—no medical coverage, no retirement plan, no disability or life insurance, not a single "fringe." Nor did he have an office, a summer salary, a computer, an e-mail account, or a card allowing him to use the research library at the University of California, Berkeley, where he earned his PhD in 1965. He was in his mid-sixties and teaching two or three courses a semester, besides supervising students in a writing lab. For these labors, he earned approximately $15,000 a year, give or take a little depending on the availability of summer courses.

How my friend came to this pass had partly to do, of course, with his own personal decisions and crises, but I think it also had to do with developments

The author is Professor of English at the University of California, Davis, and a past president of the Modern Language Association.

in public, institutional history that at the time of his death the MLA's Committee on Professional Employment had been studying for the last two years. Such congruence between Bob's private history and the public history we were examining made Bob an especially valuable member of our committee. More specifically, this poignant correlation between two histories helps dramatize the pain inflicted by the kind of academic downsizing that has lately led campus administrators to substitute low-paying, part-time and temporary "adjunct" jobs for properly compensated, full-time, tenure-track positions.

When Bob earned his doctorate, he was by all accounts the golden boy of his class. Like most worthy candidates in the mid-sixties—indeed, even like some *un*worthy ones—he had multiple tenure-track job offers from prestigious research universities. When he chose to accept an offer from Yale, nobody was certain he'd get tenure there, but it seemed a foregone conclusion that he could move to a tenured position at a school nearly as prestigious. In the event, however, he never came up for tenure, because he chose to leave his Ivy League assistant professorship before he was eligible for promotion. Partly from personal preference but also partly because of the escalating radicalism of the sixties, he decided to commit himself to a career built primarily on teaching rather than mainly on scholarship; and partly because he'd fallen in love with Berkeley as a graduate student and partly because the Bay area was then where, in the language of the day, "it was at," he took a job at the California State University, Hayward, a briskly growing campus that had started life as a teacher's college but was now part of the Cal State megasystem. And it was in the Hayward English department that I met him in 1969. I had been teaching there for a year as a beginning assistant professor—my first full-time job—and he was hired as an untenured associate professor. We felt simpatico right away and soon joined with other new arrivals on campus to try to revamp department offerings and, generally speaking, rock a few pedagogical boats.

But of course, as I hardly need remind most readers, the late sixties weren't just a time of radical idealism: the era was a fateful period of political turmoil and more specifically generational strife, with the Bay area a tumultuous microcosm reflecting macrocosmic changes on the national and even international scene. Just in our part of the world, the San Francisco State strike and the Berkeley riots were making headlines. Student rebellions from New York to Paris focused on issues that concerned us all, and soon the Kent State killings violently illustrated the vulnerability of protesters everywhere. In its provincial way our department was a microcosm of the microcosm: battle lines were quickly drawn between the senior, tenured professors—some of them holdovers from the old teacher's college—and the smart-alecky junior professors, most of whom had dauntingly superior academic credentials. And quickly, in an impressive series, many of us whippersnappers were fired (or, to use the decorous euphemism deployed by the Cal State bureaucracy, "not retained") before we could even come up for tenure. I myself was "not retained" as of 1971, and my friend Bob was "not retained" as of 1972.[1]

Again, however, let me invoke a history I imagine many readers know quite well: the early seventies represented a moment of crisis in professional employment that was in many ways comparable to the situation we face today, though the source of the problem at that time was demographic rather than economic. With the campus expansions fueled by the baby boom losing force, departments that had prospered in the sixties were shutting their doors to job applicants. Soon many departments would even be "tenured in," as the saying goes, but in any case few were growing. Those of us on the market had to be diligent, inventive, or just plain lucky to gain a foothold at almost any institution. Both Bob and I found ourselves doing part-time teaching while we were also occupied with the business of job applications—a cottage industry even more arduous in those precomputer days than it is now. Eventually, I accepted a position halfway across the country from where my husband taught, and we had to confront the logistics of academic commuting while trying to raise three young children. As for Bob, he left teaching to become executive director of what was first the UC Berkeley Faculty Association and later, under his guidance, the systemwide Faculty Association.

Bob stayed on at the Faculty Association for seventeen years, but as time passed and UC departments first got increasingly "tenured in" and then, in a worsening California economy, dwindled in size and in resources, the organization dwindled too. Some UC professors may have gotten complacent as they gained seniority; others may have simply given up hope in the increasingly strenuous fight for public funding. At the same time, the rise of a more aggressive union, the American Federation of Teachers, reflected the striking growth of a new class of academic service workers: so-called adjuncts—temporary full- or part-time lecturers—whose interests weren't adequately served by an organization focused on the concerns of tenure-track faculty members. By the early nineties, therefore, the Faculty Association had lost so much momentum that it could no longer afford a full-time director. At that point, when he was in his early sixties and it was too late to reenter academia as a tenure-track professor, Bob turned to part-time community college teaching—which is where I began his story.

And to be sure, as I noted earlier, his story is a special one. Nonetheless, in the context of current dilemmas I think it is as monitory as it is moving.

To begin with, the shifts in Bob's teaching career highlight major changes in the academic marketplace, changes both in the kinds of employment available to job seekers and in the nature of the teaching those job seekers are increasingly called on to do. In addition, however, the erosion of support for his position at the Faculty Association points not only to the evolution of a multitiered academic job system (whose various participants may have seemed at first to have clashing interests) but also to the passivity, perhaps the complacency or perhaps the anxious denial, with which all too many tenure-track professionals have reacted to a series of crises undermining contemporary study in the humanities. Finally, the indifference with which not just university and college administrators but also—perhaps even more to the point—legislators, parents, students, and others concerned with campus issues have responded to the plight symbolized by Bob's jobs casts some deeply disquieting shadows over the future of higher education in our country. For from a public policy perspective as well as from the supposedly narrower perspective of the "ivory tower," recent changes both in the academic labor market and in the climate of academia have had manifold untoward consequences, pedagogical as well as ethical, political as well as professional.

As we all know, in the thirty years since Bob earned his degree one of the most dismaying developments in the very structure of American higher education has been the growth of the academic underclass into which he was assimilated five years ago: that is, the increasing number of PhDs doing part-time ("adjunct") service work in lower-division courses. As we all know too, this extraordinary proliferation of part-time jobs is associated with a reallocation of campus resources away from full-time, tenure-track positions, draining countless departments of FTEs needed not just for lower-division offerings but also for offerings in the major, while—what is more painful still—confronting job candidates with an excruciatingly tight buyer's market in which many will be forced to perpetuate a vicious circle by accepting just the kinds of part-time positions that have replaced more appropriate full-time jobs.

Of course, as MLA and AAUP reports dating back to the seventies attest, there has always been a part-time job market: I myself first began teaching as a part-timer in New York in the sixties, when I was a graduate student at Columbia (where women were not then offered TAships), and I can remember not only the exploitative wages and conditions I had to accept but also the enthusiasm with which the composition director who hired me just after the birth of my third child confessed that he "loved mommies" because they were so eager for jobs that they'd do more work for less pay than their male counterparts. (Does this imply that "daddies" *weren't* eager for jobs?) But in today's increasingly impoverished academic economy part-time work is no longer just the dismal fate to which unlucky "mommies" have been consigned. Indeed, as the Committee on Professional Employment report notes, in the same three-year period (1991–93) in which the number of full-time positions advertised in the MLA's *Job Information List* declined by 29% in English and by 14% in foreign languages, part-time and temporary positions across higher education grew by 17% in four-year institutions and by 40% in two-year colleges. In 1970 22% of the faculty nationwide consisted of part-timers, but the face of higher education has now changed so drastically that part-timers constitute 40% of the faculty (Gilbert et al. 7–8). (For a more detailed discussion of these statistics and the history they represent, see Gilbert et al.)

Putting aside considerations of professional equity and simple ethics for the moment—temporarily ignoring, that is, the financial hardship and personal humiliation inflicted on those faced with such hand-to-mouth working conditions—the pedagogical implications of this situation are deeply disturbing. For while some of our colleagues subsist precariously as "freeway flyers"—lacking not only the economic security but also the professional support that institutional continuity provides—ever-growing numbers of our undergraduates, most often lower-division students who are in many ways our neediest constituency, find themselves in classrooms overseen by teachers who may not always be able to give them meaningful guidance when they need help *outside* the classroom. I know that, like all the other part-timers in my own circle, Bob was profoundly conscientious about grading, advising, course planning, and other pedagogical tasks. Night after night he'd leave parties and dinners early or excuse himself from movies and concerts because he had literally hundreds of papers to read, and week after week he worked in writing labs, conferring with students who needed remedial assistance, not just because he needed to supplement his meager part-time teaching salary but also because he was really *committed* to clear writing as well as to good reading. Yet, overloaded and underpaid, without any real clerical aid, with little or no departmental community, without even a significant personal space (not so much as a desk or a hat rack of his own!), how could he who was hardly present to his colleagues be present to and for his students?

Miraculously enough, without an office or computer, Bob *was* able to be present outside the classroom for a surprising number of his students. Several days after he died, in fact, a few of us who had volunteered to help organize his household found a card, from a former student, that he'd kept for some years on the mantel of his living-room fireplace. She wanted to thank him, she said, for the letters of reference he'd written for her over the last three years. His support had helped her move on from the community college where he'd been her composition and "intro to lit" teacher to the four-year college from which she'd just graduated—and now to Boalt Hall, the home of the law school at UC Berkeley, where she'd just been admitted, she wrote, thanks to his help. Not knowing he was an "adjunct," she addressed him as "Professor." He was her "favorite professor," she declared, and she'd always remember his "important contribution" to her career.

That despite all the pedagogical as well as personal obstacles he confronted Bob was able to make such a contribution to this young law student's life emphasizes a profoundly ironic *dis*junction between our use of the word *adjunct* to describe people in his position and the dictionary definition of *adjunct* that I give as an epigraph above. For what Bob and others like him bring to their students' education is hardly "something joined or added to another thing, but not essentially a part of it." On the contrary, it is every bit as essential as the contributions made by their more appropriately rewarded tenure-track colleagues. Indeed, where would the rest of us—who blithely theorize and historicize as well as enthuse about great literature—be without the thousands of "adjuncts" whose dedicated but all too often oppressed labor makes possible so many of our apparently more sophisticated accomplishments?

A few weeks ago my department met for one of several self-analytic discussions of the professional employment possibilities now available to our graduate students, a discussion inspired (as I hope others around the country have been) by the recent Committee on Professional Employment report. We wondered whether, as our newly minted PhDs emerge from the ivory tower in this era of campus downsizing, many of them will be consigned to the academic equivalent of the part-time positions scathingly described by the national media as "McJobs." Might they, speculated one especially bitter observer, be forced to labor as "McProfessors" in "virtual" or "drive-through" universities? How can we help them retool, retrain, reimagine their skills so that they can maintain their personal and pedagogical standards by joining in professionwide efforts to transform "adjunct" posts for the teaching of introductory courses into the *essential* positions such jobs ought to be?

In the midst of our debate a voice came from the back of the room—the voice of an "adjunct" in our own department who works in the campus writing center. (And yes, although he and a number of other lecturers at our university have full-time slots with fringe benefits, they are nonetheless "adjuncts.") "Maybe you should invite us to more of your meetings," he said. "Some of us have a lot to teach you."

NOTE

[1]For another account of these events, see Lazere, esp. 86–88.

WORKS CITED

Gilbert, Sandra M., et al. *Final Report, MLA Committee on Professional Employment.* New York: MLA, 1997.
Lazere, Donald. "Class Conflict in the English Profession." *Coming to Class: Pedagogy and the Social Class of Teachers.* Ed. Alan Shepard, John McMillan, and Gary Tate. Portsmouth: Heinemann, 1998. 79–93.

Letters

Confronting the Current Job Market

To the Editor:

I would like to join other correspondents in thanking the MLA for its current focus on the urgent practical concerns of those in our profession. Most particularly, writers of recent essays and letters who have gained employment outside of college and university literature and language departments not only share their experiences with graduate students anxious about attaining scarce tenure-track positions but also inform our colleagues about the value of advanced degrees in liberal arts outside of the academy.

It is perhaps natural that the bulk of the letters in *Profession 1997* discuss other teaching options; teaching is what we do, what our students learn to do, and what most of us enjoy. Lawrence Goodman makes it clear that a career in secondary school teaching can be at least as rewarding as teaching in a college or university, and this is important information for those who assume that the high school classroom is of necessity a riot waiting to happen. But the fact of the matter is that some of our students either do not enjoy teaching or would like to try something else. As our profession is just now acknowledging, academics in the liberal arts have done a poor job of counseling students—undergraduate and graduate—about employment opportunities, and I believe there are two reasons why this is traditionally the case: ignorance of the alternatives to academic work and persistent and endemic prejudice against business.

Others would object to my analysis, claiming that attractive alternatives to academic work are simply in short supply, or even nonexistent. In his response to Mark A. Johnson's optimistic *Profession 1996* essay, Mike Hill, insisting that Johnson's enthusiasm is "grossly misplaced," makes just this claim about the midlevel managerial positions PhDs would be likely to seek. It must be said that the statistics cited by Hill reporting an increase in low-wage earners as well as those cited in Johnson's reply to Hill noting a downturn in unemployment are, in common parlance, neither here nor there, being far too general to define the situation for a small, select demographic group, persons with graduate degrees in languages and literature. But an educated guess might suggest that the increasing ranks of unskilled workers (the waiters, cashiers, and janitors Hill mentions) are comprised of young, inexperienced high school and college graduates, women returning to work, and working-class persons moonlighting to make ends meet. Though overall employment patterns and increasing disparities in income distribution present a picture many of us find socially distressing, and though Johnson might be too optimistic about industry expansion, he is right to insist that a PhD distinguishes one from the general workforce.

In fact, my own experience indicates that even an MA endows one with such distinction. After earning an MA in English and Creative Writing, without a single business or business-related writing course to my name and with no directly relevant work experience, I found employment in a small industrial advertising agency as an administrative assistant and entry-level copywriter. I was greatly overqualified for most of the work and dreadfully underpaid, but after a year I accepted a position in Marketing Communications in Conrail's public affairs department paying me over twice the salary of my previous position. In my capacity as an account manager, I wrote and oversaw the production of slide presentations, brochures, proposals, and the like. From discussions with my supervisor in the two-and-a-half years I was employed by the railroad, I know that the following factors were salient in gaining my initial interview from a pool of two hundred applicants: 1) the reputation of my undergraduate institution, 2) my graduate degree, and 3) a moderately creative approach to my résumé.

I cannot emphasize enough how generally impressed businesspersons are with advanced degrees. In Conrail's large corporate office, I knew of four persons with PhDs; one of these held a degree in an area as unrelated to his daily work as my MA was to mine. Once, after I had had a brief phone conversation with this man, I mentioned his unpleasant manner to my supervisor, who immediately responded, "*He* has a PhD, you know," as though this godly status exempted him from the rules of common decorum. In this case my boss's regard for the degree was certainly misplaced, but he and other well-educated businesspersons respect advanced degrees for good reasons, for the abilities they should always indicate, sophisticated thinking, good writing skills, and independence in one's work. Corporations also like MAs and PhDs for the less good reason that they confer status on the organization, but no one who is bad at his or her job will keep it for this reason alone. If Hill is right that midlevel managerial positions are increasingly scarce, competent MAs and PhDs who appear eager to devote themselves to a new kind of work are likely to be among the strongest competitors for these jobs.

When I decided to return to school to pursue my PhD, my coworkers, from secretaries to executives, were uniformly happy for me, and I still have friends from my years at Conrail. More important from the professional and economic point of view, I had another career, better paying if in other respects less satisfying, to return to if I was unable to find academic employment after completing my graduate work. Believe me, I would not have accepted the criminal wages and conditions of a part-time university English instructor. And indeed, as a recent reading of Richard Russo's novel *Straight Man* reminds me, even tenured professors may see the day when they will need to seek occupations outside the university. There are many personal and practical advantages to a varied work experience, not least of all the likelihood that one will, in one profession or another, be decently employed.

I hope what I say here supports Johnson's point while also broadening the message. We are talking about more than options outside the tenure track for PhDs; like myself, most MLA members teach in departments without PhD programs. BA and MA candidates in the liberal arts should be encouraged to take a few courses or even a minor in areas such as marketing and engineering to broaden their background. Better yet, they should be counseled to enroll in writing internships in departments that offer them, because such programs offer actual experience, the thing most sought after by prospective employers. Finally, while those with an aptitude for computers may have a special advantage in securing nonacademic employment in our technology-prone culture, there is still room in the world for the rest of us: high schools always need talented teachers and much traditional industry is very stable. Coal and steel can't be delivered on the Internet, and no one wants to drive across a bridge made of computer chips.

Nancy L. Easterlin
University of New Orleans

FACULTY WORK

To the Editor:

Katherine Kolb's article, "Adjuncts in Academe: No Place Called Home" in *Profession 1997*, raises a number of important issues regarding universities' continuing reliance on adjuncts, the impact of this "temporary" job pool on postsecondary education, and the debilitating effect such work has on both the scholarship and teaching of part-time faculty. As a part-time lecturer in the writing program of a large East Coast university, I know first-hand the problems facing those of us not yet lucky enough to have found tenure-track positions. The combined sense of personal failure and protracted placelessness that Kolb's article registers is one I experience every minute of every hour I'm on the campus of my "home" institution. The unrooted nature of this relationship forms an unfortunate, central part of the work I do as a teacher for hire: valued enough to have been brought on as an adjunct, but not valuable enough to be given "real" work as a tenure-track faculty member.

It was with some frustration, then, that I read Kolb's concluding comments on this entire situation. Having worked out in moving detail the institutional and personal consequences of adjunct life, Kolb finally suggests that however bad things seem, the choices are finally our own to make. However, it needs to be pointed out that these choices, far from being entirely or even significantly in our control, are part of a much larger process that really leaves adjuncts with only two options: EITHER stay and teach at absurdly low pay levels (the income paid adjuncts suggests we're either independently or dependently well-off or working four other jobs to make ends meet), while waiting for that 1 in 500 tenure-track post (the odds these days, in English at any rate) OR leave university teaching altogether and look for work elsewhere. Either way, *choice* is hardly the operative term for what Kolb describes; *caught* would seem to be the more appropriate word here. Given that it's understood that once you leave adjunct teaching for work outside the academy, any chance at a tenure-track post is all but ended, whatever we do in the meantime to construct meaningful existences as teachers, scholars, and writers is linked to a social and institutional network that makes staying or leaving seem like two sides of the same coin. Kolb's sense of agency, then, needs to be seen in the context of institutional factors that all but require such work of those of us willing to forgo other career options. For how long and at what cost one goes down this road are questions that Kolb, based on her own life experience, seems both stringently aware of and painfully unable to resolve.

The relative benefits of the adjunct life (access to a university library, lack of committee duties, and so on), represent nothing more than the residue of what an intellectual and scholarly life was supposed to look like. As with Kolb and thousands like her across the country, I've come to enjoy and depend upon the intellectual stimulation of teaching, the real satisfaction of working with students in an environment that on the surface at least encourages thought. But it's exactly this disjunction between the aspirations of my position as an educator and my overwhelming awareness that we are expendable—more, that the department and university administration *depend* upon our expendability—that makes Kolb's "choice" and "freedom" seem like terms of desperation, *not* elucidation. For any of us, the move to engage, understand, and finally accept our choices is a crucial, first step toward real empowerment. But the politics of rationalization and acquiescence, as exemplified by Kolb's parting comments, has no place in a discussion meant to eradicate, rather than solidify, the kind of exploitation she otherwise rejects.

Finally, cogent as her critique is, Kolb's essay amounts to little more than another form of "head shaking." That she can acknowledge the profound problems in the way we train, hire, and employ at the postsecondary level, while defending a system that devalues *all* of our efforts as educators, suggests the pathos of a profession unable to speak clearly about its own practices.

Andrew Mossin
Lambertville, NJ

Reply:

I would like to thank Andrew Mossin, and the many who wrote to me privately, for echoing and expanding on my indictment of the academy's use of adjunct faculty members. Dire as my picture may seem, it barely begins to convey the pain of those "caught" in the system, as Mossin puts it, or the severity and complexity of the problem for those who might attempt to fix it. "Things are even worse than you imagined," a University of Minnesota colleague observed ruefully to me a few months ago; he had just begun to study the situation as part of a faculty senate–mandated effort toward reform. His committee (which I was invited to sit in on) discovered that it hardly knew which questions to ask in assembling its data, and that it was difficult even to learn how many of us there are. Since I had not been teaching during the quarter surveyed, my name did not turn up in the listings; conversely, two other long-time adjuncts in my department went uncounted because they had full-year appointments.

But even faulty data revealed much. There turned out to be wide disparities in the compensation and circumstances of non-tenure-track faculty members. In such fields as medicine, law, or architecture, part-time faculty members are often well paid, while retaining lucrative practices on the side; their example is the one invariably brought up in defense of adjunct hiring. Meanwhile the sweat-shop conditions lie close by, more intractable than ever. They are in fields where, as Mossin points out, leaving the academy means leaving the profession: literary scholars may find employment elsewhere, but rarely in the research and teaching for which they have been trained. A medical instructor can presumably return to full-time practice; a French or composition instructor has no such choice.

I have no quarrel with Mossin's exposure of the "choice" open to adjuncts in humanities as little more than a trap. For someone committed to a particular field of study, the option to quit can feel less like a choice than a death sentence, conjuring up echoes of the poet André Chénier on the scaffold: "To die without emptying my quiver!" I spoke of choice partly to preempt the question, Why, then, do you stay? I tried to own up to the seductions and delusions that induced me to stay, and I assessed the cost, both to me and to the institution—as, I hoped, a cautionary tale. And I urged a conscious choice, such as it is, for adjuncts because I think it vital to maintain the power of the few options we have. Precisely because our agency is so limited, it is essential for each of us to weigh our decisions carefully (true, I have no one-size-fits-all solution) and review them as often as necessary to stay sane. In so doing, it is crucial to know that there *is* life outside the academy, although it is ironic, as Jacques Raphanel points out in the same issue of *Profession*, to be reminded of it in academic journals.

Choosing to stay sane (or lucid, at least) under insane conditions can, of course, play into the hands of exploitive institutions. But to say "I choose to stay *although* I can choose to leave" is to cast the choice in a different light. Such choice is the basis not only of individual but also of collective power—the power that collective bargaining is all about. I glanced at a possible scenario in which adjuncts would follow the example of the graduate strike at Yale University. What if all adjuncts went on strike—all 44% of the college instruction in this country? What if—now I'm really getting carried away—all the temps in the nonacademic world joined in? Unlikely,

I said; but France in 1968 offered a precedent, and e-mail is proving an asset to far-flung political causes.

The scenario I prefer (not that it excludes the other) would have faculty senates take the lead in reforming current hiring practices. Most faculty members I know are very much concerned about the future of their profession, their institution, and their students. Many have very little idea even now of this shadow side of the profession; the eminent faculty members on the committee here were genuinely shocked to learn about it. If they succeed in shocking their colleagues, changes may occur. To have an entire faculty put its anathema on current abuses and its weight behind a demand for new positions could begin to repair a disgrace—a state of affairs in which a wealthy society desperately in need of educated workers and citizens refuses to invest long-term in students eager to learn and in teachers trained and eager to teach.

Katherine Kolb
University of Minnesota, Twin Cities

To the Editor:

The essays in *Profession 1997* are superb and open many vistas of thought on teaching, tenure, writing, and research.

There is one glaring omission, however—the role of emeritus professors in the profession. Those leaders of the 1980s and 1990s are, in many cases, still at the helm of excellence with articles, books, and activity in the MLA and other organizations. Without the burden of university teaching, long-delayed projects are more easily completed.

In my own case, if I can overcome my modesty, I have had published three university-press books since I retired in 1988 from the University of California, Santa Barbara, after thirty years of teaching. Besides these books and a new batch of articles, I have a fourth volume in final draft. Like other emeriti at the Huntington Library, I have been awarded citations for excellence; I lecture at colleges and universities and am active in several academic associations, and I write dozens of letters to support younger people for jobs, fellowships, and grants. Are emeriti destined to the wasteland, or do we fade away like old soldiers? We may fade, but not before we sparkle a bit.

Wilbur R. Jacobs
Huntington Library, San Marino, CA

Personal Encounters

To the Editor:

I have been an appreciative reader of James R. Papp's "Deconstructing and Reconstructing in a Post-Communist Country," *Profession 1997*. I admire Papp's ability to make *sense* out of his experiences and to shape them into a readable, coherent essay—something that I have not done after several appointments abroad. Like Papp, to take one example, I have discovered that many students abroad are studying English because they "like it or love it" and not because they expect it to bring them economic benefits.

One student came particularly to mind as I read Papp's final sentence ("And there is nothing a stranger and a teacher [. . .] can do [. . .] except [. . .] to care"). A male Palestinian student, apparently a second-class citizen in his new "home" country and someone who entered the university through a back door, came to see me frequently; and shortly after nearly every class, he followed up on something that I had said by putting his handwritten reactions or pertinent photocopied material in my mailbox. Naturally I discussed many things with him and was especially interested in his goals, his vision of his personal future. On one occasion, when I may have pressed too hard, he announced that after graduation he would "go home and watch television." During our last meeting he asked a haunting question: "Why do you care?" The caring itself, I fear, was foreign and probably incomprehensible to him.

In the same country large numbers of female students, called "girls," are being educated in the state university. Some are very intelligent and quite capable of responding to American methods; but they cannot hope to do graduate work or to gain meaningful employment, and perhaps (as one experienced onlooker told me) they cannot expect to marry, because they are overeducated.

Daniel P. Deneau
Fargo, North Dakota

To the Editor:

Many students want to turn poems into aphorisms or plain statements: "Why doesn't the poet just come out and say it and be done with it?" This attitude is analogous to a child on a trip who continuously asks, "Are we there yet?" Freud might have related such an outlook to the death wish—

the desire for closure, quiescence. Leonard Woolf once said, "The journey not the arrival matters." (Why doesn't an artist just take a photograph instead of laboriously creating a painting?)

Poetry is elaboration, a side trip. Strictly speaking, as Plato pointed out, it is unnecessary—even, in some ways, undesirable. Poetry is the bad boy of literature and life, the one who is always saying, "Yes, but . . ." and "Wait, look, listen"; the one who does not go along with the program; the one who causes problems. For example, Daniel Defoe's poetry landed him in the pillory and the prison. The authorities did not fool around back then.

These days the average person does not seem to recognize the fact that there is a problem with arts funding; or, if people are aware of the problem, chances are they are in favor of making it worse, cutting public funding even more or eliminating it altogether. Poetry and art in general have been so marginalized and cloistered that they have almost ceased to exist for the general public. Outside of college courses and the decoration of homes, art is merely an afterthought, a tiny glint on the spinning bubble of existence.

Here is what we need to say to students: poetry is like life—it can be enjoyed or viewed as the necessary drudgery before death. Look at Shakespeare's sonnets and Ginsberg's howls. There is a rich, exciting power there. And W. B. Yeats and T. S. Eliot certainly knew how to put words and thoughts through some hoops and somersaults. But what all these people said is as important as how they said it, so after and during our appreciation for the beauty of the form, we can look at the meanings, which coalesce around one point: If you want to love life, you have to take the time to look at all of it. There is no tool like poetry for helping you accomplish and enjoy that worthwhile task.

Jack Turner
Wesley College

The eagerly awaited new edition of the leading style guide for authors

**MLA STYLE MANUAL
AND GUIDE TO
SCHOLARLY PUBLISHING**

2nd edition • Joseph Gibaldi

1998 • xxviii & 343 pp. • Subject index
Cloth ISBN 0-87352-699-6 • $25.00
(members $20.00)

"A standard authority for scholarly style."

LIBRARY JOURNAL

SINCE ITS publication in 1985, the *MLA Style Manual* has been the standard guide for graduate students, teachers, and scholars in the humanities and for professional writers in many fields. Extensively reorganized and revised, the new edition contains several added sections and updated guidelines on citing electronic works—including materials found on the World Wide Web.

The second edition begins with an expanded chapter on the publication process, from manuscript to published work, and includes advice for those seeking to publish their articles or books. The second chapter, by the attorney Arthur F. Abelman, reviews legal issues, such as the arcana of copyright law, the concept of fair use, the provisions of a typical publishing contract, defamation, and the emergence of privacy law. Subsequent chapters discuss stylistic conventions and the preparation of manuscripts, theses, and dissertations and offer an authoritative and comprehensive presentation of MLA documentation style.

**MODERN LANGUAGE
ASSOCIATION**

10 Astor Place, New York, NY 10003-6981
212 614-6382 • Fax 212 358-9140
www.mla.org

Individual subscriptions to the *ADFL Bulletin* are $21 a year (three issues). Library subscriptions are $30.

❑ Please enter my subscription to the *ADFL Bulletin*.

Enclosed is my check for $__________ $ [   ]

❑ **VISA**   Please specify in the above box the amount to be
charged to your credit card and please authorize the
❑ **MasterCard.**   transaction by signing below.

NAME ___________________________________

ADDRESS ___________________________________

CITY ___________________________________

STATE ______________   ZIP ___________________

ACCOUNT NO. ___________________________________

EXP. DATE ______   TELEPHONE NO. ___________________

SIGNATURE ___________________________________

❑ MLA member

ADFL
www.adfl.org   *10 Astor Place*
New York, NY 10003-6981

ASSOCIATION OF DEPARTMENTS OF FOREIGN LANGUAGES

"The *ADFL Bulletin* is an indispensable tool in our efforts to build, strengthen, and expand teaching and research in foreign languages and literatures. In its pages we can share our accomplishments and learn about innovations as we focus on language acquisition at the heart of education. This is a crucial mission, and the *ADFL Bulletin* is an important part of this struggle."

RUSSELL A. BERMAN
STANFORD UNIVERSITY

The *ADFL Bulletin*, published three times a year by the Association of Departments of Foreign Languages, reports on a broad range of programs at colleges and universities and provides a venue for discussion of developments in foreign language and literature teaching. The *Bulletin* publishes articles on professional, pedagogical, and governance issues, as well as analyses of national surveys of postsecondary education in foreign languages and literatures.

Recent articles have focused on change in the profession; the disjuncture between secondary and postsecondary language teaching; the place of cultural studies, literature, and translation in the graduate and undergraduate curriculum; international studies; interdisciplinarity; and emerging technologies and language instruction. The *Bulletin* also features information on ADFL activities, upcoming conferences, and funding.

The Fall issue includes a directory of ADFL members and a directory of useful addresses. The *Bulletin* invites essays discussing such topics as faculty development, pedagogy, assessment, gender and minority issues in the foreign language classroom, teacher education, and the administration of graduate and undergraduate foreign language programs on campus and abroad.